Delbrück's Modern Military History

T0326922

# Delbrück's Modern Military History

# Hans Delbrück

Edited and Translated by

Arden Bucholz

University of Nebraska Press

Lincoln and London

The introduction incorporates materials taken from approximately three
pages of Arden Bucholz's "Armies,
Railroads, and Information: The
Birth of Industrial Mass War" in
*Changing Large Technical Systems*, ed.
Jane Summerton (Boulder CO: Westview Press, 1994) Copyright © 1994
by Westview Press. Reprinted by permission of Westview Press.

Library of Congress Cataloging-in-
Publication Data
Bucholz, Arden.
Delbrück's modern military history /
Hans Delbrück; edited and translated
by Arden Bucholz.
p.   cm.
Arden Bucholz's free translation
from the German of, or "musings
on," selected writings of Hans
Delbrück.
Includes bibliographical references
and index.
ISBN 0-8032-1698-X (cl.: alk. paper)
1. Military history, Modern.
2. Delbrück, Hans, 1848–1929.
I. Delbrück, Hans, 1848–1929.
II. Title.
D214.B83    1997
355'.009'04—dc21
96-50000
CIP

ISBN 0-8032-6653-7 (pa.: alk. paper)

For Susie with love and thanks
for thirty-four wonderful
and extraordinary years of
marriage.

# Contents

# Preface

In the fall of 1969 my father died the week before University of Chicago final oral exams. Once past these crises, I began to work on the dissertation. Frederick the Great's war economy between the Austrian succession and the Seven Years' War proved impossible: there were no accessible sources. Working on Helmuth von Moltke the elder's four Turkey years (1835–39), I came across Gordon Craig's seminal article on Hans Delbrück in the 1943 edition of *Makers of Modern Strategy*.[1] Delbrück's *History of the Art of War in the Framework of Political History* had been reprinted in Germany several years previously, to European acclaim, but the author was little known in the United States.[2]

In the early spring of 1970 Professor William H. McNeill and I settled on Delbrück as a dissertation topic. It soon became clear that Delbrück left a great many papers when he died in the summer of 1929. His wife, Carolina (Lina) Thiersch, who survived him, spent the remaining years until her death in 1943 organizing them, finally presenting them to the Preussische Staatsbibliothek, where Adolf von Harnack, the great church historian and Delbrück's closest friend, was general director.[3] A second batch of Delbrück material had found its way after World War II into the hands of another relative, Peter Rassow, professor of history at Cologne. His wife had given it in 1962 to the Bundesarchiv, Koblenz. Confronted with this material, McNeill commented to me that anything written on Delbrück by someone who had not at least looked at these papers would be sadly open to criticism.

The problem was that six years before, during the depths of the Cold War, I had been a counterintelligence special agent attached to the United States Second Armored Cavalry Regiment (the Cav) in Nuremberg, Germany. A colleague and I were responsible for the internal security of one of the key Seventh Army units in the European command. With a hundred-mile segment of the Czech–East German border under constant surveillance, flying side-looking radar and photographic scan trips several times a week, with a dozen border stations, the Cav was charged with early warning of any Group Soviet Forces buildup or, if worst came to worst, cross-border attack. We had no illusions: top-secret intelligence reports whose pages I counted and certified twice a year said that 140 Group Soviet divisions confronted the Seventh Army, and the Cav was to be only a thin screen during the first three or four days of any war. At the time, we did not give much thought to this overwhelming force. There were always the Air Force and special weapons to delay incoming forces and allow us to get back behind the Rhine River. My top-secret cryptographic security clearance, however, required me to inventory and count the pages of classified war plans and materials held in the document repository of the Cav headquarters and each of its three squadrons in Amberg, Bamberg, and Bayreuth. Thus I had "need to know" access for all Seventh Corps war plans, intelligence reports, and special weapons briefs in southeastern Germany, the potential forward edge of combat.

Another part of our job was to debrief border crossers—those who crossed the great Iron Curtain border, located sixty miles east of the Cav headquarters, with its minefields, triple wires, guard towers, destroyed bridges, broken railroad lines, and roads that ended abruptly in the middle of nowhere. There the Western world ended and another world began. In the heat of the Cold War these physical barriers were only the tangible, immediate warnings of ominous possibilities.

Border crossers were of two kinds. Mainly they went east to west, fleeing Soviet-controlled Czechoslovakia or East Germany. In that case, if they were picked up in our sector they were debriefed fully by another segment of American intelligence in Nuremberg. Occasionally they went west to east, either by accident or design. Several times during my tour U.S. soldiers and officers strayed over the border. Usually after a few days or weeks they were kicked back to us. On several occasions we had to pick up these men by helicopter and de-brief them ourselves, always trying to figure out if they had been forced or cajoled into Soviet employment. We never found any who had, and most were terrified by their experience. Once a lieutenant had fallen asleep and, probably with the connivance of the train personnel at the Hof crossing point, found himself in East German possession. We heard that the second day two KGB officers had come from Moscow and, using perfect American English, had shown him a TO&E (Table of Organization and Equipment) of his unit, classified "confidential," to begin the debriefing. We may have had more respect for Soviet intelligence agencies than they merited, but we had it.

That the largest cache of Delbrück papers was located in the Deutsche Staatsbibliothek, on Unter den Linden, about ten blocks east of the central point of the Berlin Wall, the Branden-burg Gate, was a cause of some anxiety as I prepared to go there in the summer of 1971. I wrote ahead and, when nothing arrived in the mail, even telephoned. A week before I left, I received formal written permission to use the Delbrück papers from Dr. Hans-Erich Teitge, director of the Manuscript Section of the Literary Archives, Deutsche Staatsbibliothek.

As I left New York City in early May 1971, with McNeill's charge ringing in my ears, I was uncertain what was coming. I had seen the wall and border many times from ground level and from the air, but I had never passed over it. After several days of finding my way around and tuning my ear to spoken German, I gathered myself for the great adventure: East Berlin. As I boarded the s Bahn, everything seemed normal; it was empty. The Friedrichstrasse station, however, was across the border: over the triple-barbed-wire minefields, beyond the machine-gun towers, and past the border guards with their police dogs and Kalischnakov guns. All went well. The train stopped, and we were out on the platform, confronting about two dozen heavily armed, black-booted railroad police. Fol-lowing the line, I shoved my passport through the narrow slot, through which no human face was visible, and sat down to wait in the large but run-down waiting room. Would East German officers come out and pick me up immediately or would it take a few days? Perhaps they would have to contact the Russians and tell them there was a fat chicken to be plucked right in their midst. After what seemed like a lifetime, I was called to the window and given my passport along with a one-day pass and instructions to change twenty-five West German marks into East German marks. And I was on my way.

East Berlin in those days left a strong impression on visitors from the United States and even from West Berlin. It was shabby, unreconstructed, gray: even the people seemed to be in mourning and dispirited. Buildings destroyed in World War II had not been rebuilt; ruins abounded. There were lines outside small stores for meat. The Deutsche Staatsbibliothek, right next to the old university buildings, was still imposing. As I passed beneath the tall support pillars at street level, I saw a high stone monument announcing that Lenin had studied there in 1894. Inside was a large quiet space dominated by a huge staircase in the center. I announced myself and my purpose to an official in a glassed-in office to the left, filled out some papers, and waited while the official cleared the visit upstairs. I was told where the literary archive was located and went upstairs and down several corridors. Everything was deathly still. Old wooden steps and floors creaked. The archive reading room is huge and high-ceilinged, with two or three large working tables and a long counter where requests for materials are filled out, picked up, and returned. Once inside the almost empty reading room, I was welcomed by the officials, who were delighted I was working on Delbrück. The longer I stayed, the more cordial they became. On the last day of my second visit in 1974, on a damp and cold afternoon, Dr. Teitge invited me to tea in his office, a cheerful, wood-paneled room down several sets of stairs, deep in the archive itself. A World War II veteran, he could not have been more gracious. Furthermore he facilitated the microfilming of hundreds of Delbrück's papers, sent to me in Waterport months later for a very modest cost. After a few days my fears about not getting back to the West faded.

In sum, within the Deutsche Staatsbibliothek there was no Cold War. Or were the East Germans just happy to have an American working on Hans Delbrück? Not infrequently in those days American historians were refused admission to the East German archives, with no reasons given. Delbrück's last decade of scholarly work, after all, had been very critical of imperial Germany. Hans Mehring, the great socialist writer of the prewar era, had praised the *History of the Art of War* in no uncertain terms: quoting Delbrück's passage describing the triumph of Roman civilization over the barbarians, he said nowhere was it more clearly demonstrated that the means of production had a decisive impact in war.[4]

The other requirement for using the Delbrück papers was family consent. For access, one needed to obtain permission from Frau Helene Hobe, one of Delbrück's daughters, who lived in Berlin. Frau Hobe not only granted access in 1971 but in 1974 invited me into her apartment, providing me with weeks of time to ask questions about her father, the family, and the past of her country. She shared the traditions of Prussian parsimony with me during sparse dinners and teas. Documents in her personal possession included more than a hundred letters written by Carl von Clausewitz to Count Neithardt von Gneisenau, loaned to her father during the time he was completing the Gneisenau biography, as well as other family letters and papers. She was most generous, and I very much appreciate her going out of her way on my behalf. Her sisters and son, Dr. Hans Christoph Hobe of Bremen, have also been helpful.

During the spring of 1970 I wrote a long essay on Alfred Vagts, author of the first and most famous *History of Militarism*.[5] I wrote to Vagts, initiating a correspondence that lasted nearly to his death in 1986. Vagts was the essential primary witness for Delbrück's Berlin University world. Born in 1891, attending university at Hamburg and Munich, serving as a mortar platoon officer in World War I, on the periphery of the

Munich revolutions of the early 1920s, working for Albert Mendelssohn-Bartholdy's Hamburg Institute of International Politics as he completed the second dissertation necessary to teach in a German university, Vagts experienced the last twenty years of Delbrück's life, much of it intimately. He left Germany at Christmastime 1932 to marry the daughter of Charles and Mary Beard, the well-known American historians, and he and his wife, Miriam, lived in New Milford and Sherman, Connecticut. As I began work on Delbrück, I had fewer questions about Vagts and more about Delbrück. Vagts filled in the context from his own life, sending me offprints of reviews, articles, and essays and dozens of letters describing his own experiences in Delbrück's milieu, German scholarly life.

I finished the dissertation in 1972, and it took another decade to make a book. The main problem was Wilhelmian German, forbiddingly clothed in its Fraktur script that even some contemporary Germans will not read. To bring this material to a contemporary audience, it is necessary to go down into it but then to come back out of it into American English. It was a long road. My wife, Sue Ann, struggled valiantly with my thick translations of the 1970s. My colleague, John Kutolowski, worked for weeks through this thick soup in the early 1980s. Both helped liberate me from the heavy gravitational pull of Wilhelmian German. After *Hans Delbrück and the German Military Establishment* was finished in 1985, I turned to Delbrück's great contemporary, Alfred Count Schlieffen, and the writers within the general staff who had so strongly opposed Delbrück's war history.[6] Along the way toward *Moltke, Schlieffen, and Prussian War Planning* I lectured on Delbrück and modern military history, summing up what was known, but I knew I had to go further.[7] A sabbatical leave granted by the State University of New York during spring and summer 1994 allowed the project to move forward.

Since 1985 little has been published on Delbrück. Only occasionally has any scholar in the Atlantic world tackled his work or life,[8] and there is a great deal left to do. I hope this sample whets the historical imagination of some younger historians coming along. With Germany reunited, the wall and East Germany no longer extant, visitors to the rich Delbrück papers need not confront any of the anxieties I had in the 1970s. The way is open.

Arden Bucholz
Waterport, New York
January 1996

# Acknowledgments

Sue Tally Bucholz for insight, sharing, love, support, and the best kind of companionship; for the early morning Lake Ontario walks and late evening dinners after the stars are out.

Bill McNeill for reading the rough draft on Delbrück's life with his usual rapid, economical, honest, and supportive response.

Kempes Schnell, Steve Ireland, John Kutolowski, and Neil Johnson for reading and commenting on several drafts of the essay on Delbrück's life and work and listening to the book proposal many times.

Our former SUNY Brockport history chairman Ken O'Brien and colleagues on the Governance Committee, Bob Smith, Bob Marcus, Jim Horn, and John Butz, for supporting the sabbatical in spring semester 1994.

Our current history chairman, Bob Smith, for helping maintain an environment in which scholarship can go forward and for providing a Macintosh Performa and Hewlett Packard printer to speed that scholarship.

The Deutsche Staatsbibliothek, Berlin, and Bundesarchiv, Koblenz, for sending a large quantity of the Delbrück papers on microfilm.

Bob Gilliam of Drake Library Interlibrary Loan for tracking down and obtaining hundreds of books and articles.

Holger Herwig for a surprisingly valuable publisher's reading.

The family of Hans Delbrück, especially Hans Christian Hobe of Bremen, for answering questions, loaning photographs, and staying in touch these past twenty-five years.

Copyeditor Kimberley Vivier for improving the manuscript in many ways.

Without their help, encouragement, criticism, and suggestions this work would not have reached completion. Whatever errors remain are my responsibility.

# Note on Translation

The twenty-four selections in this volume are mainly Delbrück's unknown writings. They are not really translations but musings on Delbrück's writings as I see them. In working them out, I adhere to the dictum laid down by Helen T. Lowe-Porter, translator of so much of the work of Thomas Mann. "It is necessary," she said, "to set oneself the bold task of transferring the spirit first and the letter so far as might be. Above all, to make certain that the work of art, coming as it does to the ear in German, like music out of the past, should in English at least not come like a translation, which is, God bless us, a thing of naught."[1]

I have taken great liberties of form and of content with these pieces of German, bringing to bear on them my knowledge of Delbrück's life and work, trying to reconstruct the total image and situation that is conveyed through the limiting possibilities of language.[2] Above all, I have kept in mind a contemporary audience. In fact this work is not, strictly speaking, a translation. I have edited, leaving out the ellipsis marks of omission. I have rearranged order, used wide discretion in word choice, altered tenses. I have added words needed for clarity and deleted words that confused and obfuscated. My single goal is to make Delbrück's ideas, clothed in formal, scholarly Wilhelmian German, understandable to today's audience. Delbrück expresses his thoughts in sticky, highly echeloned grammar. Reading his work in the original often makes contemporary Americans feel as if they are moving through a still pond of molasses. I have stripped away the conventions, peeled back the layers of structure to reveal the essence of his ideas as I understand them from nearly three decades of study. German-language purists will rightly be taken aback. But, to return to Lowe-Porter's metaphor, I hope readers will be able to appreciate Delbrück as they do Mozart.

# Introduction: Delbrück's Life and Work

For his gravestone in the Halensee Cemetery, Berlin, Hans Delbrück (1848–1929) wrote this epitaph: "I sought the truth. I loved my country." As the first modern military historian, Delbrück reflected in his work and life exactly this tension between knowledge and patriotism.

## The Making of a Historian, 1848–1881

*Family and Education*
His childhood and school days witnessed uncertainty, humiliation, and disappointment for his country, Prussia, and stress, disability, and finally death for his family.[1] Born 11 November 1848, the eldest son of passionate democrats, Hans Delbruck absorbed their dreams for a liberal national German state and their horror at its failure. His father, Berthold Delbrück, from an academic and bureaucratic family close to the throne in central Germany (a grandfather was executor of the University of Halle, and an uncle had tutored Prince Frederick Wilhelm IV, later king of Prussia), had moved the year before the revolutions to Rügen, an island off coastal Pomerania. Berthold's passion was tax law, for which Greifswald University awarded him an honorary doctorate a year before his early death.

His mother, Laura von Henning, was the eldest daughter of a Berlin philosophy professor who had been the favorite student of Hegel and held a patent of nobility granted under the Holy Roman Empire in the seventeenth century. Her passion was music, especially Brahms. At home the Delbrücks sang, played piano, and entertained such musically inclined friends as Professor Julius Planck (Max Planck's father), Professor Karl von Noorden, and their wives. The local university professors, chemist Ruhle and archaeologists Limpricht and Michaelis, were known as "Laura's singing companions." They had a cook, one servant, and a cleaning girl who lived in. Evenings the family read aloud such books as Alexander Dumas's *History of Napoleon* and Goethe's *Natural Daughter*.[2] During Delbrück's school days in the 1860s the family was hostile to Bismarck, rejoicing in September 1862 when the Prussian Landtag defeated the military bill. Berthold thought Bismarck a kind of laughingstock. When Hans and his younger brother Max took target practice in the backyard, the bull's-eye was a bust of the Iron Chancellor.[3]

When Hans was ten his father was diagnosed with tuberculosis. By 1860 Berthold stayed home, then was put on a respirator, and finally in 1868 died, during Hans's one year of service in the army. Before he died, Berthold went into extreme depression. His wife was serene through it all.[4] Laura gathered the children around her dead husband and addressed them. "This is your father." she said, "who is now dead." To her husband she said, "Thank you, dear, for all the happiness you gave us." She closed his eyes. Everyone cried. She and the children faithfully attended the *Totenfest* (memorial service). She and Hans found it ghastly. Whoever was not orthodox, she said, had to give up the whole thing! With her family background, marriage at seventeen, and a lack of education, she could not work. Laura planned to auction their house, but just before she sold it, her sister-in-law's family bought it and put her and the six children in the upper floor.[5]

Delbrück moved out of his family into the world in four great steps. In 1867 as his father was dying, he left home for the Royal Prussian and North German Rifle Defenders of the Fatherland as a one-year volunteer, paying for his own room, board, and uniforms. The peacetime army apparently made little impression on him. In May 1868 he returned home for the funeral and in early June left military service. His Berlin godmother, Ida von Kahlden, provided a stipend for him to spend the summer studying at Heidelberg University. Hans had attended public school in Greifswald and fallen in love with history: he told his parents he liked it better than play.

With his military service completed and his father dead, Delbrück chose Greifswald, the cheapest university and one close to home. He spent the winter and summer of 1869 there. Then his mother's close friend Noorden told him to go to Bonn and study with Heinrich von Sybel, and in the fall of 1869 he did so.[6] His uncles, who thought Bonn too expensive, nonetheless paid his way. At the time, Sybel was a leading member of the Prussian school of history. In 1859 he had founded the *Historische Zeitschrift*, the first scholarly historical periodical to survive to the present day.[7] His *History of German Nationalism* championed German nationalism under Prussian leadership. Noorden told Hans, "Do an important piece of research for Sybel as soon as you get there." Delbrück learned English, studied Greek tragedy, wrote essays in French, researched the sources for the history of Rome, and studied German constitutional history.

An outsider at Bonn, Delbrück did not join a student society but went his own way, writing that these fraternities were exactly what he sought to avoid. He did not like the lectures he heard. Athough engaging to listen to, they were full of false pathos, romance, and nostalgia. Friedrich Lange's *History of Materialism* convinced him that truth itself was unknowable.[8] On the one hundredth birthday of Ernst Moritz Arndt, fellow Rügen Islander and passionate nationalist of the Napoleonic era, Delbrück gave a talk to the "nonassociated" students. It was wrong, he said, to measure the value of an idea by experience. One idea can only be measured against another. And ideas are differentiated from phantoms, fancies, and whims by their power to control human behavior. For an idea to become dominant, it had to make an impact on the human soul. Everything, he concluded—art, literature, history, and religion— rested on ideas.[9]

In July 1870 he went to war with the Twenty-eighth Rhineland Infantry Regiment. His mother's youngest brother, Peter von Henning, also fought. At Sedan, on 2 September, Peter was wounded and his right leg amputated. He died in October.[10] Hans survived but, as his letters attest, experienced horrible sights and great terror (reading 1). The battlefield at Saarbrücken was littered with bodies, Prussian and French, as far as the eye could see. Three days after the fighting, few had been buried, leaving a ghastly sight and a foul stench. At Gravelotte men died beside him and in front of him. Bringing up reserves, Delbrück had to force them to move forward with drawn sword. He concluded that only discipline forced soldiers into battle and began to see how a small Greek army could triumph over the Persian hordes. He wrote to his mother in October from Liehon, France, signing his letter "Royal Prussian lieutenant."[11] It was the last letter he wrote before almost dying of typhoid fever. By early January he was out of danger. The last bit of idle theorizing had been scraped off, he wrote to a friend. His idealism was strengthened. He had seen reality.

Convalescence at home slowly restored his strength. He read the *Prussian Yearbook* (*Preusissher Jahrbücher*), which, like Fritz Fischer a century later, he called the most important journal of political commentary in the new German state. He wrote his doctoral dissertation.[12] His subject, Lambert von Herzfeld, an eleventh-century chronicler, had hitherto been viewed as a credible and important source for his era. Delbrück took him apart, piece by piece, demonstrating the degree of uncertainty, impossibility, and fable in his writings.

During the summer of 1872 he became associated with the European nobility at its highest levels. He was employed as tutor to the crown prince of Sweden, who was living at the princess of Wied's Schloss Monrepos at Neuwied, a few miles outside Bonn. There he was instructed in the arts of court life by the ladies in waiting and established relationships with princes, high officers, and officials.

By 1873 Delbrück was again seeking a job. He had graduated from Bonn University, "maxima cum laude," with the first dissertation in the philosophy faculty written and defended in German rather than Latin. He began to learn Russian. He took the examination for gymnasium teacher and wrote a short book on the wars of religion but found no publisher. Finally, he took a position as tutor in the Berlin family of Frau von Wedel, friends of his mother's and well-connected members of court society.[13] He attended the Berlin ball season, which began the day after the kaiser's birthday and ended the first Tuesday before Lent.[14] It was during a ball in 1874 that Professor Rudolf Virchow, the famed pathologist, asked him to tutor in the family of the crown prince of Prussia.[15]

At first he was inclined to turn the offer down, since he was still teaching in the Wedel family. But his mother, Karl von Noorden, and Hermann Grimm, son of the fairy-tale collector Wilhelm and a professor of art history at the University of Berlin, thought he should give it a try: it would open new possibilities.[16] From his two previous jobs he was comfortable with the high nobility: he knew what to wear, how to act, and what to say. He interviewed Baron von Roggenbach, Colonel Mischke, Count Götz von Seckendorff, and Countess Reventlow. He drank champagne with some, took tea and ate beefsteak with others. He asked about conditions. He would live in an apartment next to Prince Waldemar, at the time five years old, take walks with him, tutor the prince for an hour and his sister, Princess Charlotte, for two hours. He would eat with the court ladies, be paid five hundred thalers for the year, and receive the interest from two hundred thalers after the first year. He was to make no public utterances.[17] He was interviewed by the crown prince and princess. The princess, eldest daughter of Queen Victoria, spoke German with the same accent as Karl von Noorden's wife: they were both English. In early May 1874, returned from maneuvers with his regiment in Wittenberg, Delbrück lunched with his father's cousin Rudolf Delbrück, Bismarck's chief assistant as president of the Imperial Chancellory.[18] He got a sense of royal affairs and a hint of the importance of the crown prince and princess: not much! He was present while Princess Charlotte was examined by her parents in geography, mathematics, and history, and he wondered if there was a good book for the education of young ladies. He renegotiated the terms of service, increasing the salary. After all, the crown prince finally agreed, "Delbrück was my war comrade" (they had both fought in 1870).[19] The last thing he did before entering royal service was to go on maneuvers with his regiment. Obtaining a copy of Wilhelm Rüstow's *History of Infantry* from the regimental library, Delbrück said that from that time on he never again lost sight of the subject.[20]

## Royal Tutor

The Prussian court Delbrück joined for the next five years was a foreign country. In the first place it was very wealthy. In the developing German economy of the early 1870s great captains of industry had yet to overtake royalty in grandiloquent living. Despite Wilhelm I's parsimony, his son and especially his daughter-in-law, who came from one of Europe's richest royal families, looked opulent. The Neues Palais, where they resided in Potsdam, was Frederick the Great's masterpiece of 1780 with nearly a hundred rooms.[21] There were many others, including Schloss Babelsberg, Sans Souci, and the crown prince's palace in Berlin. The family dressed in silks and satins and was attended by a large entourage and staff.

Second, it was an Anglo-German household. The English side was represented by the crown princess, Queen Victoria's strong-willed eldest daughter. She sought to re-create her own family culture, guided by memories of physical and intellectual perfection, political liberalism, and English language and culture. In contrast to many female royalty of this period, she took herself seriously as an adult "mover and shaker." In fact, she dominated the marriage.[22] Family life developed a fracture: her eldest son, later Kaiser Wilhelm II, spoke English to his mother and German to his father. Unconventional gender relationships further confused the marriage. Delbrück, used to a dominant woman—his mother—was not at all put off. His school English improved dramatically, as Victoria loved to talk politics and religion. By the 1890s, when he met Lord Acton in Berlin, he spoke good English.[23]

The German side was represented by everything else. The court resided in Prussian Germany, the German language predominated, and the customs of the Prussian court were generally followed. In spite of its wealth and schizophrenia, these were familiar patterns for the twenty-six-year-old who had tutored in the courts of Sweden and in the homes of Berlin nobility. Four years after achieving unification by war this German court was filled with high officers and war veterans. Prussian kings, including Frederick the Great, had always worn military uniforms, but for several generations after 1807 the military was not in high repute and the middle class spurned it as a career path. After 1870 everything changed. The army's great feats covered soldiers with honors. Delbrück, a war veteran among war veterans, fit in well with these celebrities.

On 17 May 1874 Delbrück became royal tutor.[24] He had more leisure time during the next five years than at any point before or after. He was advised to look as elegant as possible whenever at court. He resided at the Neues Palais, Potsdam, and worked with two young and pretty governesses. At seven-thirty in the morning he drank coffee. At nine he had soup with cold roast and wine. Tutoring was done between then and one. At two was dinner with the court ladies at the Hofmarshal's table, a walk, then five o'clock tea with the children at Bornstedt. He played croquet and had long conversations with the crown princess. Although he called her a liberal in public, he said privately that she had some strange ideas about religion. In the evening there was tea with the full court in formal dress and an hour of conversation and music. Delbrück learned to ride. He had lengthy discussions with the crown prince's adjutants, mainly war veterans such as Field Marshal Count Karl Leonhard Blumenthal, General Leo von Caprivi, and General Friedrich Karl von Fransecky. He wrote later that these five years were a virtual war academy of military instruction from more than a dozen high-ranking officers.[25]

He got to know Prince Wilhelm, who was growing up during these years from age fourteen to nineteen. Delbrück retained this relationship up to World War I: in June 1914 the kaiser and the professor conversed at length about threatening possibilities during a social luncheon.[26] Wilhelm's left arm was so short and his left hand so weak that the young man could hold the reins of a horse but not pull them. He could not cut his food at the table. But he had a "very princely walk, while his brother Prince Henry walked like a commoner." When the old kaiser came to dinner, he arrived at the door at the exact stroke of the clock. The whole family met him, but at the door stood a guard and, before the kaiser greeted the family, he returned the salute of the soldier.[27]

Delbrück traveled with the court. In the summer they went to the Isle of Wight to visit Victoria's mother at Osborne. He found Queen Victoria tyrannical and very little liked. Yet here, he said, "I can see what a real court is like." He hid behind a bush while the children said their good mornings to her. He saw the legendary Elizabeth, empress of Austria, whose beauty, he remarked, was now about gone.[28]

Under royal auspices Delbrück began to think about a university career. He talked with Karl von Normann, private secretary to the crown prince, about a Berlin University appointment, bypassing the initial lecturer stage. Delbrück got along well at court. Most of all he liked Countess Hedwig von Brühl, granddaughter of Count Neithardt von Gneisenau, military hero of the wars against Napoleon.[29] Delbrück had graduated in history, and his mother's closest friend was a historian. As he began to cast about for topics for the second dissertation needed to qualify for university faculty, he came on an unfinished book that had already achieved some notoriety. In the fall of 1876 Brühl asked him to complete the biography of her grandfather, Gneisenau, begun years before by the recently deceased Georg Heinrich Pertz. He accepted, obtaining an advance from the Berlin publisher Georg Stilke. To finish it, he used all the resources of his position, taking out books from the crown prince's library and documents from the state archive in the crown prince's name. During trips with the royal family to England, Scotland, Austria, Italy, and France he carefully checked out European archives. In July 1877 the king of Belgium loaned the family a house at Ostend, and Delbrück visited nearby battlefields. He used materials gathered years before by General von Fransecky, as well as new sources such as the parole book at the Fortress of Kolberg during its siege.[30] He and Colonel Mischke walked across the battlefields at Belle Alliance and Ligny on the way to London. He talked artillery with Field Marshal Count Blumenthal, the crown prince's chief of staff in 1866. Leopold von Ranke, to whom he sent his first published essay in 1878, wrote back with advice about the Gneisenau biography. What are you going to do with the parts already written? Ranke asked. He believed Pertz had included too much in his first draft and that the continuation must focus on the really important things. He sent along an edition of his collected works, "to pass along to your prince." "The prince will see, Ranke emphasized, "that the second part is all new!"[31]

In late May 1878 there was an attempt on the kaiser's life. In early June the second attempt badly wounded the kaiser, and the crown prince had to take over his duties for six months.[32] Later that year Delbrück tried to resign, but the royal family would not have it. He renegotiated the terms of employment, gaining eighteen hundred thalers, and raised the possibility of rapid promotion to full professor once on the university faculty.

On 11 November 1878 nine-year-old Prince Waldemar appeared at two in the morning at Delbrück's bedside—the room next door—with a new pair of ice skates. "Herr Doctor, it's your birthday, congratulations!" The next spring, while Delbrück was away on maneuvers, young Waldemar caught diphtheria and died in a few days. Delbrück was badly shaken. Prince Henry consoled him from Yokohama, Japan, with his own grief, anguishing over losing his "shadow," as "Waldy" had styled himself to his seventeen-year-old brother. Delbrück dedicated his first book to and named his first child after his young charge. His first daughter's middle name was Victoria.[33]

## The Critic of Military History, 1881–1904

In 1881 Delbrück took the fourth and final step out from his family. With his young pupil dead he published the first two volumes of the Gneisenau biography. It was written in the "life and letters" style, with lengthy quotations from Gneisenau's letters interspersed with Delbrück's comments and conclusions. Now he felt qualified for a university position. Using royal leverage, he was ready to assault the university. Since he was a war veteran among veterans, whose first book dealt with a military hero, in an era of enormous prestige for soldiers, he naturally thought about military history. As he got into it, he discovered a strange situation.

The crown prince's staff pressed the Prussian cultural affairs ministry for a midlevel appointment as associate professor in military history, passing over the beginning rank of lecturer. In spite of lack of tenure and a token salary, titles were extraordinarily significant in nineteenth-century Germany. "Professor," although not denoting nobility or military rank, was probably third on the list of most coveted. To go from "princely tutor" in the crown prince of Prussia's household, which opened doors and granted access, to lecturer in the university was clearly a step down. He expected a professorship.

The ministry consulted the faculty. The faculty members opposed it: one had to begin at the bottom. They were hostile: military history was not a recognized subject of university study. If anyone should be hired to teach it, they suggested an officer from the general staff. They reacted negatively to royal meddling. But Delbrück was finally hired, perhaps without the faculty's concurrence. The university could not thwart the crown completely; it was a royal Prussian institution, after all. That Heinrich von Sybel, Delbrück's *doktorvater*, was at Berlin and that Friedrich Althoff, powerful Prussian minister of culture, had been attracted by Delbrück's earliest publications undoubtedly aided his cause. Delbrück was appointed lecturer in universal history in the fall of 1881.[34]

Right from the beginning Delbrück was an upstart. His inaugural lecture, attended by faculty and officials, was entitled "The Battle of Napoleon with Old Europe." The dean, who sat in the front row, was incensed: Delbrück had not been appointed to teach military history, so why did he lecture on it? Delbrück retained and strengthened his ties to crown, court, and high nobility. If the faculty had voted against him, he would have asked the crown prince to appeal to the ministry again.[35] In the summer of 1884 he and his new bride, Lina Thiersch, attended the cornerstone laying of the new Reichstag. They were seated by the Hofmarshal very close to old Kaiser Wilhelm I.[36] When Delbrück visited Rome on holiday, the crown princess invited him to breakfast. He met the king of Italy and had a lively conversation with him in French. Campaigning for a Reichstag seat in Rügen, he stayed with estate owners. When Prince Putbus attended his speech and sat among the commoners, Delbrück wrote his mother that twenty years earlier such a thing would never have happened.[37]

At the burial of Leopold von Ranke in 1886 Heinrich von Treitschke was scheduled to give the address but at the last moment asked Delbrück to do it. The speech created a stir. Why is Ranke not a popular historian? Delbrück asked. It was not because he was difficult to read but because he was out of step with his times. In 1824 his first books were models of objective history. But at the time, the German public did not want objectivity. It was conflicted by the great tension between provincialism and nationalism. Patriotic idealism, awakened by the uprising against Napoleon, evoked energy and passion—the opposite of deliberate, calm objectivity. Delbrück concluded that many had never read Ranke then or now.[38]

Delbrück did not set out to change the rules and rewrite the substance of military history. His naturally independent and critical nature, combined with opposition to his appointment, hostility to his lectures, and attacks on his writings, propelled him in novel directions.

What was the status of military history in Germany in 1881?

War was an aberration to the professoriat. Military history did not exist as a humanistic discipline to be taught, written about, and argued over by university scholars. If included at all, it was as an afterthought to politics. The causes and consequences were dealt with, but not the killing or the battles. German professors of the first half of the nineteenth century revered the ancient historians, the Greeks and Romans. They looked to Herodotus, Thucydides, Xenophon, Polybius, and Arrian as sacred texts whose venerability was almost biblical. What did the professors' accounts of ancient military history look like? They were full of vague, orally transmitted fables, embedded in narratives considered of classic beauty. Unwilling to criticize the latter, the professoriat accepted the former.

Thus, as Delbrück pointed out in "A Little Military History," War Academy teacher Max Duncker had a Greek force of eight hundred thousand operating in a land area insufficient for an army one-tenth that size (reading 3). Carelessness about military realities carried over into modern history as well. The magnificent portrait of the wars of Louis XIV by Delbrück's mentor, Karl von Noorden, contained so many mistakes at the militarily decisive points, Delbrück said, that it was impossible to understand how Europe could have withstood the Sun King. Johann Gustav Droysen's otherwise unsurpassed biography of York von Wartenburg was so deficient in its military aspects that it described Blucher making the same march twice.[39] Heinrich von Sybel, Delbrück's *doktorvater*, and the director of the Prussian State Archives, who thought he had portrayed Frederick the Great as a hero, made so many errors in describing his wars that readers could only conclude Frederick was a buffoon lacking all strategic fundamentals.[40]

That Delbrück publicly criticized his own scholarly mentors suggests that deference to people or positions and reverence for historical tradition were not part of his makeup. Professors, full of respect for the classical authors, projected their romantic idealism onto the military past. For Delbrück, it did not work.

Ancient historians of that day tended to treat war with heroic metaphor. In their view the army of Julius Caesar succeeded because a genius led it. For Theodor Mommsen, Caesar was the entire and perfect man; T. Rice Holmes thought Caesar the greatest man of action who ever lived. For this generation, Caesar was the apotheosis of a superman. [41]

For Delbrück, Caesar did not triumph over Ariovistus or Vercingetorix, but rather Roman civilization defeated German civilization. Culture triumphed over barbarism. "Not only were the organization and management of the army crucial, but so were the technical and material aspects of Roman culture undergirding it. Roman military success came from the ability to bring a large mass together in one place, to move it in formation, to supply and maintain it together for a long time. These things the Gauls could not do. This was the creation of a higher culture." [42]

Military history per se, that is, tactics, operations, and strategy, was the province of the army. From the beginning of the Prussian general staff in the early nineteenth century, military history had been central. A separate bureau was created for it, and general staff officers were expected to lecture, research, and write. The War Academy and Berlin University, both founded in 1810, were next door to each other, and professors from the university often taught at the academy. The results of their study appeared as lectures, as the basis for war games, as articles in the *Military Weekly*, and as books published by the Berlin firm of E. S. Mittler. [43]

Whereas the professors taught politics but excluded war, the soldiers taught war but excluded politics. Indeed, everything beyond the battlefield was left out in favor of the details of practical military life: mathematical knowledge of topography, mechanical descriptions of weapons, and long quotations from general orders (reading 4). Officers, like professors, projected their daily experiences and professional ideals onto the military past.

Overwhelmed by the sudden, unexpected, and astonishing success of the wars of German unification, 1864–70, general staff historians wrote the history of these campaigns soon after they ended, publishing a volume on the Danish war, two volumes on the Austrian war, and seven volumes on the war against France. As Helmuth von Moltke confided, in writing volumes intended for the general public so soon after the wars had ended and the dead were buried, they could tell the truth but not the whole truth.[44] With these volumes finished, the officers turned to the wars of Frederick the Great. In doing so, they applied Moltke's successful strategy from the wars of German unification: Frederick the Great and Moltke had used the same strategy! Anything but a war of annihilation they believed invalid and illegitimate. Attack and destroy became the war paradigm. This revisionism began in the late 1870s, and twenty years later the general staff image was considered standard within the army: it had replaced reality.

Delbrück could hardly believe this interpretation. All historians knew that material circumstances limited Frederick the Great's strategy, he wrote. Factors of size, space, and time had been fundamentally different in the eighteenth century. Frederick's small, long-service professional army; the lengthy training of the men, who were expected to fear their officers more than the enemy; and the huge casualties—sometimes 40 percent of those engaged—meant that Frederick fought as seldom as possible. The contrast with Napoleon and Moltke, Delbrück emphasized, could not be greater. Their armies were several times larger and made up of many citizen soldiers who had a stake in the political outcome of the war. They marched faster on better roads and provisioned themselves by seizing supplies along the way. Eighteenth-century generals often obtained results without fighting, by using maneuver, blockade, or siege. Neither Napoleon nor Moltke could use this approach. In a statement that provoked the officers' lasting enmity, Delbrück noted that even Carl von Clausewitz had recognized that Frederick regarded battle as an evil to be avoided except in necessity.

Delbrück's civilian, middle-class criticism of "official" history irritated the noble officers. They assumed they were the sole legitimate specialists to write military history. They had fought past wars, experienced contemporary military life, and assumed responsibility for future conflict. Their legitimacy and authority in society rested in part on their claim to military knowledge.[45] To invoke Clausewitz, the Bible of official theory, was an outrage!

Delbrück rejected the officers' claims. If it were true that only those with experience could legitimately write about the past, he noted, most historians—Herodotus, Thucydides, Ranke, the whole lot—became invalid. Historical reconstruction, difficult under the best of circumstances, became impossible if only those with experience could write it. The claims of practical knowledge and technical competence had to be heard, but as one voice among many.

Like the professors, the officers had their sacred texts. Knowledge of past wars is always bonded in blood. Army historians believed they had an institutionalized, professional responsibility to honor the dead and wounded of the wars they described. Armies are large public monopolies created and maintained primarily to compete against each other on future battlefields. At the outermost bounds of this competition one or both of the organizations will suffer some degree of death. Because armies serve as instruments of death, and because of their size and the way they command the loyalties of their society, they are unique among the organizations of human social life. Death always clouds objective "scientific" knowledge of past war.

In reconstructing the past, regimental historians were mindful of this. By describing honorable and courageous behavior in the past, they hoped to inspire it in the future. The paradigm of courage was a necessity in the face of the deepest and most fundamental fact of war, which was death. Men in combat needed to believe that war was endurable, an activity that earned soldiers honor and praise, even if it also killed them.

War history was vital to the new German state in other ways as well. War had created the Second Reich. Its legitimacy depended on the integrity of the image of its creation. Past and future were also linked by the German war plan. During the forty-four years between the last war of German unification in 1870 and the outbreak of World War I in 1914, Europe suffered no wars. Alfred von Schlieffen, the man who dominated German war planning processes after 1891, repeatedly told his colleagues, "We must study the past to gain the knowledge which the present refuses to give us."[46]

During these forty-four years war technology—weapons, transportation, and communication—changed decisively. Machine guns, high-velocity long-range artillery, railroads, telegraph and telephone, the airplane, barbed wire, and more contributed to a high-technology arms race fueled by imperialist and capitalist competition in a climate of ethnic social Darwinism.

Confronting these changes and attempting to integrate the new technology into future war plans, armies faced a classic problem: the impossibility of testing the plans, of finding out how the new technology worked. In place of combat, in which men kill, die, and react to death, peacetime maneuvers and war games were an imperfect substitute. Death and response to it could not be simulated. Confronted by this classic enigma, European armies disregarded, underestimated, and misunderstood the new technologies. Ultimately they fell back on tradition: the rifle and bayonet charge delivered by densely packed infantry remained the foundation of tactics and operations.[47] Except for Ivan S. Bloch, whose 1899 book *The Future of War* clearly described what was coming, few practitioners or commentators foresaw the impact of new military technologies.[48] German casualties in the six-week combat of 1870 were forty-three thousand killed and one hundred thousand wounded. No one could imagine a fifty-two-month war with two million dead and almost six million wounded.

Delbrück based his first published writings on the assumption that Frederick the Great had fought with the strategy of attrition, the paradigmatic eighteenth-century strategic form. Professional officers criticized these assumptions: Frederick had fought with the strategy of annihilation just as Moltke had done in the wars of German unification. They stamped Delbrück as illegitimate: a civilian without professional expertise could not validly write military history.[49] This opposition awakened Delbrück to the special features of government-sponsored, bureaucratically written military history. From that time until his death he and the officers fought it out.

Of what did Delbrück's military history consist? Right from the start his work sharply contrasted to the existing historical tradition, both academic and military. "German historical science," as Delbrück often called academic history, was by no means insignificant in 1881. But its methods of reconstruction may surprise us.

It was not the cold, dispassionate chronicle that is sometimes associated with Leopold von Ranke, the so-called father of scientific history. German scholars of the first half of the nineteenth century used Enlightenment rationalism, based on careful research in primary sources, but in constructing their images of the past they then took an intuitive leap into the dark, following romantic idealism. Their results astonished them! As Barthold Niebuhr described it, historians could make a complete picture from separate fragments by knowing where the parts were missing and filling them in. No one believes, he said, how much of what seems lost can be restored.[50] Wilhelm von Humboldt described two stages in writing history: first, an exact, impartial, and critical examination of the events, and second, intuiting that which was still unknown.[51] For Ranke, historical understanding began with meticulous research and study of the documents. After that the historian approached the "spiritual essence through an act of intuition."[52]

Like Niebuhr, Humboldt, and Ranke, Delbrück began with the sources. And he also used his own ideas, sometimes imagining what must have happened. But like Count Leo Tolstoy, whose *War and Peace* was published just as Delbrück was becoming a professional historian, he added to sources and intuition exact, technical details of military life, often from the bottom up. His focus on the material circumstances described by the sources was tempered by his own experience. Some examples illustrate the striking parallels between Tolstoy and Delbrück.

Tolstoy, describing the battle of Austerlitz (1806):

> At five o'clock in the morning it was still quite dark. The troops in the center, the reserves, and Bagrations' right flank, had not yet moved, but on the left flank the columns of infantry, cavalry and artillery that were to be the first to descend from the heights to attack the French right flank, and, according to the disposition, to drive it back into the Bohemian Highlands, were already up and stirring. The smoke of the campfires, into which everything superfluous was being thrown, made the eyes smart. It was cold and dark. The officers were hurriedly drinking tea and breakfasting, the soldiers were crowded around the fires munching rusks and beating a tattoo with their feet to warm themselves. They made firewood of the remains of the huts, chairs, tables, wheels, tubs, everything they did not need or that could not be taken away.[53]

Delbrück, describing the battle of Gravelotte (1870):

> Whoever said that hell is falsely painted was right. It is a paradise compared with a night bivouac in torrential downpour, with nothing to eat or drink, lying on the ground without wood or straw. In spite of great tiredness, we cannot sleep. Gradually, as we spend more and more of these nights, we are losing our good humor. Luckily, one night there was some milk, the second night a few fires were built. But now, when everyone wants above all to dry out, our endurance must be built up for more such nights.[54]

Tolstoy, writing about combat units in battle:

> A soldier on the march is as encompassed, confined and borne along by his regiment as a sailor by his ship. However far he goes, whatever strong, unknown and dan-

gerous regions he may penetrate—just as the sailor is always surrounded by the same decks, masts and rigging of his ship, so the soldier has always and everywhere the same comrades, the same ranks, the same Sergeant Major Ivan Mitrich, the same company dog Zhuchka, the same officers. The soldier is like the sailor, who rarely cares to know the latitude in which his ship is sailing, and yet on the day of a battle—God knows how or whence it comes—in the moral atmosphere of the troops the same stern note is heard by all, sounding the approach of something solemn and crucial, and awaking in them an unwonted curiosity. . . . the soldiers became aware that in front, behind, and on all sides, other Russian columns were moving in the same direction. Every soldier was heartened by knowing that wherever it was that he was going, many, many more of our men were going too.[55]

Delbrück, dealing with the same topic:

The tactical body is made up of individuals as the human body is made up of atoms. But as little as the human body is identical to the sum of its atoms, so the tactical body is not just the sum of the fighters that make it up. It is a spiritual organism, built of individuals but which in battle symbolizes and becomes the power of them all. It is the unity of the will of the multitude. The individual draws on the complete energy of his will and submits to the will of the body. . . . It cannot be created quickly or by legislation. It takes time, work, and routine. Its members must be so close that their fear of death is overcome by their allegiance to the tactical unit.[56]

Both sought to describe war from the inside out, as well as from the outside in. They wrote as practitioners experienced it but added all the technical data—machinery, time, space, size—that outside observers see. For Tolstoy as novelist, this approach continued to work well until his personal crisis of the 1880s.[57] For Delbrück, it worked as long as he was dealing with the distant past or as long as his own experience was fresh in his mind and he had access to recent technical knowledge: he retired from the army as a reserve captain in about 1885. In time and with rapidly advancing technology, his understanding changed. When he ventured into contemporary defense criticism, beginning in about 1904, things got stickier. But he still had a sure touch, because the sources were valid and plentiful, and if there was secrecy or propaganda, he could see around or through it. And he was still mainly a disinterested observer.

During two decades of peace, 1881–1901, Delbrück critiqued traditional writing on war and began to define modern military history. He published four books and several hundred essays and reviews. His work met ferocious opposition. Officers and conservatives accused him of insulting Frederick the Great and distorting Clausewitz. Classicists said he disregarded the power of the Greek gods. Nevertheless gradually he began to legitimize the military as a valid subject of scholarly work. Beyond that, he developed a following among the educated laity. Nevertheless promotion to full professor was delayed. During these years he sat in the Prussian Landtag and German Reichstag and edited the *Prussian Yearbook*. These activities evoked disapproval: professors and officers agreed that journalists and political commentators were dilettantes and amateurs. Delbrück was nearly fifty when he finally achieved full professorship, and it was in world, not military, history. He was almost fired, fined, and put in jail for attacking harsh Germanization policies in Prussian Poland and Schleswig-Holstein. And during the entire period he fought a celebrated running battle, called by contemporaries the "strategie-streit," with a series of general staff historians over the strategy of Frederick the Great and the theories of Carl von Clausewitz.[58]

In 1887 Delbrück started to work on an innovative history of the wars of German unification.[59] He began by offering a lecture course on the subject. Having had discussions with many of the leading commanders and staff officers during his half-decade as royal tutor, now he directly interviewed the crown prince on his experiences and recollections. This approach was a radical departure. At the time, royalty did not appear in historical reconstruction. Official histories buffered sovereigns, using secondary figures for praise and blame. Delbrück's notes, several hundred pages, tell us a great deal about his intentions.[60] But it was too late. Before the work was completed, both the old kaiser and the young crown prince had died. In 1888 during Kaiser Wilhelm I's death week Delbrück was with the crown prince's family. He attended family and state funeral services, as well as the marriage of Prince Henry on 24 May. During the ninety-nine days of Kaiser Frederick III's reign the new emperor frequently consulted him, and many believe Delbrück was headed for a ministerial appointment. A week after the last conversation Kaiser Frederick died, and his eldest son, whom Delbrück had known as an adolescent, assumed the throne as Kaiser Wilhelm II.

## The Cold War, 1904–1914

By the turn of the century Delbrück was established in his dual profession of historian and political commentator. He had published the first volume of his great *History of the Art of War* and settled into a chair at Berlin. Borrowing money from Bankhaus Delbrück, Schickler, his uncle's bank, he had purchased the *Prussian Yearbook* and built a new house for his growing family.[61] At that point the greatest challenge of his life began.

The decade 1904–14 was the cold-war period that preceded World War I.[62] Delbrück sensed the danger of this period. But he did not fully comprehend it, and as was the case for nearly all his generation, his understanding was slow in forming, fragmented, and ultimately incomplete.

In 1905 Delbrück described the first Moroccan crisis and the Russo-Japanese War, emphasizing their strategic interrelationships (reading 5). Relying on English and Russian sources, he described the blindness of the Russians and the daring risks of the Japanese. Logistics, he wrote, was the key. The naval victory at Tsushima gave Japan command of the sea, whereas the Siberian Railroad was much too thin and long to supply the Russian war front adequately. He warned that Russia, if defeated, might turn with a vengeance to the Balkan theater, which would not bode well for Germany's ally, the Turks. He cautioned that Russia employed only 350,000 troops in Manchuria, retaining at home a standing army much larger than that of Germany and Austria-Hungary combined. He dismissed English sources which reported that in the heat of the crisis, German army leadership had proposed war against France.[63]

Delbrück did not know that Alfred von Schlieffen, chief of the Prussian general staff, had sent agents over the border into Russian Poland for a month-long reconnaissance. They ascertained that the area was virtually denuded of troops. Schlieffen undoubtedly counseled an attack against France. Only Kaiser Wilhelm II's innate timidity and the nervousness of a few high officers over French artillery prevented the execution of the Schlieffen Plan. Schlieffen saw a 960-hour "window of opportunity" between the time Germany mobilized and the point when substantial Russian forces would cross the East Prussian frontier. With most of the Russian army fighting in the Far East, this window was even larger. He planned a modern Cannae, the complete destruction of one national opponent and the annihilation of two other armies of several hundred thousand, on opposite geographical frontiers. Only railroad technology offered the possibility that this daring gamble might succeed.[64] But in 1905 it was a risk not taken.

By the time of the Bosnian crisis of 1908 Delbrück began to understand that war might break out at any time (reading 6). English, French, and Russian politicians and generals were visiting one another. The German fleet had concentrated off the Azores, and the European mass media were in a frenzy. He compared the peacetime strengths of the great powers, noting the rising storm of anti-German press in England. He emphasized the near impossibility of completely destroying and occupying France but concluded that if Serbia began a war against Austria, hopes of peace depended on Austrian restraint.[65] Although clearly recognizing the dangers, Delbrück only alluded to the countervailing partial mobilizations of Serbian, Austrian, and Russian forces and did not realize that two German ultimatums in March 1909 finally backed Russia down and ended the crisis.[66]

In 1911 during the second Moroccan crisis Delbrück directly confronted the immediate danger of war (reading 7). He warned that Europeans lived in a "discontented atmosphere" dominated by wild nationalist ambitions. He cautioned his countrymen not to bring the most terrible fate on themselves without absolute necessity. Frederick the Great's wars had been affairs of kings and princes, small and limited. But a war today would be different. National states would use the new, lethal technology to run all over one another. The Russo-Japanese War was only a minor colonial skirmish compared with a European war of the future. Economic life would come to a standstill. Oak trees would no longer bear fruit. Factories would rust as men were called away to battle. By water and land, thundering bombs and tongues of flame would destroy what generations had built. The renter would pay no more rent, the believer give no alms, the corporation pay no dividends, the state collect no taxes.[67]

Delbrück was unaware that German military attachés were reporting hourly on military preparations in France and that border crossers had been sent both east and west to report on immediate border activity. The kaiser and his general staff chief Helmuth von Moltke the younger ordered negotiations with France to continue with no breakdowns so that the upcoming army maneuvers could be held. The navy, partially alerted for war, conducted exercises while in constant touch with Berlin. France called off its maneuvers, keeping troops in camps from which they could most effectively mobilize. England canceled fleet maneuvers and held the navy in readiness for war concentration. Belgium and the Netherlands partially mobilized.[68] Moltke wrote his wife that he was fed up. If Germany once again crawled away with its tail between its legs, he would quit, abolish the army, and put the Reich under the protection of the Japanese so the Germans could concentrate on making money.[69] Again, as in 1905 and 1908, no war erupted in 1911.

By 1913 Delbrück had become thoroughly frightened (reading 8). He appealed to his readers. The greatest danger for Germany was to be seduced into war when necessity, honor, or the future of the nation was not at stake. He cautioned that a limited conflict, pitting Germany against France, was out of the question: Russia and probably also England would fight. He recognized that the centennial celebrations of Germany's 1813 war against France threatened to turn national idealism into national fanaticism.[70]

In 1912 and 1913 southeast Europe erupted with war along the frontiers of the Ottoman Empire. In October 1912 Russia ordered a highly provocative trial mobilization of its forces in Poland. In November Austria countered by putting its troops in Bosnia and Dalmatia on war footing and bringing its garrisons on the Russian frontiers up to war strength. Archduke Franz Ferdinand, Austrian heir apparent, arrived in Berlin seeking confirmation of the 1908 German pledge of support. Against this background both Germany and Russia summoned councils of state. Russian war minister V. A. Sukhomlinov said that war would occur anyway, it was unavoidable, and sooner would be better for Russia. German general staff chief Moltke told his colleagues that war was inevitable. The sooner it came the better![71]

The July 1914 crisis began as an act of traditional nineteenth-century terrorism, the grotesque, almost comic-opera assassination of visiting royalty. It ended as the modern mechanical launching of the first industrial catastrophe of global proportions. The crossing point from traditional to modern came with the forty-eight-hour Austrian ultimatum to Serbia of 6:00 P.M., Thursday, 23 July. With this event the time clock of the war plans began to tick.

In this science-based social Darwinist finale every action was quantified by time and space. As General Joseph Joffre said on 31 July, every delay of twenty-four hours in calling up reserves meant an initial abandonment of fifteen miles of territory. As opponents began to mobilize against each other, all European general staffs felt the urgency of time. When news of Russian partial mobilization reached Berlin on 26 July, German and French war planners probably ordered into effect the first two stages of their war plans, "state of security" and "political tension."

The impact of military technology on political decision making was in reality the impact of the specialist on the dilettante, of more knowledge over less or no knowledge. In worst-case scenarios political leaders deferred to military officers whose plans appeared absolute and certain because based on the mathematics of engineering. Although relatively unclear in peacetime, this dependence became highly evident by the end of the July crisis, especially in Germany.

On 28 July, 120 hours after the Austrian ultimatum to Serbia, German general staff chief Moltke sent a secret situation assessment to his chancellor. Moltke stated that Germany's options were now gone. As a result of Austrian and Russian mobilizations the direction and movement of events were out of control. Only the speed could still be determined. The next 72 hours were crucial. Germany could not allow them to slip away without acting, or the most grievous consequences would befall her.

Finally, on the afternoon of 1 August, after the mobilization documents had been signed and the implementing orders were being processed, Kaiser Wilhelm II changed his mind. Having heard from his ambassador in London of the possibility of English neutrality, Wilhelm ordered a halt to the west front deployment and a redeployment of all forces against Russia. Moltke finally convinced the kaiser that this change was impossible. The final war plan, the product of a year's work, could not be altered. The result would be to send a swarm of disorganized troops to the east front while at Germany's rear a fully war-mobilized French army threatened. Moltke said he would take no responsibility for this chaos. They telegraphed

London, saying that the deployment could not be stopped, for technical reasons.[72]

On Sunday, 19 July, Delbrück entertained Professor Paul von Mitrofanoff, of the University of St. Petersburg. A former student and regular contributor to the *Prussian Yearbook*, he had just been to Paris and London and appeared to have some semi-official political mission. But such was not the case. They spoke about war but did not believe it was coming.[73]

By 2 August a strange quiet pervaded Berlin. The previous night the unrest in the streets had been indescribable, an explosive rapture by endless masses of people pushing down Unter den Linden. Three of the Delbrück children, two cousins, and their nurse went down to watch and were astonished. The telephone rang the whole day. At noon they heard from the Naval Ministry that Russia had mobilized. At ten that night rumors flew that the German crown prince had been assassinated by Russian agents![74]

The third of August, the 114th Founder's Celebration of Berlin University, became the mobilization day for most of its student body. Max Planck gave the speech; they sang the national anthem. Delbrück was elected dean of the philosophy faculty.

Nine days later Delbrück's cousins began to die. "Now the voices of destiny have spoken, we cry with you and are brave with you," he wrote to the widow of one.[75] Fear of spies grew to epic proportions. Delbrück's eldest son, Waldemar, returning to duty at midnight on the second day of mobilization, failed to stop fast enough at a roadblock, and his car was riddled with bullets. Newspapers carried stories of foreigners fleeing the country in cars filled with German gold (reading 9).[76]

### World War I, 1914–1918

Delbrück's writing during the next fifty-two months took two great turns. By the first Christmas he had concluded that this was a war without precedent: Germany had to follow a different strategic philosophy than it had adopted during the forty-four years of European peace (reading 10). By 1915 he compared the world war to Frederick's eighteenth-century wars, describing both as wars of attrition. He argued that Germany had won everything it could expect to win and should begin peace negotiations, promising at the onset to return conquered Belgium to complete independence. If any territory were to change hands as a result of the war, he warned that it should be either in the east, in Russian Poland or the Caucuses, or in colonial areas, but above all, not on the west front (reading 11).[77] By 1916 he foresaw American intervention as a result of submarine warfare, a potentially decisive strategic weapon (reading 14).[78] Through it all, Delbrück tried to describe the great battles—Gorlice-Tarnova, Verdun, and Caporetto (readings 12, 15, and 19). He compared the Russian and German armies, described the changing technology, dealt with the relationship between submarines and food supplies, and deplored the absence of wise and intelligent German political leadership (readings 13, 17, 18, and 20).

The suggestions for peace negotiations based on giving up Belgium and avoiding a war with America through unlimited submarine warfare provoked a storm of protest. Delbrück was accused of lacking patriotism, of aiding the enemy.[79] In an environment of rigid censorship he made use of every source he could find, including neutral and Entente writings. Alien sources provoked his opponents that much more. As the war worsened, the rhetoric and the passions it engendered grew desperate and malevolent, inflamed by censorship, propaganda, and increasingly huge numbers of dead and wounded.

Early on, Delbrück was singled out for attack. In 1915 he was attending an imperial reception in the garden pavilion of the chancellor's palace in Berlin, along with Reichstag delegates, media figures, leading party men, and professors, all influential in public life. The kaiser was late. Delbrück stood talking in a small group near the entrance. The kaiser arrived and bounded forward into the pavilion with quick steps. The hall fell silent. The first person his eyes fell on was Delbrück. Before a greeting or salutation of any kind, the kaiser walked up to Delbrück and said in a voice that was heard by everyone, "Don't talk with this man. All he wants to do is to attack my government."[80] Delbrück said it was the most humiliating day of his life. Later he admitted that if he worried about all the people who wanted to insult, malign, and vilify him, he would have to carry a pistol everywhere.[81]

Delbrück and Erich von Falkenhayn, chief of the German general staff from November 1914 through August 1916, held similar views on the war.[82] By December 1914 they had both concluded that the war was unwinnable under the strategy of annihilation, that a political solution to the war should be sought, and that it should begin by renouncing annexations in Europe, especially Belgium. Falkenhayn pursued this goal consistently throughout the war but was unable to win over the key political leaders—Kaiser Wilhelm II, Theobold von Bethmann-Hollweg, and Reichstag leaders—or public opinion. Falkenhayn was an ineffective public political figure. He was a Prussian aristocrat, arrogant and sarcastic. He understood clearly and absolutely what was happening, especially before August 1917, but was unable and unwilling to act on this information. Delbrück had carved out for himself a clear public role before the war, but, during the war his information became unreliable and he could never trust it. This distrust, combined with his relativist historical philosophy and his feelings of public duty to the government as a spokesman, kept him from pushing his views to their logical conclusion. It should be remembered that public opposition to the war not only was treasonous but, as Delbrück himself recognized, weakened morale. For a professor and noted public opinion maker, this sort of opposition was simply inconceivable. For a general and chief of the general staff, it was equally impossible.

Delbrück and Falkenhayn met several times during the war years. In August 1915 Delbrück visited army headquarters at Pless, Upper Silesia, to confer on Falkenhayn an honorary Berlin University doctorate. Falkenhayn's resilience, workmanlike attitude, and quick, lively comprehension made a strong positive impression.[83] In mid-January 1916 Falkenhayn telephoned Delbrück and invited him for a talk. They met in Berlin for an hour.[84] The gist of these conversations was that Germany was in a war of attrition. Wearing-down actions, not great offensive attacks, had to persuade the enemy to open peace talks. A few months later Falkenhayn was removed as commander in chief.[85]

By summer 1916 press leaks by the high command that Germany had a secret weapon that might end the war had encouraged public clamor for unrestricted submarine warfare. Delbrück wrote that an accident of technological development had created this crisis (reading 17). Historically, warships had been able to approach commercial vessels for examination without danger. Today, with commercial vessels armed against submarines and with submarines vulnerable to defensive action, even a lightly armed ship could damage a U-boat. Thus submarines could not approach for inspection without risk of destruction. This technical problem was tied to German-American relations. He asked if a ruthless submarine war would force England out of the war without bringing America into it. Did Germany have enough submarines to attain this goal before the United States intervened? Delbrück suggested it did not.[86]

The statement that Germany had insufficient submarines for an effective war of annihilation at sea brought a stiff reprimand from the censors and the order that henceforth all *Prussian Yearbook* articles be submitted to the government before galley proofs were made up. Delbrück had had trouble with the censors before. Many times they had forced deletion of specific details, and he had always acquiesced. Now Delbrück protested. If it was implied that Germany had enough submarines to force England out of the war quickly, public opinion would be whipped to a frenzy against a government that did not use available means to end the war.[87]

In the spring of 1917, with a group of journalists, Delbrück took a "front tour."[88] They set out from Warsaw in a sleeping car, sharing meals with a division, a reserve inspector general, and the general staff of a *Landwehr* (territorial reserve) corps. At Baranowicze they were so close to the Russian lines that an artillery shell landed forty feet away, spraying their windshield. Delbrück ate with Hans Hartwig von Beseler, governor-general of Poland, and his staff: they were closely following the Russian Revolution. Later that year Delbrück was the guest of Polish noblemen on their estates outside Posen.[89] When he returned to Berlin, his recommendations for German Polish policy were laid on the kaiser's desk. Wilhelm II read them and made marginal comments, and the document was returned to Delbrück, marked "secret."[90] Delbrück's message in all this was clear: an independent Poland would become a German ally. Instead, Poland was treated as a conquered enemy.[91]

His eldest son was severely wounded in May 1917. Waldemar was operated on and seemed on the road to recovery. He dictated a letter but contracted pneumonia and died a few days later. By the time his baggage and clothes arrived the following week, his Guard Jaeger battalion had been attacked and overrun. Many of Waldemar's comrades, who had written in grief to Hans and Lina, were themselves killed. Delbrück read the *Nibelungenlied*.[92]

In July 1917 the Reichstag passed its Peace Resolution, based in part on arguments Delbrück had been presenting in the *Prussian Yearbook* for a year. Peace negotiations should be sought, beginning with the public renunciation of forced annexations.[93] Belgium had to be given up completely.

In January 1918 Delbrück had urgent consultations with Rudolf von Valentini, the kaiser's closest political adviser.[94] They were both worried about the conservative incitement of popular enthusiasm to end the war by military victory. A week later Valentini was forced to resign. In a scathing *Prussian Yearbook* editorial, surprisingly allowed by the censors, Delbrück asked if the supreme command was coming out from behind the kaiser's back to dictate the politics of the Reich. Was Germany moving so far away from its monarchical tradition that the kaiser could no longer choose his own advisers? A proletarian revolution had always been a phantom in Germany. Was the monarchy now in danger from the right?[95]

In February 1918, accompanied by Kurt Hahn and Paul Rohrbach, Delbrück traveled to neutral Holland to lecture. He talked with German embassy staff, Dutch professors, the international media, retired Dutch officials and legislators, and the Swedish ambassador. His purpose was to try to open channels leading to negotiations. He failed and concluded, "One of my main purposes here has been accomplished. There is nothing that can be done! Just to know that is useful."[96]

Later that spring, as the last German west front offensive was being prepared, Delbrück had several long conferences in the German Foreign Office. The next day he was walking on the Wilhelmstrasse when an officer came up to him. "Don't you remember me?" he said. "I'm Prince Max von Baden!" They went up to Baden's hotel room, talked for an hour, and found themselves in complete agreement.[97] That week Delbrück dined with Admiral Henning von Holtzendorff, commander in chief of the admiralty staff. German Foreign Office official Friedrich von Payer was also there.[98] In June, Delbrück met August Count zu Eulenburg, the kaiser's close personal friend, on the street and that afternoon wrote to him. A new liberal government should be put in place, Delbrück said, to open serious negotiations while military operations were going successfully. He suggested Max von Baden.[99]

It did no good. Few in Germany understood what was happening.

Toward the end of the war Delbrück maintained an increasingly frantic schedule. In June 1918 he went daily to the atelier of Herbert Garve to pose for a seventieth birthday sculpture. His secretary, Elsa Klose, went with him and he dictated furiously from the pedestal.[100] Delbrück's university lectures directly foreshadowed his writings, interviews, and travels. His lecture "The Development of Modern Strategy from Gustav Adolphus to the Present" outlined the gist of his confidential memorandum, advocating peace negotiations and a German withdrawal to the Maas River. It was sent to a variety of German leaders.[101]

In March 1918 the last German west front offensive commenced with a seven-mile pentration of Allied lines the first day and a five-mile sweep the second. The offensive slowed through April and May, with huge casualty lists. Official publications and the conservative press prepared German public opinion for a coming victory.

Delbrück wrote to Lina that "as splendid as the military news is, my enthusiasm evaporates as soon as I see the huge casualties undergirding it. The very magnitude of these tactical victories puts us on the road to strategic defeat" (reading 21).[102]

Among the letters he received in the last week of June 1918 was one from a reader in Krotoschin, Silesia. This local judge described his monthly court day in a small town near his city. At court appeared a woman whose child had been killed in the same battery as the judge's son. There were women whose husbands had met death, mothers whose sons had died, daughters whose fathers and brothers had been killed. The courtroom was an inventory list of those galvanized by repeated suffering. After court, while waiting in the railroad station for six hours—the trains were not running in order to save coal—the justice came across Delbrück's question in the June 1918 *Prussian Yearbook*: Why do these great military successes evoke no joy in the German people? "Exactly!" responded the judge. "Among our people there is a great numbness. Everyone has gone away and perished. The whole younger generation is dead, and their loss cannot be made up from this sea of mourning that dominates human lives in my region of the country."[103]

According to his wife, Delbrück was a daily participant in the government of Chancellor Max von Baden in October and early November 1918. On October 28 Lina wrote that "tomorrow the allies would have the German answer to Wilson's overture. Hans knows what the content of this answer is." But all was in vain. Armistice Day, 11 November, Delbrück's seventieth birthday, was "a day of sadness and terror."[104]

World War I posed the most severe crisis for Hans Delbrück: to what extent could a historian of the military past become a current defense critic? Despite insights that were consistently clearer than those of most of his contemporaries, by November 1918 Delbrück had achieved only limited success in his new role, for a variety of reasons.

The sources available to him were poor in quality and quantity. Government censorship and official propaganda worsened the situation. To try to overcome this lack, Delbrück regularly quoted English, French, and American publications, comparing them with German, Austrian, and Swiss. Although that improved his understanding, it also aroused the antagonism of both censor and conservative. In their minds Delbrück associated himself with the enemy foreigners.

Delbrück was forced to disregard the important historical quotient of distance. Before the war the "fifty-year rule" had dominated German scholarship. No topic that had occurred within the previous fifty years was considered valid for research. The sources were thought incomplete and the writer too subjective. In violating this rule, many believed, Delbrück described the war primarily as a publicist, not as a historian.

Delbrück himself resisted the application of his historical methodology to the analysis of operational warfare. He recognized that there had been no forum for public opposition to defense policy in peacetime, and war conditions made that discussion dangerous and illegal. In spite of difficulties with the censor on numerous occasions, his wartime statements were carefully executed to stay within the bounds of what was allowed. Delbrück was primarily a historian and only secondarily a political commentator. His political views were derived from his historical understanding. As historian he was never sufficiently convinced of the validity of his conclusions to move to political action. He remained skeptical, never forgetting the relative and tentative nature of historical knowledge.[105]

**Postwar, 1919–1929**

More than seventy years old when the peace was signed, Delbrück lived for another decade.[106] It was the most painful period of his life. His eldest son, Waldemar, namesake of his royal student of the 1870s, had died in combat in Macedonia in 1917 and was buried in an unmarked mass grave. His country changed forms of government, and the new republican leadership, forced to conclude the lost war, eight months later was compelled to sign the Treaty of Versailles. It stated publicly that Germany had caused the war and the war damage and would pay the victors for this unparalleled destruction (reading 22). Having been told to anticipate victory in May, the Germans could not believe their defeat in November. Instead, they were told that the German army had not been defeated in the field but stabbed in the back by the treacheries of the liberals and new republican government. Shame at losing infused the grieving Germans with intense hostility.[107]

In March, Delbrück was visited by a former student, Arthur Conger, an American, who had heard Delbrück's lectures at Berlin University in 1909–10. Conger, now chief of the political intelligence section of General John J. Pershing's headquarters, was sent on a fact-finding mission. He wanted to know the mood of Germany. Delbrück immediately cleared the air: Germany would in no case resume the war. On returning to American headquarters, Conger reported directly to Pershing, and his written report reached President Wilson's desk.[108]

In May 1919 Delbrück went to the Versailles Peace Conference, summoned by German foreign minister Count Ulrich Brockdorff-Rantzau to answer the war guilt charges of the Allied powers.[109] He traveled with General Count Max Montgelas of the Bavarian army, accompanied by a French army major who was cordial but spoke not a word. The treaty was presented to the German delegation, which worked frantically to translate it, send it to the government in Berlin, and draft a response. German technicians, worried that the deliberations were being overheard, played two large gramophones during the heated discussions within the delegation. As they were finishing their task, Delbrück wrote to Lina that the most that could be obtained was to save Germany's life, but a life barely worth living. On 24 May, their work done, Delbrück saw only black ahead, for Germany and for the world.[110]

Max Weber, his colleague at Versailles, wrote to Delbrück when they had returned, wishing to discuss the teaching and study of military history. Weber emphasized he could discuss this only secretly and in person. In spite of the ban put on military studies in Germany by the Treaty of Versailles, Weber believed military history had to be studied and in a different way than before. It must be fundamentally changed from the ground up.[111] Weber soon died, and the teaching of military history was expurgated from the one German university in which it was then taught.

Delbrück retired from Berlin University in 1921. The faculty ignored pleas to continue his work. Military history, they said, was not an important subject of university research and teaching. It was superfluous: an ancillary, nonessential "helping science" that could be learned by any professor in his spare time.[112] Delbrück sold the *Prussian Yearbook* and bought a house in Bloney, Switzerland, which proved a pleasant refuge for the family after 1950.[113] But in 1923 his youngest son, Max, who was to share the 1969 Nobel Prize for medicine as a professor at the California Institute of Technology, had to work as a common laborer to get enough money for his university studies during the period of hyperinflation.[114]

In 1921 British military commentator Charles à Court Repington visited. Delbrück, who had been the last German to take a meal at his house in London before the war. Aged and greatly saddened, he was badly off. Repington thought Delbrück, a moderate during the war, now deeply hated the Allies: "The iron has entered into his historian's soul."[115]

Picking up where they had left off in the 1890s, Delbrück and the military fought a stormy public battle over German strategy, this time over World War I. Delbrück accused General

Erich Ludendorff of satisfying his own ambitions by playing a deadly game with the future of Germany (reading 24). If Ludendorff had been brought to trial for mutiny in 1916, Germany might have been saved. Ludendorff and his supporters attacked Delbrück for joining the enemy foreigners to slander his war leadership. Delbrück, they said, was no historian but only a journalist and armchair strategist who lacked the intuitive understanding of war that came from technical training and practical military experience (reading 23).[116]

At the time of this controversy Delbrück fought another battle over military history. He was part of the minority voice on an advisory commission to the German National Library (Reichsarchiv), whose job it was to research and write the official German history of World War I. Officers and conservative officials on this project saw the civilian members as aliens. They believed the Reichsarchiv was a continuation of the old military history section of the general staff and should act as such. The old army had fought the war, they said, and its members should write its history. Delbrück's directly opposite views were dismissed.

Failing to convince either the university or the army of the validity of his history, in the last years of his life Delbrück entered the public forum. He tried to convince public opinion of the decision-making mistakes of World War I, particularly at its end, condemning the military leadership for dishonorable, self-serving, and disastrous ambition. He said that the last German offensive failed because of basic shortages of men and matériel and because of the technology and terrain of the battlefield. Delbrück repeated Ludendorff's own statements that the German army lacked adequate munitions, food supplies, horses, and gasoline. The army was drafting men forty-five years old with four children. By the spring of 1918 restoration of railroad lines to support a swiftly moving attack was impossible (reading 23).[117]

He also fought against the war guilt clause of the Treaty of Versailles. In a speech written a few days before he died, he described his country as beaten and defenseless, while its enemies

savaged its democratic foundations, doomed its citizens to unending economic slavery, shamed its national honor, and
marked the German people as criminals (reading 24).
At his death, on 14 July 1929, the words he wrote for his
gravestone—"I sought the truth. I loved my country"—evi-
denced his belief that he had failed to convince others of his
quest for knowledge or of his patriotism. Perhaps he was for-
tunate to die in the summer of 1929, for far worse catastrophes
were to come for his family, his profession, and his country.

## Military History since 1929

At his death Delbrück was not unknown. Felix Gilbert, who
studied at Berlin in the 1920s, remembers being told that Delbrück was an eccentric but important historian.[118] But if he was
well known, it was more for his political involvement than for
his historical work. After 1933, history in Germany underwent
a process of Nazification. In the military it continued to be
used for war planning purposes.[119] Delbrück's voluminous papers were scattered among two archives, and even forty years
later few historians knew the contents of both of them. His former students, Emil Daniels and Otto Haintz, published a fifth
(1928) and a sixth (1932) volume of *The History of the Art of War*.
Two festschriften appeared the year before he died.[120] But the
editors soon emigrated from Germany. Delbrück was dead,
and the development of modern military history had apparently stopped.
Then it slowly revived. During the years 1936–39 the Soviet
Union's People's Commissariat for Defense translated *The
History of the Art of War* into Russian. In 1941 Edward Mead
Earle, of the Princeton Institute for Advanced Study, orga-
nized a seminar on American foreign policy and security is-
sues, and a young assistant professor, Gordon Craig, wrote a
seminal article on Delbrück. More than twenty years after
World War II *The History of the Art of War* was republished in
German. The European historical community hailed the vol-

umes as "a masterwork of German historical literature."[121] In 1961 Theodore Ropp, whose graduate program in military history at Duke University was one of the few in North America, noted on the first page of his standard *War in the Modern World* that Delbrück's *Art of War* was "the classic in the field."[122] The next year, Michael Howard, creator of the first War Studies Department in England, at King's College, University of London, described Delbrück as "perhaps the greatest of modern military historians."[123] Commentators said it was Delbrück who took military history out of the confines of the army and made it understandable and important to the ordinary educated citizen.

As Paul Kennedy has pointed out, however, the Vietnam War caused a collapse of interest in military history in the United States. There were widespread protests and deep-seated mistrust of anything to do with the military. Enrollments dropped off, graduate students changed fields, and publishing houses sought other ventures. New fields of study, such as gender history and ethnic studies, attracted attention.[124] By the early 1970s it looked as if military history would be limited to government institutions such as West Point and the Naval War College and those few universities such as Duke and Ohio State which had influential writers and teachers.

Just at that point military history underwent a broad-based renewal. Defined as the "new military history" or as "war and society," courses burgeoned, fellowships multiplied, publishing houses revived their interest, and new journals proliferated. Kennedy comments that increasingly Americans "recognized that war was an important aspect of history which could not be ignored just because it was unpleasant."[125] Scholars concluded that the integration of a broad range of military topics instead of concentration on the battlefield would enable them to use social science methods for better understanding. In addition to political scientists and sociologists the Pentagon and the army and navy war colleges turned to military history to aid in their analysis of contemporary strategic and operational issues. American military history of the 1980s was not a return to the pre–World War II variety but in fact fully Delbrückian: paying attention not only to the military's combat performance but focusing on contextual, social, and economic aspects as well. All this interest is evident in the growing reputation of Delbrück's writings. By 1983 a West Point officer had translated the first four volumes of *The History of the Art of War* into English.[126] In 1985 *Hans Delbrück and the German Military Establishment* appeared, aided by Gordon Craig's suggestions to the author and generous review for the publisher. Peter Paret opened a conference at the Institute for Advanced Study by noting that the conference title, "War in the Framework of Political History," came from Delbrück's best-known work. Archer Jones's best-selling Oxford University Press book *The Art of War in Western Civilization* made liberal use of Delbrück for several of its sections.[127] In 1990 the University of Nebraska Press brought out an elegant paperback edition of the *Art of War* that in 1994 was made available through the Military Book Club.[128] Delbrück's *Art of War* is so well known on active-duty U.S. Army posts that it reportedly sells out as soon as shipments arrive on the shelves.

Modern military history, as first defined and practiced by Hans Delbrück, has four elements. First, it contextualizes military events into their appropriate place as a normal aspect of politics, economics, and society. Modern military history sees the foundations of armies and war in normal peacetime activities. It describes war within the full framework of routine and common human affairs. It was not only the organization and management of the army but also the technical and material aspects of Roman culture that led to Roman military success: the ability to bring a large mass together, move it in formation, and supply and maintain it for a long time.

Second, modern military history describes and analyzes the material and technical aspects of armies. While not neglecting morale and ideas, it carefully defines what is materially possible and impossible in war. Quantities as well as qualities of armies are important. As Delbrück noted, "a movement that is made easily by a thousand soldiers is an accomplishment for ten thousand men, a work of art for fifty thousand, and an impossibility for one hundred thousand."[129]

Third, modern military history is universal, using comparative and paradigmatic methods to analyze armies in war and peace across large distances of time, space, and culture. Neither Pericles nor Frederick the Great could practice war of annihilation. Their strategy was restrained by their social and political systems and by the material realities of the Athenian state and Prussian kingdom.

Finally, modern military history is a part of public discourse. Its forum includes universities, the active and reserve military, and the mass media as well as educated laypersons, veterans' groups, and often elected public officials.[130] Contemporary historians realize that questions of war and peace are critical for all modern national states, for the electorates from which these states are derived, and for the world community in which they must coexist.

*Part 1*

# The Making of a Military Historian, 1870–1904

Delbrück in 1884. Kindness of the family of Helene Hobe (née Delbrück)

# Letters from the Franco-Prussian War

*1870*

This reading is from the typescript "Hans Delbrück in Briefen, 1848–1880," 134 pages of Delbrück's letters to his mother assembled by his wife, Lina Thiersch Delbrück, after his death. A copy is deposited in the Delbrück papers in Deutsche Staatsbibliothek, Berlin. My copy was a gift from Helene Hobe, one of his daughters, who was so generous during my two long working periods in Berlin.

Delbrück entered the Twenty-eighth Rhenish Infantry Regiment in July 1870 as a sergeant and was promoted to lieutenant after the battle of Gravelotte on 18 August. His letters reveal his first intense relationship with war: lack of sleep, bad food, and experiences with fear, chaos, and death that cannot be understood in terms of normal civilian life and do not relate to war as described in history books. He recognizes that, in spite of the extraordinary nature of these experiences, the popular media further distort and sensationalize them, and he concludes that under worst-case circumstances discipline alone motivates soldiers. In late November 1870 Delbrück came down with a severe case of typhus. Taken to a field hospital near Compiègne and then to a hospital back in Bonn, he was not out of danger until January 1871.

## Maring on the Moselle, 29 July 1870

Dear Mom: You would laugh if you could see us march. I am the only NCO who carries his own knapsack and revolver. In spite of which, no boils yet! On today's march, thirty or forty men from our company fell out and lay on the roadside, mainly because the food and quarters in this Eifel region are so poor.[1] Many went two days with only commissary bread to eat. Today we have a rest day in a wealthy village with excellent wine, and this has restored the company a bit.

I am living with the village secretary in a very small bungalow but with excellent food. In the evening I chat with the man and his lively wife, and he has introduced me to the whole community: the mayor and secretary, the tax assessor and collector, the pastor and schoolmaster, who are Jesuits. We have lively discussions, not about the war but about the unity of the church. The meetings of the village council are often so stormy that the members almost come to a fistfight. Finally yesterday they came to me to ask advice about the village quartering situation.[2] The first pair of socks is about worn out. You can send me another pair in a letter, perhaps with a little chocolate.

These hungry days have produced excellent service from the soldiers. They are angry at the French and want to get home as quickly as possible. Overall, morale is good, even among the villagers. One woman said she would rather the village be destroyed than turned over to the French. We do not hear a thing about what is going on in the outside world.

There is a good deal of confusion. Our fusilier battalion got the order to pick up ammunition and food in a village nearby. But when it got there, there was no magazine in sight. Still, the motto is, On to Paris!

### Field Postcard, 9 August 1870

We crossed the French frontier today with wild jubilation and marched across the battlefield near Saarbrücken.[3] It was a horrible sight. The French were crushed from two directions with enormous casualties. Our troops attacked their fortified positions four times with unheard-of bravery: we lost nearly all our officers.

### Bivouac, 11 August 1870

Whoever said that hell is falsely painted was right: it is paradise compared with a bivouac in a torrential downpour, at night, with nothing to eat or drink, lying on the ground without wood or straw. In spite of great tiredness we cannot sleep. Gradually, as we spend more and more of these nights, we are losing our good humor. Luckily, one night there was some milk, the next night a few fires were built, but now, when everyone wants above all to dry out, our endurance must be built up for more such nights. War stories are told by everyone, especially those who have seen combat. The men all confess that they go into combat the second time with much less enthusiasm than the first time and have even less courage after that. In many places the dead covering the battlefield lie unburied two days later.

## Gravelotte, 19 August 1870

The first battle is passed. The terrible bullets have whistled close by, but none touched me. Yesterday evening I thought we were lost and would have to attack the French positions again: it made me more uneasy than at the beginning of combat. According to all accounts, yesterday was as bad a day as war brings: a combat experience such as never happened in the Austrian war.[4] Two days ago I was guarding a field dressing station in a castle and helping with the wounded. The next morning we did not know what was happening and had sent out a reconnaissance party when suddenly shooting began. I was standing with several other men, drinking some wine to fortify myself, when all of a sudden, bang! a bullet hit right between us and a second killed a sergeant nearby taking a nap. The French were nowhere to be seen. We rejoined our corps, which was assembling, and the main battle began with an artillery barrage. After a while we went forward. Shells screamed over our heads, and the cannonade grew louder. Quickly we took cover in a village, then moved out across an open field that stretched away toward a woods. We ran across the field as far as we could, through terrible shell, machine gun, and rifle fire as far as a deep, wooded ravine at the edge of the forest. Here we were safe with the French firing over our heads. Our officers tried for ten minutes to gather the men to finish the attack, and a great many men fell in this attempt.

The run across the field completely disorganized the regiment. The confused mass in the ravine hunkered down, scarcely moving. They could not be urged forward. There were two or three hundred men from different companies. It was a quarter hour before some order was restored. Either leadership did not exist or it was poor: the soldiers were frightened and lacked direction. It was a mournful sight. Finally we advanced to the edge of the woods but confronted an almost unclimbably steep hill. As we emerged at the top we met a murderous fire, forcing us immediately to retreat and duck down just below the ridge top. The French were a hundred feet in front of us, invisible and firing from protected positions.

Luckily there was a deep gully, about thirty paces from the edge, which was absolutely safe. Bullets rained over us like hail. With our small numbers an attack on the strongly protected French position was unthinkable. So we halted in front of the forest, waiting until we could go around it, with about thirty men returning the French fire, the rest huddled down in the gully. A reserve lieutenant was in command, and he sent me back three times to bring up reinforcements. I had to take out my sword and threaten to use it. But soon even the lieutenant became apprehensive. Officers crouched in the gully waiting anxiously to see if the French would make an attack, for there were scarcely enough men to repel it. Our captain had courage enough, but he had lost his head; the colonel was the same. The major was not there and, in any event, had acted so without sense and understanding that the men thought him drunk. The French shooting was generally poor and few shots actually hurt us, but we could not return the enormous volume of fire and remained in this stalemate all afternoon, waiting for help from Frederick Charles.[5] Finally we heard heavy fire on the left flank. The French retreated, but an attack was still unthinkable. We remained where we were but stood up and looked across the battlefield when suddenly shots fell around us. I heard a ringing in my ears, and we got down and crawled on our stomachs.

Finally there came heavy fire from the right wing too. To collect ourselves, we retreated. Scarcely had we gone a thousand steps back when the signal for a general attack was heard. It was nearly dark, and burning houses gave a grotesque light to the whole scene. The colonel gathered together the troops he had and sought to lead an attack, but we did not move forward with the mass of troops. Soon soldiers came back with the terrible news that Prussians were shooting at each other by mistake. In the confusion I joined the Ninth Pomerians. Then suddenly there was a terrible salvo, and the whole mass turned around and fled down the hill helter-skelter.[6] I tried vainly to stop this melee and finally assembled as many of the regiment as I could in a nearby village. I did not know if the burst of fire was from the Prussians or the French. I was completely in the dark.

After this everyone was completely exhausted and thirsty, but there was no water. After wandering around for a long time I found the collection point of the regiment, where about five hundred men were assembled. I wrapped myself in a coat and slept. I was awakened by a series of loud explosions quite nearby. It was morning. I drank some dirty water and saw that the main part of the regiment had come back together. An officer brought the news that the king had arrived and the French had retreated.

Why they retreated I had no idea. As I had seen the day before, their position was terribly strong. Many of our men had killed each other. As we moved about, our very movements were hindered by the thick explosion of our own grenades. As for the strategic success and the outcome of the battle as a whole, I was completely lost. If we won, it was due to the great cowardice of the French. That sounds very different from the newspaper accounts, but my understanding of war has changed since yesterday.

That our troops were so poorly led accounts for the complete disorder and chaos in front of the woods. Machine guns worked terrible havoc. Dead French soldiers lay across the battlefield as far as the eye could see and many Prussians as well.[7] Our company lost eleven killed, thirty wounded, and ten missing in action, even though many did not come under fire at all. A French civilian was hanged for shooting at passing troops from his house. We passed a dead body tied up by the side of the road: a captured and wounded soldier had been executed.

## Camp near Metz, 24 August 1870

My last letter was not very cheerful, but it was the unvarnished truth. Some write vague descriptions of camp life. Naked reality looks very different. It goes without saying that I have lost some of my enchantment for this war. In the end our morale changes with events. Our troops are heroes for attacking French positions defended with such weapons. Of the battle itself you are probably better informed than I. All we know is that we are with the Sixth Army Corps in front of Metz, with dirt and disease, while the rest of the army marches on Paris.

## Camp near Chatel in front of Metz, 5 September 1870

The day before yesterday in the evening we heard a great shout from the next battalion. We came out of our tents and asked what had happened. We were told the crown prince is in Paris, Metz has surrendered, Napoleon is captured. We thought they had gone crazy. We believed the news, however, when the adjutant arrived in the company of General Maltzin.[8] "Now, children, there is very good news: the battle of Sedan has been won," he told us.[9] Two reserve officers, sent here full of fighting spirit, lost their enthusiasm after they had spent a few days with us. This is the twenty-ninth night we have camped out, and although we arrived at the front with 227 men, there are only 155 left, including seven dead officers.[10]

In camp strict order must be maintained by continual "spit and polish" work to keep up morale. Discipline is the only reason men go into combat: the same individuals used as a mobile force would completely disappear at the first gunfire. For our unreliable troops, the same as mercenaries in the last century, the closed-line attack is the only possibility, even for very noble-minded soldiers. Now I understand how ten thousand closed-ranks Greeks could defeat a hundred thousand Persians and how the city of Rome could conquer the world.[11]

## Jony aux Arches near Metz, on the Moselle River, 11 September 1870

We are again in poor quarters only a few hundred yards from the French lines. The worst is that in good weather we must stay awake half the night prepared for an attack, especially from three in the morning on. But nothing ever happens. I received my uncle Peter's letter regarding the battle of Gravelotte.[12] The bravery of the Prussians in this fight was admirable. But I cannot agree with Peter's conclusions on the objectivity of the war reports. We have had the same stories of bravery in our regiment, but it seems to me that some men go forward fine, whereas others have very little courage: only discipline and organization moves the mass of men forward. I myself have seen how badly our newspapers lie, and I no longer believe them. For example, the two shots that killed a sergeant on the morning of the eighteenth about which I wrote became, in the Cologne newspapers, a great attack with salvos and all. In news accounts it is written that "Gravelotte was seized," but there were no French there to defend it![13] In spite of all this you must understand that my fundamental views on the war have not changed, but as a historian one must be objective.

# Prince Frederick Charles

*1885*

---

Frederick Charles, prince of Prussia, was Kaiser Wilhelm I's nephew. Educated for the army, he commanded the Prussian combined forces in the Danish war (1864), the First Prussian Army against Austria (1866), and the Second Prussian Army in the war against France (1870). He wrote extensively on the problems of command, cavalry organization, and other questions and, according to Gordon Craig, was a careful and methodical commander but one who also demonstrated energy, will, steadiness of nerve, and undauntedness in the face of difficulty.[1] Michael Howard describes the prince as a solid professional soldier but cautious to the point of timidity.[2] Delbrück, a veteran of the prince's last war, compares writing military history and commanding armies in war and goes on to discuss the importance of the army organization behind the commanding generals. Written on the occasion of the prince's death, the essay has certain features of a funeral tribute.

---

All the newspapers in Germany and Europe have published obituaries of Prince Frederick Charles which have tried to convey his importance as a commander. Yet nothing is more important than to ask in the quiet of one's heart, Was he really so great a general? The question is not posed with doubt. Nor is it asked in ignorance. The number of victories that the prince fought or took part in, the encomiums with which his maneuvers have been adorned, such as "clever," "genius," "masterful," say enough about him. But they do not answer the question, How much credit should be given to the prince and how much to his staff?

The answer is that the prince generally was regarded as a

careful, powerful personality but that the official publications that we know him by do not allow us to understand the personal aspects of his leadership. As more memoirs and letters come to light, the prince appears less important than he did at the time. Here and there newspaper stories dealing with him conclude that successful war today is achieved by heroism and genius. To bring off such victories as 1866 and 1870 requires men of quite extraordinarily sharp dialectical understanding, with an unusual combination of spirit and logic. Did the prince really have these gifts? Is it not more probable that out of the mass of ten thousand Prussian officers a few will stand at his side and second the words "Let the general staff do the worrying and the field marshal take the credit"?

It is fundamentally false that war today is a matter of intellect or indeed that it is a science. If war were a matter of scientific understanding, the teacher at the War Academy would be the best commander. But war is never the subject matter of the leading intellectuals and it can never be. The genius of understanding that is given to the commander is completely different from scientific understanding. A criticism of war fighting from the writing table is comparatively easy. But what the general does is done in the face of danger and under the pressure of time.

The work of historical understanding is related to the decision making of the commander in war as a movement in air is related to a movement in water.[3] In the open field a man can easily run four miles in under thirty minutes. When he is up to his face in water, the same movement can be done only slowly and with great exertion and only an especially strong man can do it. If the ground is full of sharp stones or the water is turbulent, the possibility of forward movement is reduced. That is the difference between a decision at the study table and a decision on the battlefield or in the commander's tent. The latter is more difficult because here the combinations of possibilities are mixed with imagination to a much higher degree.

With education comes understanding but not wisdom. The same is true for the unique essentials of the commander, such as imperturbability in the face of enormous danger, chaos, suffering, fears, and hopes for the future. To cut loose from these elements and issue military orders is difficult. Again and again biographies and war history the genius of military operations is spoken of. But when one gets closer to it, to carry out a quite simple exercise is often fraught with so many possibilities that any one of them appears almost equally valid. Because of the nature of war, the commander is usually in the dark on a number of important factors. Even when espionage and reconnaissance are used, there are always many things commanders do not know. Intelligence initially accepted as valid often proves to have been false.

What help is there to correct judgment? War history teaches us that many great operations and battles that resulted in splendid victories, whether of Frederick, Napoleon, Gneisenau, or the most recent ones, were led and often fought through to the end on the basis of incorrect expectations or assumptions. Thus Prague, Torgau, Jena, Rossbach, Königgrätz, Wörth, Vionville, Gravelotte.[4] To deal with these imponderables, commanders need good insight into the fundamentals of strategy. A general needs the qualities of bravery, boldness, determination, tenacity, alertness, faithfulness to duty, bodily vigor, and finally, as a secondary feature, learned understanding. The combination of these factors is so important that it often constitutes the origin of success or failure.

A striking example is the battle of Königgrätz. The arrangement of this battle was based on the calculated risk that half the Prussian forces would fight against the Austrians alone for many hours before the other half under the crown prince came to help. Taking this risk cannot really be called an error, because it was unavoidable. It was a mistake in judgment only in that the Prussian headquarters expected the crown prince to arrive much sooner than he did. The danger in the Prussian troop distribution did not prevent a victory; in fact it ultimately made it easier. For the entire morning the Austrians saw no Prussians on their right flank, so they moved the troops positioned there ready to fight the crown prince to the opposite side against Frederick Charles. When the crown prince arrived, he found the door, through which he had to enter and which he had expected to be heavily fortified, open and undefended. No coordination in the world could have brought about such a situation, yet it was in no way just a lucky accident. It was the reward for the boldness of the Prussian command and Frederick Charles, who had to fight the enemy with half power, although the other half was only hours away.

They could not know what success this boldness would achieve. Frederick Charles did not know if he faced a few Austrian corps or the whole army. If the former, his attack might have pushed the Austrians over the Elbe River. If the latter, he was best advised to wait until the arrival of the crown prince. W. W. Rüstow judged the premature attack of Frederick Charles's army a mistake.[5] If Frederick Charles had realized he had the whole Austrian army before him, he might have waited a few hours. But that is the unique character of war. They did not know, they attacked prematurely, they accepted the danger of fighting for hours against an enemy twice as large as they, and in so doing, they opened the door by means of which the Austrians were attacked in the rear.

Why did the Austrians not fall on Frederick Charles's army with all their forces? That is the difference between the Prussian and the Austrian leadership. The Prussians risked it; the Austrians did not. If the Austrians had attacked, it was in no way certain that they would have been successful, considering the tactical superiority of the Prussian troops. At first Benedek waited for a Prussian attack behind his positions.[6] After he had fought them a bit and weakened them, he wanted to attack himself. But because he had waited, with every step forward the possibility of success dwindled. It is not necessary to speculate about what would have happened if he had attacked the army of Frederick Charles before the arrival of the crown prince. It is sufficient to make clear how this victory was won. Not by the clever decisions of a far-ranging combination but by less daring here, more daring there. Boldness that wins battles if it is risked also loses battles if it is not.

The education of the general staff in our century has not wavered from its concern with the foundations of strategy. In order for the commander to operate amid the unending complications and rapidity of modern war, he needs good subordinates. They support him not only with the preparation of the mass of war planning materials but also with counsel, advice, and suggestions. Under certain circumstances this assistance can be decisive. Without capable general staff officers a modern general is like an artist without arms. There can be situations in which the commander is factually corrected by the chief of his general staff. Nevertheless victory and defeat always carry the name and the reputation of the commander, not those who advised him or gave him the idea but he whose will brought the idea into reality.

We must take into account all these elements when we consider how many generals in world history have been men of princely status. High birth, which, among other circumstances, ensures high social status, does not guarantee the character able to reach decisions needed to carry out war strategy, but it is an advantage in the creation of an able commander.

There is a second building block in the creation of an able commander which can be seen in the Prussian officer corps. That is the empowering of natural abilities with a theory. This is the most important of all unique features of a commander and also one of the fundamentals of war command.

The Prussian army has Clausewitz to thank for its theory.[7] In truth Clausewitz is the schoolmaster who won the battle of Königgrätz. Through the medium of Clausewitz, the teachings of Scharnhorst, Gneisenau, and Blücher spread throughout the Prussian army. They can thank him that there is a unified theory of strategy throughout the army and that neither the silly half-truths of Jomini nor the logical spiderwebs of Willisen have caused any doubt or disagreement.[8]

In Frederick Charles's last great operation, the battle at Le-Mans, the Prussian army came together from many divided roads.[9] The communications between them was very difficult because of terrain, the time of year, and the circumstances. On a few roads the Germans were victorious; on others they could not break through the resistance. The generals on both sides concluded that if their neighbor retreated, they could be attacked in flank and rear. What happened? The Prussian generals went forward in the assumption that all Prussian troops would do the same. The French retreated from the positions they had initially won, for fear that their flanks would not be protected: they did not trust what the other French troops would do in that situation. Thereby the French, who retreated separately, lost the battle, and the Prussians, who moved forward together, won it.[10] This marvelous unitary spirit of our officer corps is the reason that individual personal relationships are less important. Everyone, in similar military circumstances, draws roughly the same conclusions.

What do we know about the personality of Prince Frederick Charles? How sharply the great personalities of the war of 1813 stand out from the rest: Scharnhorst, Gneisenau, Blücher, York. They are all individuals. Even men of the second rank, such as Grolmann, Boyen, and Müffling, are not just names but flesh and blood.[11] The great commanders of our own time are certainly no less distinct individuals, but they do not appear to us in the same way. That is partly because of our information: it is incomplete. Also today personalities play a smaller part. An original such as Steinmetz we know well from a few anecdotes.[12] But the wars of liberation, 1812–13, were a much more complex situation: the unending complications of the allies; the fighting between the old and new schools of thought in politics, strategy, and organization; lots of disagreement in which everyone played to win. How different is our epoch! No parties on the inside, no uncertain or prideful allies, no defeats. Instead, a string of unbroken victories in which one general, one officer appears like the others. Few fail to measure up to the standard set for all. The most extreme test that any officer faces, the bad luck of a great defeat, has been spared these men.

As for Frederick Charles, one finds that he cared a great deal about the peacetime preparation of the army. In the Prussian army, during a long period of peace, a unique, very special

style of command evolved. It was based on the free development and exercise of the commander's own intelligence and
wisdom.[13] Military memorandums laid heavy emphasis on individual knowledge and experience at the point of command
and fought against reliance on specific, eternally valid rules.
The main example of the latter pedantic form was the Guard
Corps. In direct contrast, the prince, as commanding general
of the Third (Brandenburg) Corps, inspired his men to use
their own intelligence and wisdom, and soon his example
spread throughout the whole army.

If one sees this uniqueness as the boldness of natural genius,
such as Seydlitz or Blücher, one errs.[14] One must here speak of
study and self-instruction in the decision-making process. The
prince had a thoughtful, deliberate nature, but he was fully
conscious of the need to take risks. The terrible onslaught of
the guards at St. Privat was carried out with his agreement.
During the battle of Königgrätz there is another example. The
prince wanted to attack Benedek. He put his Third Corps, the
Brandenburgers, into motion with this in mind. He was riding
with the regiments and urging them on when Moltke's order
not to attack arrived. The attack undoubtedly would have
failed, as at St. Privat. Benedek had behind his powerful artillery line two corps at the front with two additional corps in reserve. Moltke's prudence was without doubt correct, in contrast to the daring of the prince. But we may not judge this
undertaking as a mistake without further information. A mistake that springs out of daring is not really a mistake. Mistakes
very often derive from a lack of boldness, an absence of decision making. But mistakes, in the sense of a wrong understanding of the material conditions of war, are typical of every
commander. Even prudence can misfire. The battle of Königgrätz itself is the antithesis to every rule. As the Austrians were
in full flight, the crown prince ordered the Fifth Corps, under
Steinmetz, a command that hardly fired a shot, to follow it. In
a second, as the order was given, Moltke stopped it. His error
was that from the viewpoint of the headquarters and the First

Army, the magnitude of the Austrian defeat was not understood.

The word "genius" should not be used as an element of originality and personality. That it is not. Genius, here defined, is the genius of the Prussian officer corps and the Prussian army. As Gneisenau wrote in his daily orders after the battle of Belle Alliance, "To the brave officers and soldiers of the army of the lower Rhine. Never will Prussia lose when her sons and grandsons act as you have acted."

# A Little Military History

*1887*

---

This reading is a review essay of a some works by Prince Kraft
zu Hohenlohe-Ingelfingen, commander of the Prussian Guard
Artillery in the Franco-Prussian War of 1870 and of the reserve
artillery of the Prussian Second Army at Königgrätz in 1866.
Hohenlohe also wrote a celebrated memoir of these wars.[1] The
essay contains a summary of Delbrück's arguments why military history should be recognized as valid for university teaching and research, as well as an interesting capsule biography of
Eduard von Hindersin, one of many still little known but significant leaders of the Prussian army in the decade of the 1860s.[2]

---

Today there is an extraordinarily lively interest in military history and in the military, far outside army circles. And there are
a large number of military works written for those outside the
army, for the educated public. They include several by Prince
Kraft zu Hohenlohe, general of infantry: *Essays on Strategy, Essays on Infantry, Cavalry, and Field Artillery*, and finally *Conversations on Cavalry*. Although they may be read by anyone with
a general interest, these essays were written with a practical
military purpose in mind. The prince is not writing history
and is not writing to instruct laymen. He is writing to military
men about their own profession. But for general readers his
work's interest is twofold.

First is the historical background. This part includes personal experiences of the author in three great wars, plus de-
tailed descriptions of specific aspects of the work of the general
staff, with characteristics of individual personalities and useful
examples of their work. In other places are his observations on
foreign armies and fruitful comparisons with earlier military

forces, such as his contrast of cavalry tactics under Frederick the Great, in 1806 and today.

Second, Hohenlohe's work contains something even more valuable for the historian or history buff, and that is unusual clarity about the nature of military operations. This side of war appears very seldom in military literature. To the historian it is mostly unknown, whereas to the military it is so well known that it is assumed and does not need to be mentioned. Included are elements of daily military life, for example, the art of issuing orders for large formations, the work capacity of troops, and details of horses, supply, and intelligence. All are essential for the historian to understand.

Historians must make judgments about strategy and battles, commanders and weapons. We want to know how the Greeks thwarted Xerxes, and Hannibal triumphed over Rome, if Caesar or Pompeii was the greater commander, how Frederick the Great held out against the world, and what finally defeated Charles XII and Napoleon. But the history from which to answer these questions has not been written.

Soldiers who consult our history books are rightly mistrustful. Historians who have dealt with military affairs, for example, Mommsen in his Roman history or Duncker in his Greek history, make fundamental errors. Mommsen, in his presentation of the battles of Cannae, Zama, and Pharsalus, completely overlooks the decisive moment. Duncker has a Greek army of eight hundred thousand operating in a land area insufficient for an army a tenth that size. He describes Greek hoplites running for a quarter mile when their maximum exertion was about three hundred steps. These are not just unimportant details but turning points in world history. In modern history there are similar examples. Noorden's magnificent picture of the battles of Prince Eugene and Marlborough are so faulted at their militarily decisive points that it is impossible to understand how Europe was able to withstand the universal monarch Louis XIV. Droysen's otherwise unsurpassed biography of York is so lacking in its military aspects that he describes Blücher making the same march twice. Sybel has just published a study of Frederick the Great's campaign of 1757, in particular the battle at Prague, in which Frederick's ideas are so confused that readers must conclude Frederick was the fuzziest strategic thinker.[3] Sybel himself did not recognize the consequences of his depiction. On the contrary, he thought he had portrayed Frederick with a new greatness. I have intentionally described only the most enlightened, respected men in our science, to emphasize this deficiency and to bring up the urgent necessity for a professional interest in military history, the same as with economic history, the history of art or of literature.

When science focuses, it does so by specialization. But specialists cannot rely only on their own knowledge; they must make use of the knowledge of other specialists to fill in those areas about which they do not know as much. A complete picture of a single period can be improved by a cross-cut view: three or four perspectives from different specialties. To this cross-cut belongs military history.

Military history has as little to do with the practice of war as any other branch of knowledge. To study military history and to lead armies are as different as to write about portraits and to paint them. Military history exercises have as little in common with leading troops as archaeology has to do with building houses.

But academic history has its own unique approach. We cannot therefore be satisfied with the military history work of the army itself. As it is impossible to write history without contact with experience, without the ideas that derive from life, in the same way the work of the practitioner also has its weaknesses. We must bring the two sides together. Military history needs both perspectives.

For the historian some of the richest revelations come from Hohenlohe's book on field artillery. Once you begin to read it, you will not be able to put it down. For example, take the portrait of the reformer of the Prussian artillery, General Gustav Eduard von Hindersin.[4] The son of a pastor, he was a well-educated scientist, a master of mathematics, physics, and chemistry, and he spoke English and French. But he approached things not from the standpoint of the learned but from a practical point of view.

Living by the old standard "The day has twenty-four hours of service," he was a very intense personality. His anger and impatience had its origins in his conviction that he would die an early death. His father and all his brothers had died prematurely of heart attacks. He expected to die every day. But as long as he lived, he expected to shape artillery doctrine.

Like all passionate men he was fundamentally good-natured. He had a big heart for humanity and for his own family. But he thought it unmilitary to show it. Therefore he presented himself as coarse and heartless, even to his family. When his eldest son died after months-long suffering following wounds received at St. Privat, Hindersin's response was characteristic.[5] "Youth is very much to be envied. There is no more beautiful way for a young officer to die. In one hand he has the Iron Cross, in the other the heart of his mother."

Hindersin was full of mistrust regarding the troops and his subordinates. His principle was not only to watch carefully but to wait suspiciously, because he always thought it possible that they might not follow his orders and make an X instead of a Y.

Once he came to watch troops shooting under Hohenlohe's orders. Hohenlohe wanted to show him a certain maneuver, but Hindersin said it was not necessary: eight days before, he had watched that maneuver and was satisfied. Hohenlohe had not seen him eight days before and told Hindersin that he had not been aware of his presence. You were not supposed to see me, Hindersin replied. I was over in the woods watching through a telescope. I wanted to see how you were doing, all by yourself.

Another time he had ordered an inspection for six in the morning. It was a hot spell in the middle of the summer. The night before, he went into the woods and watched everything through a telescope: preparations, mobilization, presentation, and the rest. The next morning, when Hohenlohe saw him and reported the brigade was ready for inspection, Hindersin replied that, officially, he was not there. Report to me when the brigade is ready to fire, he said. I am only taking a ride in the early morning freshness.

According to Hindersin, organizing the battery was always best done at night. He did not care for inspectors who looked things over once early on and then went home. He stayed the whole night and saw the battery firing at first light. In this way he emphasized that organization was not just a secondary activity.

Although he was a man of the old school, he went to all the military science lectures in Berlin and took advantage of the newest ideas from younger officers. One winter he spent many evenings in the Berlin Artillery School and the Artillery Examination Commission, listening to officers talking about the newest research and experiences. It was the beginning of a restless passion.

In 1864 during the Danish war he was assigned to command the artillery in the attack at Düppel. After the victory he was named assistant inspector general of artillery.[6] As the inspector general was ill and died a few months later, Hindersin soon took his place. During the siege of Düppel the superiority of guns was greater than anyone had experienced before. The Prussian army in Denmark had one-fourth rifled field guns and six-pounders. Hindersin's first conclusion was to increase the number of rifled field guns.

It was at this time that Hohenlohe first came into contact with this unique man. Hohenlohe was surprised that Hindersin, an old general, came to him, a young staff officer. Hindersin said that since he had been appointed inspector general of artillery he had been kept awake at night thinking about certain problems. He asked Hohenlohe to give him a good night's rest and put his mind at ease. Hindersin feared that rifled guns were so far superior to smooth bores that Prussia needed all rifled guns. Prussia at that time had 75 percent smooth bores. He feared that if a war came and Prussia went up against a power with rifled guns, Prussia would lose. Losing meant for him the destruction of the fatherland. This thought dominated his thinking and disturbed his sleep.

Hindersin presented his arguments to the monarch. Various other personages also took part in this discussion. Although many arguments in favor of smooth-bore guns were made, including the great American Civil War, which employed only 25 percent smooth bores, Hindersin's arguments finally prevailed.[7] In June 1864 Hindersin ordered as many four-pound rifled guns as the factories were able to make. The process went slowly, as steel was used. By the time of the next great campaign, the Austro-Prussian War of 1866, only half of Prussian artillery was rifled.

At that time it was an operational fundamental that in combat one always held back a certain reserve, including the rifled guns. Hindersin believed that the coming war would be won with a single great battle and that since they had so few rifled guns, they should use them right at the start. Shortly before the beginning of the war each corps was given two batteries of rifled four-pounders. In this way 63 percent of Prussian field artillery was rifled as the war began. There was scarcely time for practice: they had one day with unloaded grenades, then off to war.

Hindersin was right as far as the war was concerned. One large battle, Königgrätz, decided it. Batteries with rifled guns did well. The general staff history of the Austro-Prussian War concluded that rifled batteries did better than the smooth bores. After 1866 all batteries were changed over to rifled guns as quickly as possible.

Another of his accomplishments was the founding of the Artillery Practice School. As early as the siege of Düppel Hindersin had seen that troops with rifled guns did not do half as badly as expected. But at his first inspections of 1864, he saw that the troops did far poorer than the potential of their weapons. In conversations with commanders he discovered that other batteries were not doing any better. Finally he asked, Why does the infantry shoot better? He concluded it was because they had a practice school.

From the beginning of his assignment as inspector general, at the conclusion of every talk, he said, "We must have a practice school." His sharp criticism of the shooting ability of the batteries provoked new thinking and new ideas about shooting, correcting, and using the rifled guns. But he always asked, How do we know this? We need a practice school.

Approval and funding had to be granted by the Prussian Landtag, and it was a period of budgetary and constitutional crisis in Prussia: the systematic opposition of the majority at that time prevented any increase in the military budget. That did not stop Hindersin a bit from doing what he felt necessary. He created a school from volunteers. The first school convened with old and young officers of varied experience.

But it was not good enough. As every artillery officer knows, along with correct service of the guns, the main difficulties are with observations, measurement, and command. And to learn these skills, one needs to use an operating artillery battery.[8]

The victorious war of 1866 broke the budgetary block, and the Prussian Landtag quickly approved funds for a practice school. But it was a while before the whole system was in place. Many trials and errors were made before it was perfected. Hindersin believed that the firing system had to be not only mathematically correct but also simple and easy to operate so that in moments of danger it would not confuse the artillery men.

Hindersin did not know which system would eventually develop as the right one. In order to come to some conclusion, he went out to the school to acquaint himself with all possibilities. There one could see him, days on end, observing the shooting, asking questions, listening to the critiques. He disturbed no one, but every day he learned something. Before he changed the firing regulations, he allowed the school to try out many possibilities. By this means he not only trained a whole cadre of teachers from each regiment but spread the word among the troops as a whole, encouraging not only obedience but compliance.

From that time on he pushed his own views that troops shoot as well as possible. Training exercises aimed at landing a number of shots near the stated firing goals.[9] That this caused many problems is self-evident. Hindersin was a man of such coarse ways, so naturally mistrustful and easily irritated, that he was not loved but feared by the troops. But he did not expect to be loved. As long as he lived, he wanted only to carry out his duties.

Hindersin's impact on fortress artillery was equally important. Under his leadership artillery brigades that had fortress units converted into independent fortress artillery regiments. Hindersin changed the whole approach of these units. Up until then they practiced their procedures on the drill field but never in the fortress in which they were expected to operate in war. Hindersin allowed them to carry out maneuvers in and around the fortress. In 1869 came the first regulations for fortress and siege service. No foot artillery regiment, as they were later called, can now go without such practice and training. Before Hindersin there was nothing.

Considering the replacement of all these smooth-bore guns by rifled guns, and what an enormous material transformation this was, and how much resistance there was, and that all the regulations of the artillery, field as well as fortress, had to be rewritten, and that Hindersin controlled every word and that every rule was tested in the field before it was issued, we have some idea of the accomplishments of this man during the seven or eight years he was at the leading edge of this weaponry. In the war of 1870 the test came. The results were so spectacular that everyone noticed them, and the artillery assumed a position of equality with the infantry and cavalry.[10] Hindersin saw the fruit of his work, and as the victory year 1871 came to a close, his life ended.

His fear that he would die prematurely of a heart attack was unfulfilled. One day as they ate the evening meal, he said to his family, "The next time the family gathers, it will be over my coffin." Eight days later, on 23 January 1872, he died.

# Moltke

*1890–1900*

---

This reading is collaged from three essays: one published at Helmuth von Moltke's ninetieth birthday (1890), one at his death (1891), and one on the hundredth anniversary of his birth (1900). Delbrück's insights as participant in Moltke's last war and as observer of Moltke's nearly twenty-year tenure as general staff chief thereafter are blended into his comparative knowledge of war history. Here is an early description of one of the most famous military figures of all time, an account full of politics, armies, and personalities. It suggests that Moltke was a pioneer of industrial mass war based on specialization of knowledge.

---

Along with his predecessor, Scharnhorst, Moltke has one of the most difficult personalities to characterize in all of world history.[1] It is the enduring modesty within the greatness that makes it so hard to understand him. Greatness has the right to step self-confidently onto the world, powerful, empowered by successful actions, the master. Such persons appear so attractive they take this right freely. We can understand them. But if we admire quiet modesty, it is very difficult to understand modest persons.

Not all the paintings of the master Lenbach are successful.[2] As he tries to portray his subjects from within, not only as we see them from the outside, for Lenbach as for historians there are difficult and easy personalities to characterize. The titan Bismarck and the less famous intellectual Döllinger are both valid images for Lenbach's eye.[3] A hundred years from now people will stand in front of the Bismarck portrait and say, How wonderful! The founder of the new German Empire!

Not so with the picture of his embattled colleague, Moltke. Moltke told us that once he went to the National Gallery, and as he stood in front of his own portrait a group of people from the countryside came up. They did not recognize him as they stood before his portrait. "He doesn't look so angry," said one to the other. "That," said Moltke, "results from the fact that Lenbach portrayed me as something of a hero, but I have none of the heroic in me."

There is nothing more beautiful than words from Moltke's own lips, but can we believe him? The goal of art, whether painting or history, lies exactly in this: that those qualities which remain the highest values are brought forth. Master Lenbach had the right idea in mind, but he could not quite bring it off.

Moltke is different from other great commanders with whom one might compare him in that he was exclusively a soldier. Alexander the Great, Gustavus Adolphus, Frederick the Great, and Napoleon were also kings. Hannibal, Caesar, and Cromwell were like kings. This is not simply an exterior culmination of different actions but a deep interior difference.

As Clausewitz said in a famous definition, war is the continuation of politics by other means. The best of all situations is therefore the union of politics and war command in the hands of that person who holds supreme power. The interchanges between war actions and other political actions characterize great kings. After a victorious battle Frederick wrote as many diplomatic notes as military orders. The greatness of Napoleonic warfare lay in the fact that at that moment when the emperor had achieved military success he employed political negotiations to reach his goals. The advantages of the victories from Jena to Tilsit, the success of the battle of Friedland were made possible only by a peace that made former enemies allies of the victor. To the victory of Austerlitz over the Russians and Austrians belongs the simultaneous diplomatic negotiations with Haugwitz, the Prussian ambassador.[4] Without this brilliantly handled political art, the strategic success of Napoleon would have been impossible.

Those commanders of the first rank who did not hold royal power, such as Themistocles, Epaminondas, Scipio, Prince Eugene of Savoy, and Marlborough, had eminent statesman-like powers, and this strength also characterizes the two Prussian generals who may be compared with Moltke: Scharnhorst and Gneisenau.[5] They not only fought the wars of liberation but carried with them the spirit of freedom. Wellington, a leading commander, was also a very active statesman.[6]

Moltke is different from all these others in that he was exclusively a soldier.

We can carry this distinction even further. Moltke was exclusively a strategist. He did not personally lead troops, he was not placed at the head of fighting forces in the midst of extreme danger, and he did not experience the bravery and reluctant fortunes that finally brought victory. His feeling for command came entirely from his position as chief of the general staff.

In the rich memoirs in which Konstantin Rössler in the *Berlin Post* memorialized the field marshal, he says Moltke directed war in a methodological way.[7] What he meant was that of all great commanders Moltke is the most theoretical. The art of war that Napoleon practiced with naive genius Moltke practiced systematically. Moltke directed his ideas toward practical conclusions. The public has some idea of this relationship when they call him the "battle thinker." I do not like this expression because it implies that strategic value lies only in planning operations. That is only one part of strategy. Underlying Moltke's decisions there was the steadfastness of will, strengthened not only by pure instinct but also by the doctrinaire correctness of his judgment. Although theory and doctrine sometimes weaken practical capacity and sureness of action because they are not in tune with reality, in Moltke's case this was not so. His theoretical understanding coincided so closely with reality that he operated easily and effectively in the real world. As Prince Frederick Charles with caution and slowness backed out of Bohemia, Moltke, knowing the value of the initiative and the offensive, urged him on by telegraph to Gitschin.[8] As General Werder hesitated in front of Belfort, undecided if he should risk battle against his threefold larger foe Bourbacki, Moltke in Versailles understood that psychologically Bourbacki assumed he would soon be attacked in the rear by Manteuffel.[9] Moltke knew that large masses of troops had to be clearly led when they attempted operations of great magnitude. As older men in his position hesitated, he had the self-confidence to move forward and get the job done. In this way he developed his art confidently, based on two opposing tendencies—strong leadership from above and spontaneous action from below.

Moltke came from an old Mecklenburg noble family. His grandmother was of French blood, a Huguenot. His father, one of ten brothers, was a Prussian lieutenant who married the daughter of a rich Lübeck patrician, Paaschen. Following the wishes of his father-in-law, he left Prussian service and became a farmer. Moving frequently, he lived for a time in Parchim, where his brother was a Mecklenburg officer, and here Helmuth was born on 26 October 1800. Thus, like his family, he was also a Mecklenburger by chance. He lived his youth partly in Lübeck, partly in Holstein, and at age eleven he joined the Danish cadet corps in Copenhagen. His father had found his calling in the army as his grandfather had. To help bring up the large family, his father took service with the Danish crown, in whose army he rose to the rank of lieutenant general.

In 1822 the Danish lieutenant Moltke, after three years in the Rendsburg garrison, transferred to Prussian service. He had visited Berlin with his father and there saw Prussian soldiers for the first time. His aunt was married to Geheimrat Ballhorn in Berlin, and a younger brother of Helmuth lived with them. The reason for the transfer Moltke has never said. It was not nationalism. Moltke had no contact with the circles and forces in which nationalism was then moving, and the officers of the Schleswig-Holstein regiment of the king of Denmark did not feel very much the national differences among Prussian, German, and Danish. The reason why Lieutenant von Moltke sought Prussian service was none other than the reason why

other able soldiers such as Blücher, Scharnhorst, and Gneisenau had made the same decision: the fame and the greatness
of the Prussian army, which set high ideals, inspired consciousness of powerful deeds done, and suggested the possibility of great deeds to come.[10]

Within a short time it was demonstrated that even in that
gloomy era the Prussian army recognized talent. A year and a
half after beginning with the Eighth Regiment in Frankfurt am
Main, Moltke was called to the War Academy, and after he
studied there three years and spent a few months in company
service, he was appointed director of the officer training school
of his division. A year later, at age twenty-eight, he was called
to the topographical section and then into the general staff itself.[11] He remained there for the rest of his life and in 1857 became its chief.

It was one of the first official acts of the prince of Prussia, after he took over the regency. Had he recognized already the future army commander of his wars? No! and it is a curious piece
of history how Moltke really became the Prussian-German
commander.

It is clear that Moltke did not lead the general staff in 1857
in the sense that he later did. The general staff at that time was a
kind of academic institution headed by a learned general.
Moltke, who had no family or personal ties to the king, first
joined the circle of the royal family as chief of staff to the Fourth
Army Corps commanded by Prince Frederick Charles. In 1845
he served as adjutant to the old Prince Henry in Rome, perhaps
as a result of his learnedness, as reflected in his delightful letters
from Turkey, 1835–39.[12] The special interest of our hero in
Rome was topography. He spent his time in scholarly studies
of the city and, with the help of Alexander von Humboldt,
aroused the interest of the prince in these studies.[13] After the
death of Prince Henry he was again a general staff officer and,
as a colonel, was named in 1855 adjutant to Prince Frederick
Wilhelm, later Kaiser Wilhelm I. This position was much
more complicated and delicate. The king had appointed Moltke,
but the prince did not want anything to do with him. He was

not against Moltke the person but against the position. The first meeting of Moltke with his future warlord was painful.

Why he finally accepted Moltke is not clear. It was a time of great tension between the brothers. Perhaps the king wanted to provide an older, more conservative mentor to his brother, a move the prince of Prussia saw as unnecessary. Moltke's personality soon equalized the situation. Nothing lay further from Moltke's mind than to push his ideas on someone who did not want them. In the crown princes' household I was told that Moltke rode into the country with his prince as quiet as a mouse. An adjutant asked Moltke to talk more with the prince. Moltke replied, "He could ask me questions." After half a year Moltke wrote to a friend that he was getting along with the prince and princess. On 7 October 1857, the death day of General von Reyher, fourteen days after the proclamation of the regency, General Adjutant von Gerlach wrote in his diary, "Another important position to fill. Moltke is the best candidate." Edwin von Manteuffel, chief of the military cabinet and adviser to the regent, did everything he could to get Moltke named as the chief of the general staff and was finally successful.

By directing maneuvers and by his actions during the Danish war Moltke gradually moved closer to the king. On 14 March 1865 Manteuffel wrote Roon, "The king has great confidence in Moltke as chief of the general staff and deep down wants Moltke to be the commander in chief of the army."[14] Nevertheless it was a long time before Moltke was in a position to do this job. In his 1862 essay "The Italian Campaign of 1859" Moltke himself characterized the problems of his position: commanders in the field must all hold the strategic viewpoint of a single person.[15] If the commanding generals are not all of the same mind, moving together toward a single certain position, the goal will be threatened. But in fact what happens is that the commander is given a group of generals who are independent men. Thus he hears this from that one and that from another one. One piece of advice following one set of rules leads to a certain conclusion, a second set of rules supports another position, the thoroughly correct point of view of a third

leads in a different path, and the advice of a fourth goes somewhere else. With all these instructions it is likely that the commander will lose the campaign.

Preparing for war in early 1866, Moltke was one of many in
the circles of King Wilhelm. But now came the most important moment. The modern art of war decrees that the mobilization and concentration of the army is perhaps the most significant strategic act of the war.

It is important to all armies that they be mobilized. But the
larger the armies grow, the greater the work capacity of the
transportation system, the more rapidly mobilization is carried
out, the higher burn the fires of war, the more important becomes the first move. As Moltke himself once said, fundamental mistakes in the mobilization cannot be corrected during the
rest of the war. We can turn this statement around: the mobilization sets the first great action and therefore determines the
whole further course of the war. To prepare and organize is today the exclusive peacetime job of the general staff, and it is the
job of the chief to carry their plans out in wartime. The insep-
arable unity between peace and war was first seen with full
clarity in the war of 1866. At that time it became clear that only
the chief of the general staff should direct the army in war.

But Moltke's ideas were opposed by others. At the time,
even very insightful observers did not recognize that Prussia
had found in General von Moltke a brilliant strategist. He was
sixty-five years old, had never had a command, and except for
the brief Turkish-Egyptian campaign and the Danish war, he
had no combat experience. Moreover, his opponent, Field
Marshal Benedek, enjoyed the fame that comes from practical
war experience.[16] All who knew Moltke realized he was a man
of extraordinarily clear and cool judgment, but for a strategist
there are many other necessary qualities. Could study and maneuver direction be transferred to real war command?

It would have been much easier if King Wilhelm had wanted
the war. In that case he would have one day ordered the mobilization, and the army would have marched into Moravia or
Bohemia without facing any resistance. Prussia would have

had many advantages over Austria: shorter lines of communication, tighter organization, and a well-developed railroad system. Concentration would have been so rapid that Austria would hardly have been able to defend its borders.

But King Wilhelm did not want the war. At first he opposed the whole idea.[17] A few preparatory actions were carried out. Five army corps were mobilized, then two more, and finally the last two. The result was that Prussia not only lost the advantage of an early mobilization but had to be prepared to defend its own territory and even its capital against attack. Because of the way the territory of Prussia and Austria interlock, there were many possibilities for attacks from Silesia and Bohemia and from Austria's allies. The Austrians could have fallen on Mähten from Silesia or from Bohemia; they could have moved through Saxony up the right bank of the Elbe River to Berlin; they could have linked up with Bavaria on the left. Austrian forces in Holstein could have connected with Hanover for an operation. The Austrian main army could have forgone the offensive and instead mounted a defensive in its own country. Moltke had to consider all these possibilities, all the while thinking about what the French might do.

Finally Prussia seized the initiative, and Moltke carried out his great decisive plan. He knew that the Austrian main forces were not yet concentrated, that they were marching toward Moravia, and he concluded that Prussian forces could arrive in front of the Bohemian Mountains before Benedek came to the spot and attacked his isolated forces. Was it clear that this plan could be carried out?

In the immediate circle of the Prussian king there were grave doubts. General von Manteuffel and General Adjutant Gustav von Alvensleben both had the king's ear. Manteuffel was far away, but Alvensleben accompanied the king and wrote Moltke three letters (19, 20, and 22 June) warning him of the dangers. It was too much of a gamble to pull off, he said. The assembly of the forces on the other side of the mountains was just what the Austrians wanted. The Austrians were near enough to both Prussian armies to defeat one and then the other. The Prussian armies were spread so far apart that even the Bavarians might attack them. Colonel von Döring, one of Moltke's assistants who had been entirely committed to Moltke's plan, began to doubt it after reading these letters.[18] Alvensleben wanted to concentrate Prussian forces on the north side of the mountains, seize Dresden, mobilize further, and then take Hanover and north Germany. By following this plan Prussia lost nothing and gained strength and support.

It is not known if Moltke responded to these letters. Probably he did not, for what could he say? From the standpoint of pure strategic logic Alvensleben was right. But Moltke was more than a pure operational mathematician. His Clausewitzian education taught him that it was false always to choose the completely safe way in war, and he had the courage to follow this conviction. He was confident that even if the Austrians reached Bohemia on inner lines between the Prussian armies, the Prussians individually were strong enough at least for a time to withstand Austrian pressure, long enough for the other Prussian group to arrive, and then the Prussians could move from a strategic disadvantage to a tactical advantage. Even as I write this I have a new book by General von Schlichting, *Moltke and Benedek*, which clearly portrays this idea and supports it with examples.[19] Nothing shows Moltke's genius more than this: taking the tactical advantage from the start by splitting his forces and thereon cold-bloodedly accepting the strategic dangers. Schlichting further argues that Moltke's method should not be called encirclement because it really depended on the opponent's actions. Why did Benedek adopt the deep formation, with narrow front? He did it out of cautiousness. The commander would have complete control of his troops; there would be no separations; everyone would stand fast for the decision of battle. Benedek lost the battle not by some great mistake but exactly in these small details of cautious assemblage. And Moltke won it by the advantages of an attack from two fronts.

Along the way, however, there were places where Moltke came close to complete and terrible annihilation. His plan was clear and correct, but its execution depended on the actions of many others, and a few of them failed. Most important was Prince Frederick Charles, who, like Benedek, was very anxious to keep his forces together and as a result did not move forward. He did not trust his three corps to go forward until Herwarth's forces had joined him, even though he knew he was facing only two or at the most three corps.[20] He took seven days to move the forty miles from the border to Gitschin although he had only a hussar squadron in front of him. Moltke wrote him to move forward rapidly, join up with the crown prince, and close with the main Austrian force beyond the mountains. Moltke expected him to arrive at Gitschin by 25 June. The prince arrived only on 29 June after repeated direct orders from the king and Moltke in Berlin. If Frederick Charles had arrived two days earlier, the crown prince's crossing of the Silesian Mountains would have been much easier. Now instead of that the crown prince had to move in the opposite direction toward Münchengrätz, and along the way the mistakes of one of his generals, Eduard von Bonin, put the whole operation in jeopardy. Near Trautenau, Bonin was opposed by equal forces, corps against corps. He moved out of the pass and was attacked while moving. A great part of his force never fought at all. He lost fewer than 1,339 men; his opponent lost 4,787. Nevertheless Bonin retreated, and it was a day and a half before he considered his responsibilities to the other Prussian forces.[21] On the next and decisive day the crown prince had only two and a half army corps to confront the entire Austrian main army.

But Moltke's strategy was based not only on size, space, and time factors but also on the belief that Prussia had brave and able soldiers and generals. What one promises, one delivers. The crown prince, advised by Blumenthal, held fast, and Steinmetz, who had been standing by at Nachod, fought and won the decisive battle at Skalitz in a beautiful union of heroism and prudence. With this stroke everything was about done. On the day before, Prussia had fought at Trautenau and Langensalza and the Italians had won the battle at Custozza, so that the victory of Skalitz virtually sealed the campaign for Prussia. Moltke's operational ideas were so strong that they were good enough to overcome the greatest misfortune in execution.[22]

For all other great commanders, war was only a means to their political goals. Moltke thought of his victories in another category: priceless strokes of fate created by a general staff which gave the politicians, such as Bismarck, room to operate. His modesty, serenity, and length in office made possible his greatness. Here we are at the point where he appears the man of pure intellect, who never falls into the temptation to operate outside the bounds of his competence.

The study of topography and the general staff educational system formed the basis of his career. In his letters he describes the world as an artist. His profession was to organize all the thousand wheels of the machine: to get together every troop unit and prince every evening in the right quarters, with the right horses and right provisions. At forty years old, as a weatherbeaten veteran from Turkey and the adventures of the Syrian campaign, he became engaged to the 15-year-old Marie Burt, stepdaughter of his sister. They had a happy marriage. As long as they lived, they remained fond of teasing and vivacious, and even though reserved nobles of the highest position, they could always laugh. His letters are filled with humor, displaying his sense of the natural world, art, humanity, and history. Thus humor is prominent in his character, and without this warm, golden light his quiet would appear cold.

Earnest and wise, duty true and a hard worker, these qualities are the cornerstones of Moltke's character. Heroism is hidden and wisdom and humor are united with an image of grace. The director of the wild wars stands before us as a man with no enemies.

# Part 2

# The Cold War, 1904–1914

# The Russo-Japanese War
## 1904

---

Here is an example of "contemporary history," a contradiction in terms but a direction Delbrück was repeatedly forced to go after 1900. As cold war spread across Europe, Delbrück described it as it was happening, a chancy situation for a historian who relied on the validity of sources and a degree of separation from the events they describe. These two cardinal principles of Delbrück's philosophy of history are missing from his "current events" essays. Nevertheless his roughly seventeen hundred *Prussian Yearbook* readers each month, a diverse circle of the ruling elite, admired Delbrück for independence, nonpartisanship, and clear, effective analysis from a moderate national point of view. This reading is a good example of all these things applied to a war going on at the time.

---

When a great war unsettles the political scene, people at home and abroad believe one side will be defeated, the other will be victorious, thereby moving the wheel of world history forward. It appears unavoidable: a historical necessity. But things do not happen that way. In every case there is the interplay of personal passions, the bravery and patriotism of the people and their leaders. There are simple mistakes made and, instead of objective causality, many unintended consequences. Take, for example, the Crimean War. We are uncertain if it could have been avoided, because it had no aftermath or consequences. It broke out as the leaders were unaware of all the possibilities: Czar Nicholas did not understand the earnestness of the great powers, and the prince regent and a few ministers in England did not expect the czar to compromise.[1]

Today it is asked whether the Russo-Japanese War was unavoidable. I doubt it. If it is true that the Japanese wanted to lead a war of the yellow races against the white, to make themselves rulers of China, and to lead the way to an Asia for the Asians, then the war was indeed unavoidable. But if intelligent Japanese statesmen had looked ahead, acting only to obtain for Japan equal treatment with the European powers, it is possible that an acceptable agreement could have been reached between Russia and Japan. It is quite false, as the German newspapers were saying, that Russia could not allow Korea to be taken over by Japan because of its naval advantages. That is, Russia wanted to avoid creating another Bosporus situation with access to the sea closed off. But the sea between Korea and Japan is forty miles wide even in its narrowest place, much too large to be dominated from the shore. It can be blocked only by a fleet with bases on both shores. Korea by itself has very little value for Russia.

If Japan simply wanted to be recognized as an East Asian great power, she could have gone about it more easily by asking for other concessions. Why did not the Russians, as soon as they noticed that the Japanese were thinking earnestly of war, offer them whatever was of value in Korea, instead, as it appears, of withholding Seilchen und Klauseln? It seems that nothing but Russian pride was injured. It is also possible that Count Lambsdorff, anxious over domestic politics, really wanted a war and stretched out the negotiations only in order to gain time to mobilize.[2] But that is probably incorrect. It is more likely that the leaders in St. Petersburg were totally surprised by the war's outbreak. One might say as surprised as the editors of the *Norddeutsche Allgemeine Zeitung* (*North German News*). Right up to the last minute they did not believe it would happen.

Whichever is right, it was a major mistake of the diplomacy of the Russians that they were not more forthcoming with the Japanese. It was obvious that Japan would have an interest in Korea, but Russia expressly demanded the use of various points on the peninsula for strategic purposes and neutrality for the rest, north of the thirty-ninth parallel. In the eyes of the

Japanese such demands were a joke, and it is undeniable that responsibility for the war rests now on the Russians. They gave the Japanese very few concessions. As for Manchuria, the Japanese expressly said it was out of their sphere of influence. The Japanese, who are much more interested in being a land power than a world naval power, had already taken the Liaotung peninsula and Port Arthur from China in 1895.

A very instructive article of last July tells us what Russia believed about Japan and its relationship with the czarist empire.[3] It contained sentiments of boundless Russian self-confidence and an absolute disparagement of Japan. This article demonstrated that Russian diplomats had no idea what Japan wanted. If Count Lambsdorff wished to provoke a war with Japan, which is not entirely out of the question, he could not have gone about it any better. Likewise, we do not know if Japan wanted to provoke a race war in the Far East or not. As it stands, it is Russia that provoked Japan by deceitful negotiations, and Europe therefore has no reason to stand firm behind Russia in this situation.

Japan began the war with an attack when Russia had not yet achieved a major goal of its war preparations, namely, concentration of its fleet. The Russian battle fleet was divided among its northern Siberian harbors of Ozean and Vladivostok; Chemulpo, the harbor of Seoul and the Korean peninsula; and Port Arthur and the southern tip of Liaotung. After an attack against the fleet at Port Arthur, carefully led with nighttime torpedo boats, both great ships in the harbor at Chemulpo were also destroyed and the Japanese won a great victory. If the Russian main fleet was warned, the success of the Japanese is even greater. Whereas before the attack the two fleets were considered roughly equal, now it is clear who has the upper hand.

This naval victory cannot be overestimated. Up until now it was unknown if one or the other of the great powers could appear from the sea and mount a great land invasion. Japan has now begun its invasion of Korea unhindered by the Russian navy. The Japanese army is on the attack north of Seoul, marching to where it can attack the Russian main force at the

Yalu, the river border between Korea and Manchuria. An advantageous and workable location for the landing is on the east side of the Liaotung peninsula, but there the coast is often covered with ice and a landing might be foolhardy. The Russian fleet in Port Arthur is indeed weakened, but it is not entirely out of the game and might still fall on Japanese transport ships. But the Japanese have chosen a location so far from the Russians that their landings will probably not be disrupted and their approach march can move forward to the border.

From Seoul to the Yalu River is 260 miles as the crow flies, and a few weeks will pass before the great land battles begin. The Japanese are not losing anything in these weeks, because the Russians can neither increase their forces substantially nor bring their fleet up to strength. In other words, they cannot materially improve their position. Naturally Russia cannot think of an offensive into Korea lest the Japanese attack them in the rear.

By naming a Japanese prince as regent of Korea, Japan has taken into its hands the whole government of Korea.

As extraordinarily favorable as the beginning of the war is for the Japanese, one cannot at all predict the final outcome. Two quite different scenarios may be suggested.

The Japanese are brave, concerted, and ambitious. But they are also rash and unpredictable, and their organization may be overextended. It is therefore possible that before the war is over, their strength will wane. It could happen that after a while their ships will not be able to transport enough coal, and their munitions stockpiles, food supplies, or means of transportation will become insufficient. A great combined land and sea operation needs lengthy preparations. The attack of Bourbaki against Werder at Belfort in 1870 failed partly because Gambetta's army organization had not paid sufficient attention to details, namely, ramps to unload the horses from the railroad cars, and ice horseshoes, without which the horses were unable to move over frozen ground.[4]

Such shortages ultimately result from a lack of discipline. Until they are tested, one cannot speculate about the administrative and organizational undergirdings of the Japanese army. It is also difficult to say if Japan has the financial strength for this war. The English army administration ultimately overcame its shortages in the Crimean War by spending two hundred million pounds.[5] The Greeks began their war against the Turks in 1897 with a good strategic idea. There was no lack of personal bravery or patriotic feelings, but the attack soon came to a halt and finally failed because of administrative shortcomings and material deficiencies: munitions for the warships were not on hand and could not be produced.[6]

A second scenario is the military or economical defeat of Russia by Japan. For Russia it might be a bit of luck in the sense that it was lucky for Prussia that Napoleon cut off the Polish provinces after the peace of Tilsit. In the 1890s Russia turned to East Asia and built the Trans-Siberian Railroad as it became clear to her that obstacles stood in the way of her traditional Balkan policies. Without giving up these policies entirely, the Russians sought a different method to open up national feeling.

What an open-ended province for action these broad ocean areas seemed! One could imagine a close relationship between the Chinese and the Russians, both very authoritarian, and a future joint aegis over the whole of Asia. But rabid nationalism on the Russian side has run out. The new Russia on the Amur River and the old Russia in the west do not have a working economic relationship. The lines of the Trans-Siberian Railroad are much too thin and long. Freight costs by sea to Hamburg are much less than freight costs by railroad, even with a very low fixed rail rate. The *Kreuzzeitung* recently published an instructive article on this.[7] Russian industry, not yet ready to compete with western Europe, can compete on the Yellow Sea. But the Siberian Railroad, which cost many million marks, remains almost entirely for military use.[8] Also it is possible that the Russian finance minister might think in the quiet of his chamber, If the Americans bought Alaska from us, they also might want the whole of east Siberia!

If the Asian war has made an enormous impression on Europe, calling forth a general economic depression, along with it comes new possibilities, new combinations, and sudden revisions of Far Eastern and Near Eastern politics. It is noteworthy that the immediate result of a Russian–Japanese war was that powers such as Sweden and Spain took precautionary war measures.

But it is a long way from these uncomfortable moves to a full world crisis. We must not forget that in spite of all the tension a fairly strong alliance exists between Russia and England. With its strength in East Asia, England cannot wish for a nativistic movement to break out in China. As soon as that happens, the desire will arise in England to take the upper hand without an overflowing of the wild waters of world war. On the basis of this wish we can again expect a long, secure period of peace. At least we may not give up this hope while also preparing for the opposite.

# International Tension

*1908*

---

This reading was written about forty days before the outbreak of the Bosnian annexation crisis, the second Cuban missile–type crisis during the nine years immediately preceding the outbreak of World War I. This crisis, which lasted from October 1908 through April 1909, reached its climax in Austrian and Serbian countermobilizations and two German ultimatums to Russia, threatening "to allow matters to take their course" unless Russia restrained Serbian hostility.[1] With hindsight we can see that Delbrück missed a lot; nevertheless he recognizes the clear possibility of a European war, sketches out who will most likely be on each side, discusses the impact of Germany's bad press image in England, and analyzes the potential of a sea blockade against his country. He ends by describing the specific role of Russian mobilization. Over the years many observers have seen the 1908 Bosnian crisis as the precursor to the events of July 1914.

---

As King Edward and Czar Nicholas meet in Reval, international tension is high.[2] The French president will soon make the same trip, raising the tension level. Kaiser Wilhelm has given up his usual North Sea trip, and the entire German war fleet, sixteen battleships and ten cruisers, is maneuvering in the Atlantic Ocean off the Azores. Germans are apprehensive. What does this apparent encircling of Germany mean?

Is it only a diplomatic game, or is war about to break out as in 1870? A year ago one of the leading English military figures, General French, visited eastern Europe and traveled through the Russian garrisons.[3] Now General von der Goltz of Prussia goes east to see his old friends in Constantinople.[4] Journalistic hatred against Germany, quieted down for the past several years, has stirred up again, fraying the nerves of the French people and giving the usually robust English the jitters. An enormous English fleet sails along the Danish and Norwegian coast and works on the fantasies of the northern peoples. A Pan-Slavic congress in Prague stirs up the Slavic peoples of Austria against the Germans. In Morocco the French assure us they are strictly carrying out the Algeciras accord.[5] Nevertheless their troops remain in Algeria, occupying new areas, inciting one pasha against another, and waiting to see if Germany will raise questions.

If it comes to war, Germany and Austria will be allied with the Moroccans on the one side and the Turks on the other. A new complication is that the Young Turk movement has caused a great mutiny to break out in the Turkish army.[6] The Young Turks want modern European ideas to be incorporated into the Islamic empire, especially constitutionalism. At the same time, they want the Turkish state to be decisively strengthened. The plan of the English and Russians, who want to sever Macedonia from the body of the Ottoman Empire in the process of reforming it, is opposed by the Young Turks and the sultan. It is questionable if this movement is doing more to weaken the empire further or will give it renewed powers of resistance.

It is not calculable how far the war will go if it breaks out in Morocco or Turkey. Persia will be dragged in and India, and England, from its unassailable island, will have to defend Egypt and the Suez Canal. If Austria and Germany reinforce the sultan's hand, the railroad from Damascus to Mecca, which the sultan built, makes possible the movement of a large Turkish army through Syria.

Why the sinister tension? Where does the specter of world war originate? Is it really possible that the great cultural peoples will destroy themselves over Morocco or a few Turkish provinces? If the fire spreads to the United States and Japan, it will be an enormously enlarged example of a constellation created two hundred years ago, when the War of the Spanish Succession and the Great Northern War wasted and finally transformed Europe.

The invention of the dirigible airship has increased English nervousness. The technical experts are clear that this invention is not important either as a weapon or as transportation. It is an invention of reconnaissance. The enormous range of modern weapons and the extension of the modern approach march have made timely reconnaissance, always an essential part of strategy, more and more difficult. The dirigible provides a new method for this. The popular mind, however, sees armies flying through the air and attacking enemy lands from above. When a zeppelin from East Friesland flying the German flag crosses the North Sea, makes a circle over London, and comes home, the English people fear that the age of sea power hegemony is past and the age of air power has arrived. They fear that Germany has armed itself with a new and terrible weapon.

What plans do they attribute to Germany? Earlier they thought we wanted a German Austria or a German Switzerland or the annexation of Holland. Next they thought the German kaiser sought a European alliance system under his hegemony. Now they believe we are preparing to land in England. We laugh about this and see in such suspicions only ill-willed prejudice, but it is necessary to look further and see it as a symptom of fear for our future. This fear is a real fact and a real power. It is a basic and foundational source of war danger. The English, who fear the future Germany, can think of nothing else but that this danger must be prepared for: the German trade and battle fleet must be destroyed before it gets too strong. In this way England destroyed the fleet of the Netherlands in the seventeenth century and Napoleon's French navy a hundred years later, leading to hegemony over the sea and sovereignty over a quarter of humanity.

Bismarck founded the Triple Alliance to protect Germany against a simultaneous attack from Russia and France. At that time the only rival of England in the other parts of the world were these two powers. Germany counted on the benign neutrality of England in any continental war. How the world has changed! It is correct that we are now in danger, but no Bismarck could warn us of this danger because we are the relatively strongest power and weaker powers naturally ally against the strongest. But we cannot and do not want more of the European continent.

The decision to go to war lies with Russia. In a war against us, England, in alliance with Russia and France, has so little to risk and so much to gain that her ministers do not have to stop for humanitarian reasons as long as there is a possibility of successful action. No less than one-seventh of British trade goes to Germany, but what is that against the possibility of securing the naval hegemony of the world for all time! The French, if their feelings of revenge have strongly receded, will not stop as long as their alliance with England and Russia ensures them of superiority. In Russia itself there is so much hatred against the Germans it will not be difficult to incite public opinion to war. It depends on the decision of the czar and his advisers. At the end of the 1880s no one doubted that a danger to Constantinople meant danger to Berlin sooner or later. The Russo-German Reinsurance Treaty seemed to provide some security. Then in 1894 came the change. After that, instead of the Near East, the Russians looked to the Far East.[7] Then they were beaten by the Japanese. Have they resurrected their old plan about Constantinople? Earlier, England was their main opponent. Now, with Egypt and the Suez Canal in secure hands, they look at Arabia.

The attempt of Russia, supported by England and France, to become politically active again, is significant. England will provide money, and it will not really be necessary for Russia to fight the German and Austro-Hungarian armies. It will be enough for them to block the way, while English ships close off every route for Germany to import food. We cannot feed our people forever by ourselves. In Austria-Hungary the situation is dangerous but not as serious.

In alliance with France and England, Russia is risking war. But is not the fighting power of the central European armies terrible? And will not the ultimate winner finally be England? Will not France be destroyed and a large part of Russia be overrun by German, Austrian, Romanian, and Turkish troops and domestic revolution? All set in motion before the starvation of Germany by sea blockade is accomplished? Is such a blockade capable of being carried out?

While I have been writting, the news announces that the Russian prime minister Stolypin is meeting the German chancellor in Norderney and in fourteen days the English king Edward will visit the German kaiser.[8] These meetings are signs that we may expect peace to continue for a while. At the same time, the Young Turks have negotiated with the sultan and the December 1876 constitution is to be renewed, an event whose influence and significance gives us a little security. It may be an accident without meaning; it may be an alternative, giving the empire extended life for a short time; or it could be the beginning of the end.

# Danger of War

*1908*

---

Here Delbrück describes the 1908 Bosnian crisis right in the middle of it, before any resolutions. He lines up both sides and compares the possibilities of war in 1908 with earlier coalition wars. In a novel approach for his day he introduces a preliminary analysis of the media coverage and its consequences. As in 1996, Serbia figures in important ways here. It is essential to note that, before the advent of its twentieth-century industrial mass format, war was considered a normal, natural, and legitimate method of politics. Delbrück's generation, not having experienced anything like what came after July 1914, regarded war in a totally different way than has been the case since 1918 and especially since 1945, with the arrival of nuclear possibilities.

---

Fear of war, which occupied sensitive politicians but not public opinion in Europe for a long time, has returned. Austria has engaged Russia in the Balkans, and Austrian-Turkish tension has returned. But the real war danger does not come from the Turks. We must seek it elsewhere, namely, in the Serbs. What do they want? What are their claims—historical, legal, or moral? They have fought bravely for their freedom against the Turks, but the kingdom contains only a small part of their nationality. The main part of it lives under Hapsburg sovereignty. Every Serbian relationship, political, economic, or cultural, is subordinate to Austria-Hungary. The Serbs base their hopes on Russia. Although officially the Russian government disclaims the Serbian plans, at the same time, the Russian press is filled with more or less extreme Pan-Slavism against Germany and Austria. From this background we may begin to understand Serbian aspirations.

How can a people sit by quietly when it is bottled up by Austria-Hungary on one side and by the Adriatic Sea on the other? Meanwhile, the Russians are offering help to unite Bosnia, Dalmatia, and the coast of the Adriatic, to conquer Croatia and re-create a larger Serbian kingdom.

Serbian goals are much more realistic if they are seen in relationship to Italian and English politics.

The Italians are filled with a growing jealousy over Austro-Hungarian Balkan policy. In the Middle Ages the Venetians and the Hungarians fought over the eastern part of the Adriatic Sea. When Austria today claims Dalmatia for herself, she does so remembering that it was part of the territory of Venice that she lost in 1797.[1] These traditional antagonisms multiply themselves with the arrival of Italian irredentism: the desire of Italians to bring into their national state the Italian parts of Austria, Trient, and Trieste. The natural tension between Austria and Italy is so great that these two great powers must be either allies or enemies. As compensation for the annexation of Bosnia, Tittoni demanded from Austria the Montenegrin railroad and a coastal policy based on rights given Italy in the 1878 Berlin Treaty.[2] It is questionable if Austria is willing to comply, after giving up Novi Pazar in compensation to the Turks. But even so, for the Serbian and Montenegrin national future, it is irrelevant if the Austrian holding of Bosnia begins a war. In that case public opinion in Italy will surely not be satisfied to sit back.

Even more important is the position of England. In Balkan policy England can just as well side with Austria as with Russia. But England stands today as a special opponent and rival of the German Empire, and there is a party on the island that believes it necessary to risk armed conflict with Germany in order to prevent future dangers. In the Seven Years' War there was not just a simple tension between Prussia and Austria within central Europe but also the complication of this tension in the fight of England and France over North America. So today the Balkan question's unique framework is complicated by the far-ranging competition of England and Germany at sea. For years King Edward VII has built a ring of alliances large enough to strangle us. This summer's meeting of the king and czar at Reval appeared to have behind it the fact that the czar's personal meeting with our kaiser in Cronberg was unsatisfactory.

Then came the Balkan chaos, and everything changed. Undoubtedly neither Czar Nicholas nor any of the statesmen he met with had a wish or desire for a war with Germany, but what if they are compelled to it? If the Serbs and Montenegrins in wild passion begin a war against Austria and are beaten as expected, will the national feelings in Italy and Russia not rise up as a storm-tossed sea? If she beats Serbia, can Austria again give up territory to forestall a later attack, and can Italy and Russia accept the fact that Austria has moved into the center of the Balkans? Is not Nicholas II a feeble man, and was not Alexander III drawn into the Turkish war against his will by the Pan-Slavist movement? How easy it is to nurture such popular movements with money and favorable press reports, and then, when the popular mood has been raised, minister and king enter in with an alliance and subsidies. Mr. Izvolski's policies are under pressure from Pan-Slavism. But Germany cannot put up with the possibility that Austria might be attacked and overwhelmed by Russia and Italy together. That would dishonor our allegiance bond as well as our politics and national interests. It would be a final expulsion of German influence in the Orient, and in spite of the great majority of Slavs, Magyars, and Romanians, it is the German element in Austria-Hungary that is always the strongest. A defeat of Austria by the Russians or Italy would also be a defeat for German cultures.

For German policy there is no higher law than its bond to Austria. Because fortune decreed the expulsion of our Germanic brethren from the Second Empire in 1866, it is our responsibility to stand behind them in international affairs. In return, our own national future depends on Austria with its

Germanic culture. If Russia and Italy enter the lists against Austria, we stand with Austria. Meanwhile England protects the coasts and has her will carried out. The general alliance against Germany is here: four powers against two.

Do the English really want this? Whence comes the confidence that enables small Serbia to make demands of powerful Austria? Where does the money for Serbian arms come from? Why the continuing talk of Serbian compensation without any idea of where it will come from? Why is it that the great English newspapers are full of the wildest hate articles against Germany, and English journalists cover the land with a flooding waterfall of fantastic tales describing the nearness and largeness of the German danger, the maliciousness of German character, and the insatiability of German lust and intentions? All the recent German-English diplomatic visits have had only momentary success. Without anything bad said or done on our side, English newspapers vent their rancor against Germany.

When small Serbia bares its teeth against Austria, one is inclined to laugh. But as the whole European scene carefully crosses in front of one's eyes, the sarcasm leaves and one asks, What kind of situation do we live in that the peace of the world depends on this small, hotheaded band of people?

Is the danger sweeping over our leaders really so great? Let's review the factors that could break up this thundercloud.

First it is clear that the four other great powers will risk war only if they all ally against Germany and Austria. If only one of them—for example, Italy—steps out, the other three are not strong enough to defeat us by themselves.

There is no doubt that the majority of Frenchmen do not want a war against Germany. The feelings of revanche are so lessened that even ten years ago they would have turned away from this in alliance with England. France is the banker of Europe. The welfare of its people depends on loans to Russia, Austria, and the Turks. A general European war could result in a large monetary outflow, which would affect France most sharply. The differences over Morocco are much too unimportant for so great a nation as France to pitch itself into a war against Germany. But if it comes with the possibility of a great Europe-wide coalition to break Germany's superiority for all time and, by the recovery of Alsace, France achieves parity with Germany, the French people would surely not oppose such an attempt.

The Russian government has never had direct tension points with Germany. Yet among the Russians lives a fanatical hatred of Germany.[3] They want to emancipate themselves from our intellectual and economic superiority. They hate Austria, which prevents Russia from taking all the Slavic people under Russian hegemony. But these factors are not strong enough to lead directly into war. The Russian army is disorganized, and revolutionary tensions simmer below the surface. But if England provides the money, Russia is capable of putting an enormous army into the field. The completion of the constitution has increased war tendencies. Naive liberals believe that, by definition, the completion of popular representation will ensure peace in Russia. If that representation was chosen by a free election, perhaps. But now the Duma in Petersburg is moving in a nationalist direction. If Pan-Slavist agitation in 1876 was one reason for the outbreak of war, this agitation has an even more powerful organization in the Duma. If a crisis comes, this Duma will be not a retarding but a stimulating element, suggesting that passion instead of rational political reckoning will drive Russian politics.[4] The great mass of the Russian people are peacefully inclined, as are the French and the Germans, but that gives us no assurances.

The great mass of the English people certainly do not want war, but they are filled with fear and antipathy against Germany, and fear is perhaps the greatest cause of war throughout world history. As I have said over and over again in this journal, this fear is unfounded. As long as they possess ships and as long as they can build them much faster than we can, England is completely secure. Not only are the English tormented with patriotic fantasy about future combinations and accidents that might remove this security someday, but above all, English taxpayers find the rivalry very painful to their pocketbooks. If

Germany built no warships, England could also shrink its fleet and would not need the enormous funds that are now ever increasing. We can begin to understand their antipathy when we see how expensive it is to build such a fleet and how zealous are those protests against our own new tax laws, be they inheritance, beer, electricity, or social services. Our daily newspapers teach us that such demands are made on us for our country's sake. Comes a European combination that appears to allow England with security and without great cost to destroy German sea power, undoubtedly the mass of English people would support it. Certainly it would greatly harm England's own trade, since over one-sixth of our exports are sent to England. But this loss would be made up, as the large export market dominated by German industrial production would be taken over by England. Recently a new motivation has arrived which pushes England toward war. That is the ever growing danger of a revolution in India. We have noticed exceptional laws and, in many parts, prisoners and exiles being rounded up. According to the former police commissioner in Bombay, Sir Edmund C. Cox, the tone of British India today is like that in Lombardy-Venice under Austrian hegemony: the Italians did not want improved Austrian rule; they wanted the Austrians to leave.[5]

Given all these factors it is clear that England will do all it can to avoid a general European war. But if the English are of the opinion that the situation in India can be put off a year, they might conclude that it is in their interests to provoke a European war as soon as possible, to free their backs to take care of the Indian situation later.

Finally there is Italy, stronger in its popular inclinations toward war than anyone else. On the one hand, the Italians would be prevented only by feelings of weakness or, on the other hand, by doubts about which alliance would gain or lose the most for Italy.

Ultimately our best guarantees for peace lie in these political considerations. The Quadruple Alliance, united only in its desire to defeat Germany-Austria, has among its individual members too many different aims to come together easily. These discrepancies within the alliance will be an advantage for us if it comes to war. Allies never work together completely harmoniously, and the more allies there are, the more that is true. How many tensions and inner doubts there were among the Russians, Prussians, Austrians, and English in their fight against the French hegemony of Napoleon.

Simply adding together the military strength of the four powers shows that they are far superior to the Dual Alliance, even if France becomes engaged in an unpleasant secondary war over Morocco. The peacetime strength of the Russians is 1,305,000; the French, 530,000; the Italians, 273,000; together, 2,141,000. The peacetime strength of the German army is 585,000; of the Austrians, 379,000; together, 964,000.[6] The Austrian army must fight against Italy, Serbia, and Montenegro, while Germany must go alone against the English-supported French on one side and against the Russians on the other side. That we can overrun France quickly cannot be the point, because their alliance is larger and we can scarcely occupy France, especially if we have to send half the army against the Russians. In addition France, because of its powerful system of forts, border fortifications, and camps, is defended in a nearly unbreakable way from the North Sea to the Alps. Overcoming each individual fort by artillery is a difficult piece of work, and before it is completed, the French army can counterattack. If the army breaks out and seeks victory in open field combat, it takes time. Meanwhile the enormous mass of the Russians and the other allies draw near, so that the French can defeat us with a large numerical superiority. Beyond a successful defense of our own borders perhaps we might take the chance at the beginning of defeating the Russians in Poland, before their mobilization is completed.

It is foolish to delude ourselves with illusions over these power relationships. The matter is serious but possible. We have nothing to fear. With the addition of reserves we are strong enough to stand the course. But prospects for an ultimately favorable outcome depend on politics. We may be sure that under no circumstances will the four-power alliance stay together to the end, and because of that, we may hope that the alliance will not stand together in the first place. Only if Germany and Austria are fully defeated will France, Russia, and Italy have reached their goals. If it turns out to be like the Seven Years' War, with both sides fighting a war of attrition and the borders unchanged at the end, the whole continent will be ruined and the only winner will be England. As soon as Germany's sea power and domestic economy are sufficiently weakened, England will have no more interest in continuing the war. The leaders in Paris and St. Petersburg are fully aware of this and are not inclined to make great sacrifices entirely on behalf of England.

If politics depended completely on the diplomats, we could sleep peacefully. But, to return to our starting point, they depend also on public opinion, which enters into every aspect and must be considered in every reckoning. If the Serbs begin a war with Austria, all hopes of peace depend on Austrian restraint. It is no small thing when a great power of this magnitude remains quiet, as the people of Serbia, armed and angry, mobilize on its borders. If Serbia with Montenegro proceeds to attack, the interests of European peace demand that the enemy borders where possible are not crossed and that the troops who do cross over are intercepted and made harmless or, if this is militarily impossible, that the land is evacuated as soon as the military goals are achieved. The French did this twice, in Belgium and Holland in 1831 and 1832 when they were suspected of wanting to keep those lands. Certainly the issues between the Serbians and the Austrians are different. Austria would be the attacked party, and it is unreasonable to demand that a great power, attacked by a smaller state, not act so that such an attack will be impossible again in the future. But behind Serbia and Montenegro stand Russia and Italy, and behind Russia and Italy stands England, and England is allied with France.

The danger is great. Let us hope the wisdom of the statesmen succeeds in exorcising it.

# The Second Moroccan Crisis

*1911*

---

At the close of the second Moroccan crisis Delbrück considers the possibility of industrial mass war. Although he suggests that everyone underestimates a future war's full potential for destruction, he goes on to present arguments for decreased German naval expenditures but increased German army expenditures, which is exactly the course that was followed.

---

During wars, as long as the fighting goes on, both parties can claim victory. In diplomatic wars people are no less zealous. There are always those fanatics, self-confident and cocky, who are sure that with a little more skill, a little more power, a little more bravado, much more could have been achieved. So has it been from time immemorial. We have recently experienced this situation in Germany, just as in France, and although French criticism of the ineffectiveness and cowardliness of their government has finally abated, we can say neither that the French in fact had a better outcome nor that they are a more mature and prudent people but simply that they kept a tight rein through their parliamentary system of collective responsibility.

In France those politicians who are critical must at any moment be ready themselves to be called into the government, and this is a relationship of inestimable value. As superior generally as the German monarchical-constitutional system is to the French constitutional system, the pedagogical value of the latter cannot be denied, whereas we in Germany must accept the unenlightened reasoning of the masses.

But if I see the Moroccan agreement as a bloodless victory, and the election as essentially calm, there remains one great cause for concern that casts its dark shadow very far.[1] The danger of war, which this summer was exorcised, has retreated only temporarily and stands on the horizon, irrepressible and menacing.

There are enough people in Germany today who look on this possibility without dread. For most people war is something unnatural, even unhealthy. But it also creates moral value of unending power and brings great changes in human affairs: the fight of the Greeks against the Persians, the unity of all the ancient peoples against the Roman Empire, the destruction of this declining empire by the Germans, the Christianization of the Saxons by Charlemagne, the creation of Prussia as a great power by Frederick the Great, the destruction of the ancient state forms by the French Revolution and Napoleonic Wars, the uprising and new birth of Prussia in the Wars of Liberation, the founding of the German Empire after 1866 and 1870.[2] But it is also certain that in the future the sufferings of war will remain. War is the most terrible fate that mankind can envision. Men must bravely face it when it comes on us with iron necessity but at the same time recognize that it is a crime to encourage it unnecessarily.

War engenders heroism, but it destroys culture. The suffering that a great European war would bring to us today would be horrible. Frederick the Great said that war is an affair of kings and their armies, and the middle class had to be saved as much as possible from it. Today the army is the people and the people are the army. War used to be small and limited, but the next war will run over everything, using the terribly murderous weapons of the new technology. The Russo-Japanese War, with armies the size of those that fought at Leipzig and Königgrätz, was only a colonial skirmish in comparison with a European war of the future.

Economic life will come to a standstill. Oaks will no longer bear fruit and grow; factory machines will become rusty as thundering grenades, mines, and tongues of flame destroy what generations have built. The tenant will pay no rent, the believer no alms, the corporation no dividends, the state receive no taxes. The war will come as a thief in the night. "The Germans will one day wake up," said an English lord long ago, "to find they have a fleet." Then the English fleet will mount an ambush that will open all the gates of hell and spread terror over the whole of Europe.

Is it any wonder the German people are deeply stirred and ask how they can be protected from such terror? Their anger is directed at England, which, while we are engaged in a legitimate competition with France, meddles and mixes in our affairs in a brutal way. Naturally the cry goes up, Strengthen our fleet!

But let us pay attention, lest we take a false path!

Essentially two demands are raised in the press and from the Navy League.[3] First, that beginning in 1912, we should launch one more large cruiser a year, that is, instead of the current fleet law, three ships instead of two, and furthermore, put one more squadron into service, thereby increasing the overall size of the navy substantially.[4] The second point—that we need more sailors—is more important. The danger of this autumn has brought attention to a gap in our sea defenses that must be filled. As a result of the fact that at the end of September a third of the sailors complete their service and are replaced by new recruits, there is a span of a few weeks or months when the navy is unprepared for war. But England, with trained men provided by a twelve-year service requirement, does not have this weakness. We can get over this deficiency only by increasing the number of sailors, half in the fall, half in the spring, with the goal of launching one more ship a year.

There is good reason for building more large cruisers. But many are against it. A cruiser costs fifty million marks and takes four years to complete. During this period our navy marks time without getting stronger, until the Kiel Canal, the harbor at Helgoland, and the four ships that are to be built are ready. Meanwhile the position of England in India and Egypt, as much trouble as they have caused over the years, does not get stronger but only more uncertain. Time is on our side, and we must wisely avoid anything that brings us to a crisis soon.

One hears it frequently said that if we were stronger at sea, the English would not have risked using the menacing language they did last summer. It seems to me that this opinion is a severe misunderstanding of the psychology of the English people. If we were a little stronger, then the impulse to attack us before we are ready would only increase. Our strategic position regarding England is not so strong as to allow us to attack England directly, but only strong enough so that England respects the damage that a war could bring. That is the basis of our fleet law. We have the right to go beyond this law, first of all because every state sets its own defense needs and second because of the English threat. But if we do so, we enter a new phase of defense building and with it the danger of creating new crises against our own interests. What we will gain is small, if the superiority of the English fleet, allied to the French, remains overwhelming or if the English, instead of declaring immediate war, only increase the number of their own ships. Finally it comes down to technology and the development of oil-fired and diesel motors, with which ships can move both forward and backward. If the largest ships are so equipped, there will be no future need for coaling stations, as the ships will be able to cruise for months. The relationships of sea war will then be fundamentally changed, and the ships that we are building now will be outdated.[5]

Enlarging the fleet also reduces what we can do for the army. France, which has less than two-thirds of our population—39 million against 65 million—puts into the field an army about as large as ours, 585,000 men. That is possible because France from its smaller population takes more men and because all fit for duty are conscripted, whereas we leave many thousand healthy young men at home. The German army has a significant material superiority of weapons and equipment. This deficiency the French make up for by great fortified positions along most of their borders; from the North Sea to the Mediterranean, fortified camps such as Verdun, Toul, Belfort, and fortified lines are joined to each other with fortress work. Behind all these positions Paris is no longer surroundable.

Now the Russian peacetime army is much larger than ours and the Austrians' combined; the Austrian army without officers is about 400,000 and the Russian army 1,384,000. If the Russians also come at us, insufficient building of our army could indeed be fateful. Experience has taught that with the two-year service requirement, something over 1 percent of the population is the minimum figure for the training of the qualified young men. Today our army trains only 0.94 percent of its young men. That is true neglect. We can easily increase the size of the army by 30,000 to 40,000 men.[6] To bring those men into the reserves who do not now go through military training would be a moral victory for our political and military world position. If we build more ships, England is able to build twice as many, and we would not be any stronger than before. But if we strengthen the army, we do something neither the French nor the Russians can do, the one from a lack of men, the other from a lack of money.

As earnest and naturally appealing as are the arguments to increase the size of the navy, it seems that an increase in the size of the army is the more important and necessary. It is not filled with political dangers, it will not slide us into a crisis against our own interests, and it secures us against an English attack better than the navy because it makes us stronger than England's allies.

I would advise us to use the favorable climate of public opinion and set all our energies to raise the recruitment to 1 percent of the population for the peacetime standing army. Every levy beneath this figure means a weakening of the basis of general conscription and a mistake from the standpoint of public education. It is therefore the only fundamental way to eliminate the continuing parliamentary conflict and legal wrangling.

As self-evident as I see it that new taxes are demanded for increased defenses, taxes on travelers and on consumer goods for the broad masses are impossible right at the start. Only a real property tax, the death tax, at best in the form of a graduated inheritance tax, may be considered.[7]

# The Pan-Germans

---

By December 1913 Delbrück worries that in the cold war climate of European public opinion, a radical extremist group of one kind or another can pitch the Continent into war. His example is Germany and the Pan-Germans. He realizes that popular celebrations of the 1813 German victories over the French have gone too far. In a paranoid world filled with fear of foreign invasions and domestic revolutions Delbrück discounts the latter and raises the former to the paramount place most historians have given it since 1945. Here again Delbrück takes up the question of media responsibility for cold war tensions. I have found nothing to indicate, however, that he understood his own role in helping create these tensions.

---

The *Post* is beside itself because I said that danger for the future of Germany lies not in the Social Democrats and not in the Center Party but with the Pan-Germans. For this statement they threaten me with government action, imprisonment, and libel. They say they have heard this danger mentioned by no one else. The *Daily Review* also sees this as a mistake.[1]

I do not see a mistake at all. In fact I see such a danger that it cannot be repeated often enough.

The only really great danger for the future of the German Empire lies in foreign policy. We can be seduced into a war that will not only be unnecessary, an unspeakable misfortune for us and the entire cultural world, but whose outcome for all of Europe is unpredictable and uncertain. We must go into such a war only when necessity, honor, or the future of the nation is at stake. Such is not now the case.

France is so well defended that even an isolated clash of

weapons would be very difficult for us to win successfully. We would ultimately overrun our western neighbor, but only after a long, very tenacious resistance. But an isolated fight between us and France is really out of the question. If we entered a war against France, we would undoubtedly have Russia and probably England to fight also. Russia has rebounded unbelievably quickly from the destruction of the Manchurian war and 1905 revolution. Its peacetime army is larger than Germany's, Austria's, and Italy's combined. The military power of our allies is not as large, and in many aspects it lags behind that of the Triple Entente.

The political goal of Germany in the world can be nothing less than to strive unflinchingly for a larger colonial empire and not to tolerate further partitions or shearing off of special-interest areas unless we are consulted. And at the same time, to maintain our defenses only as much as needed to fight a war if other honorable methods fail. German policy must be goal oriented and tough but also armed with patience. An unnecessary war or one at the wrong time is the most dangerous and terrible action we could take. The highest duty of national leadership today is to point Germany into the future based on these fundamentals.

I agree with the Pan-Germans that we should strengthen our defense system. This measure not only will keep the peace but may serve to accomplish positive goals. But they are not satisfied with that. They push forward, threatening and impulsive, urging and harassing us into dangerous politics and militant adventures.[2]

May I give examples? A few weeks ago a leading member of the Pan-German League wrote an article entitled "German Heroes and German Followers," in which he said, "German policy has preserved the peace, but the German people are unhappy with this policy, because the other great powers are continually expanding their power. World history and world developments are bypassing Germany. Either the German Empire should follow a policy such as Holland's or Sweden's, in which case we do not need a reserve army or a large fleet, or we should follow a policy like that of the other great powers. Germany will soon have a much different position among them if we put our shoulder to the job."

Similarly, but in much sharper tones, the Pan-German press repeatedly raises the cry that our military should be made ready for a great war of attack on land and sea. But instead of being intimidated and backing down, the Triple Entente has united against us. If Germany did not achieve as much as we expected in the Morocco-Congo agreement, the blustering of the Pan-Germans is partly to blame. Authoritative sources in England tell me that English officials really believed we were about to start a war against France. That was the reason England sided with France during the Moroccan crisis in 1911. If Germany had made a different impression, England might not have stood behind France, and we would have gotten a much larger piece of the Congo. The main responsibility for this outcome lies naturally with the diplomats, state secretaries, or ambassadors. But equal responsibility falls on the press, which defines public opinion in Germany as well as elsewhere in the world and sets the goals that we have erroneously followed. In this situation a hypernational press did not aid but impeded national goals.

No less destructive are the fanatical patriots at home who celebrate monarchism. In reality they are undermining monarchical authority in every way. The Social Democrats fundamentally spurn the monarchy and carry on their business only to fight against it. But what shall we say about the monarchists, who try to persuade the general public to accept the idea that the Reich is to be ruled not in the interests of the general welfare of the state but according to dynastic and family concerns? Suggested here is the idea that in the highest counsels of the empire the right willpower and decision-making attitude do not exist. We can resist the Social Democratic instigations, but the treacherous inciting of the people against the government by the Pan-Germans is much more difficult to stop, and the *Post* has engaged in a great deal of it.

Because this revulsion by the Pan-German demagogues cannot be directed, their criticism must be contained. Every single policy of the government must by necessity be criticized, and I myself have often done that. What is to be rejected and fought against is the systematic nurturing of mistrust of the government allied with a nationalist incitement to adventure.

A few years ago we might have said the Pan-Germans were a joke, a small sect without influence. Today that is no longer true. The Pan-German press has a wide distribution and a broad following. The *Post* is indeed not the direct organ of the Imperial and Free Conservative Party but stands in very close relationship to it. No wonder that Pan-German agitation has touched and influenced broad social circles.

I realize that many people say we should not exaggerate the Pan-German danger. Here the national ideals are presented in a sort of caricature, but it is impossible to do anything else. The people must be informed if it is to be swept away. Warnings are necessary. France was pitched into misfortune in 1870 by chauvinistic passions that were not properly counteracted by responsible people. A Social Democratic revolution is not the danger of the future. The danger of the future is a European war undertaken without necessity.

In the great ceremonial speeches of this year, the hundredth anniversary of the wars of liberation against Napoleonic conquest, one speaker after another has taken pains to say the same thing. Is this a general conspiracy to use the anniversary of 1813 to awaken conservative nationalism? That is hard to believe. But we must admit that among all these speakers and all these listeners, idealistic nationalism is in danger of turning into fanatical nationalism. This is a great danger to the health of the people. Therefore, leaders of the people, pay attention. It is an important issue.

# Part 3

# World War I, 1914–1918

Delbrück in 1917. Kindness of the family of Helene Hobe (née Delbrück).

# The War:
# Origins, Possibilities, and Goals
*1914*

This reading is Delbrück's first public pronouncement on World War I. Recognizing that his information is incomplete, he nevertheless describes fairly accurately the opening days of combat, the economic undergirdings, and the general strategic situation, although much is left out. His perceptions of counteractive mobilization are clear. He compares the German organization and mobilization with that of France and Russia. Delbrück cannot hide a certain "cheerleader" quality: he is German and those fighting are his countrymen.

A compromise between Austria and Russia over the Serbian question could not be easily reached. The satisfaction demanded by Austria for the murder of the monarchical successor could be accomplished only if Serbia came under Austrian authority. That would have meant a great political defeat for Russia and the end of her role as protector of the Slavic peoples in the Balkans. In spite of this difficulty, I did not want to give up hope of peace. It seemed to me always possible that England could have declared to Russia, after Russian Pan-Slavist policy had encouraged the Balkans assassination, that England was morally unable to go further and that, if a war came, England would remain neutral. In such a case Italy would have remained in the Triple Alliance. Russia would have seen her defeat, and the peace would have been maintained.

The special position of Belgium is clear. Chancellor Bethmann-Hollweg often said that Germany does not desire the destruction of a neutral Belgium.[1] We have violated Belgium because of strategic necessity. The border that Germany and France share is not much more than 120 miles long. For modern reserve armies, which stretch themselves far and wide, that is a very small front. In the Russo-Japanese War, where roughly three hundred thousand men fought on both sides, outflanking moves of up to 95 miles were made. The 120-mile Alsace-Lorraine frontier is secured by forts and fortifications. In front of me lies a 1913 book by the French general staff, *Our Frontiers on the East and North*.[2] It maintains that a German attack through Alsace-Lorraine would be very difficult and that the Germans therefore would have to move through Belgium, and it describes the various routes. A march through Belgium alone gives us enough front and maneuver room to make possible a decisive field battle. If we had avoided Belgium, it would have meant spending a long time on the west border while the Russians completed their mobilization and began attacking across our eastern frontier. Perhaps we could have done it differently if England had remained neutral and Italy had remained allied. But it did not happen that way. England was determined to go to war with us. The destruction of Belgian neutrality was only an excuse. In spite of everything, we took this difficult step because Belgium was the only way to victory. The disadvantages are great, but the advantages are greater.

Let us consider our strengths and weaknesses and suggest how we can believe in victory in spite of an enemy superiority of numbers.

Germany has a population of 67 million, France 39.5 million. Nevertheless France's army is the same strength as the German army, because of aggressive recruiting techniques and a three-year service law. France also has about as many reserves as we do. Our advantages lie in the defense we can put up against the Russians, Belgians, and French and against an English landing. Our superiority lies not in numbers but in better organization and leadership. France has talent and patriotism, but it is doubtful that an army with forty-two war ministers in forty-three years can be a well-functioning organization. It is unlikely that everything will be prepared and directed so that the mobilization and concentration will be carried out with the speed and certainty that ours has been. How can the French railroads, nearly all privately owned, work hand in hand with the general staff, as the German government railroads do? Even so it is inconceivable that the leadership will be the equal of the German. General Joseph Joffre may be a good man, but he is not independent in his leadership.[3] The president of the republic, the war minister, and the other ministers stand near him, and behind them stands the all-powerful public opinion. In war there are many ways to achieve one's goal. To use a well-known phrase of Clausewitz, it is not so important that the unquestionably best way be chosen as that the choice made be pursued with single unitary will. Under the leadership of the kaiser we Germans are sure of this union between strategy and politics. The French are not.

Already we can see why the French leadership has doubts. As the news came that the Germans had passed through Belgium, they asked themselves if their defense line should be lengthened or a counteroffensive mounted in Alsace. If they decide for the latter, should a cross-Rhine invasion be mounted or should they violate Swiss neutrality? Alternatively a breakthrough might be tried between Metz and Strasbourg. Along the Belgian border the questions are how far should the left flank extend, and should they risk a great battle on the border, fight on Belgian territory, or do nothing and await the landing of the English?

Is General Joffre free to answer these questions purely in terms of strategic considerations? As in every strategic decision, politics and the military must work hand in hand. Joffre's conclusions are often half-conclusions. German leadership is free from such uncertainties. Here also differing opinions are often put forward, but the final decision is carried out with clear, unequivocal authority.

If it turns out that the French split their forces, they will have no reserves, and a part of our western army can be turned against the Russians.

A French military writer a few months ago said that the Russians needed six weeks before they would be ready to attack us. After they have completed their deployment along the Brest-Grodno-Kovno line, it will be a few weeks before they are able to appear in front of our lines with full force. Meanwhile we will have mobilized the enormous reserve forces of our citizens, made up the losses from our fight against the French, and increased and strengthened our troop units. Substitute reserve and war volunteers must be at least 1,200,000 men. Thus, united with the Austrians and with an enlarged army, we will enter the fight in the east with new fighting power.

Aside from the numerical and organizational relationships, there is the question of morale. What a difference between us and our opponents! As we have seen, the French are divided between their passion for revenge and blameless patriotism. Of 166 million Russians nearly a third are foreigners who are conscripted into the war against their will. Among the Russians themselves the old ideals of holy Russia, the naive, religiously based patriotism, are separate from the new Pan-Slavism, widely dispersed among the masses. The English people are also divided. The war party is opposed by the party of humanism and culture, which finds the war not only false but horrible. To the humanists England is allied with the Russians and the Japanese against their brother cultural people the Germans. We must not be deceived by the English government itself. For political-strategic reasons and to protect the Adriatic Sea, it must declare war not only against Germany but against Austria as well. As the reason for this declaration they put forth the fiction that Austria had acted as an enemy against France.

In 1870 the Prussian-German mobilization was carried out in some villages only with force. But this time there was not the slightest amount of resistance. That is because today everyone is part of an organization and follows its direction. The union of social power with governmental authority results in the enormous mobilization power we have seen with our own eyes.

Alongside these aspects is an important technical factor to be noted: the achievements of our field and light artillery. General Maitrot, in writing about the defenses of Liège, closed with the sentence, "The city is ready for a long, hard defense." With our artillery this resistance was broken in a short time. The rapidity of the fall may seem strange to those who do not know much military history. But the Belgian war preparations might have been incomplete or the garrison not up to full strength. On the other hand there is the heroism of our troops and the excellent work of our artillery. I was assured by our military long ago that in heavy artillery we were far superior to our opponents. This test has proved it.

And it opens up an entirely new perspective. The French not only built up their defenses in several long rows but put up a stiff line of border fortifications. Now it appears that in the fighting between missile and fort, the missile is the stronger weapon, at least for the moment. Of Namur, General Maitrot said it was as strong as Liège. But of the fortresses at Lille, Maubeuge, and Reims, the main part of the French north border defense, he remarked that they were not located on the heights and specifically that Maubeuge might be attacked and encircled. Perhaps we can conclude that Maubeuge is not quite as strong as Liège. I will not awaken false hopes, because a strong garrison can have a great effect on what happens to a fortress. But we can see that this is a weak part of the French defense.

Against these strengths there are also weaknesses that we may not hide or deceive ourselves about. The great energy needed to overcome our opponents' numerical superiority in the field may need to be increased, cutting into our economic life much deeper than is the case for France, Russia, or England. Russia has a huge treasury, and England has been a commercial power for a very long time. The danger of the war lies not so much in the fact that we might sustain a defeat—

from which we could soon rebound—but in the possibility of a long war. There is the danger of enormous hunger for the German people, as the great peacetime magazines are used up. The war came at a time of good harvests. Food will not be a problem for two years, but raw materials for our industry will not be so easily obtained. Germany uses an enormous quantity of wool, silk, cotton, flax, wood, oil, copper, lead, and leather to keep our factories going. So many men are in the armed forces and so many in war industries that we are concerned about labor shortages, without saying anything about the women and young ladies, who do not at present serve. England has declared our harbors blockaded. To carry out the blockade they must venture near our dangerous mines, torpedo boats, and submarines. But the capabilities of a seafaring people give them the potential to carry it out. There is a great-power convention in which most of the above-named materials are not listed as war-controlled contraband. But the English House of Lords blocked this convention and thus England did not ratify it. England can thus declare wool, silk, metals, and rubber to be contraband and seize them, even on neutral ships in neutral harbors, and in this way inflict significant damage.

In the process England can run into difficulties, for example, if the Americans are harmed by a cutoff in trade of cotton and copper, enormous quantities of which are used by Germany. But if England decides to follow this course, they cannot avoid a conflict with the United States, and that would put them into a dilemma. Even here we can rest easy, for large quantities of these materials are on hand in Germany. But the economic side of war will remain: there may be shortages of labor and raw materials, and they will become worse the longer the war goes on.

The first difficult battles have been fought. As we have moved beyond Brussels to the French border, the great French counterthrust south of Metz and Belfort has been broken. The German army has moved forward on every front. On the other side the Russians are already in East Prussia. It is not possible that they have all their armies there, at full strength ready to fight, but they have responded to the French cries for help by putting their forces in motion. Such politically motivated actions often do not work out well as strategic operations. It remains to be seen if the Russians will succeed as they move forward. We cannot be turned away by them but instead seek the great decision against the French.

We must look at the whole line from Switzerland to the North Sea as a single front, divided into sectors. In many places this long line is packed with troops, so that ultimately we must break through in one place or seek a flank to go around.

# The War
# from August through September

*1914*

This reading is Delbrück's first war commentary based on reasonable if very incomplete information. Framing his analysis within the history of war since the early modern period, Delbrück describes the west front through the early days of September, the end of the battle of the Marne, and the battle that became known as Tannenberg in East Prussia. He then discusses the question of raw materials and concludes by outlining broad fundamentals necessary for a peace treaty between Germany and her opponents. Raising the possibility of peace caused Delbrück to be attacked by the conservatives, who accused him of faintheartedness and lack of patriotism.

Information on the war situation is so fragmented that it is impossible to understand clearly all the strategic relationships. A few fundamentals are certain, however.

Since its creation with the Swiss militia, modern infantry has developed in ever larger and thicker formations. Beginning with the powerful square formation, it was then made smaller and longer. Maurice of Nassau made it flat. Prussia in the Seven Years' War used three rows deep, with two or three formations behind one another. Linear formations were broken up by sharpshooters, but for the final charge, deep columns were used. Today, as a result of enormous increases in firepower, thin lines face each other, with columns shrunken and reserves reduced. The front on which the first German attack was made stretched from upper Alsace to Maubeuge, overall a distance of roughly 250 miles. How large our army was in the initial attack no one knows. If it was 1,200,000 men, that is one man per foot; if 1,600,000, one and a half men.[1]

Under any circumstances it is an exposed body in an unprotected setting. In some places the troops stood closer together, behind them the first reserve line; in other places there were much thinner forces with gaps in the lines. Commanders of an earlier age fought against such thinly defended lines with a massive attack and, once having passed through, tried to roll up the line from both sides. Such an operation is not out of the question, and French theoreticians have especially recommended it. But today the defensive power of modern weapons is so great that even the thinnest line can hold out against a frontal attack for a long time and finally withdraw without many losses. Meanwhile, however, the widely planted flanks of the defenders can bring such a concentrated fire on the thick mass of the attackers that an initially successful assault can be turned into a rout.

The French did not anticipate that we would march through Belgium, nor did they expect us to open an offensive on the Scheldt River and stretch out our lines as thinly as they are. Our extreme right-wing army (the Kluck army), on both sides of Maubeuge, foreshadowed an annihilation for the French, as there were only territorial troops defending it and the main front did not extend there.[2] The French could not prevent the pushing back of the English, and both armies retreated together.

To increase the power of the right wing, the German leadership offered the left wing, in Alsace, as victim. Here they allowed the French to overrun Mulhausen and occupy Colmar for a week. The similarity between the incursion of the French in the south and the Germans in the north is that each had to be quickly stopped or they would have gone farther.

Along the whole front under the crown prince of Bavaria, the German crown prince, and the prince of Württemberg the armies of Hausen and Bülow have fought in a powerful ring and won.[3] A few of these actions, namely that of Crown Prince Rupprecht, were fought as battles throwing back a French attack. The French did not rush these attacks, as their basic idea was not to seek a decision in the west until the Russians had made their power felt in

the east. But as the incoming assault moved forward in northeastern France, General Joffre believed he had to attack the Germans in the south where they were not so strong. For such an attack the area between Metz and Strasbourg seemed suited. But it
was defended by the Bavarians, and with a powerful counteroffensive they threw the French back into their fortress and defense lines.

Northwest of the Bavarian army the army of the center was
under heavy attack, and it was there, farther to the north and
west, that the offensive was pushed with heavier and greater
force.

As the right wing of the German army approached Paris,
meanwhile, behind the German front, French forts and fortresses
fell one after another. When these forts capitulated after a brief
siege and no fewer than forty thousand men surrendered, it must
have begun to feel in the whole French army as if its morale had
started to crack. In ever broader attacks the French were defeated,
and the German army attacked and moved forward, putting
Paris to its right as it moved across the Seine south and east of the
city. Meanwhile on the other wing the crown prince's army approached Verdun and pushed the enemy south. If one drew a line
from Verdun to Paris, one could believe the two wings of the
German attack would stop there, with its center on the line from
Vitry to Sézanne, eighteen or twenty-five miles to the south.

In reality the French were not nearly so beaten as it appeared,
and General Joffre had the elasticity and resolution to use geography and the French railroad network to bring a large force
quickly to Paris. From the west came English troops; from the
south, French-African and English-Indian; and from the south-
west, troops from the Voges and Alsace. These forces attacked
the flank of the German position, the army of General von
Kluck, whose headquarters was in Coulommiers, thirty-two
miles directly east of Paris. As soon as the German commander
recognized his danger, he retreated over the Marne and Aisne
into the vicinity of La Fère-Laon. According to French accounts
the Germans suffered heavy casualties; according to German accounts they took their guns with them and retired in good order.

In any event the Germans avoided encirclement. Their rearward movements, begun on 7 September, apparently halted a few days later, and now they have attacked the French from favorable positions and with reinforcements. Rearward movements of the extreme right-wing forces have brought them alongside their neighbors, who also retreated to a position north of Verdun. These movements aligned the front. Our losses have naturally been very great, especially of officers.[4] As we cannot be sure, we must be very careful on this point.

Along the right flank the French seemed to have moved back. On the left wing near Verdun, the French have not moved. If they had, they would have opened themselves up to a flank attack. They are carefully protected under the guns of the fort. On the other wing, however, they have sharply attacked and continue to try to move forward. Around the middle of the month came the action that in the French press was trumpeted as the driving away of the invaders from France. But the Germans remained in heavily defended positions with the French untiringly attacking. The decision is still up in the air and depends on which side can reinforce more rapidly.

In 1866 Moltke put everything on the decisive battle: the main army went to Bohemia, and against the smaller German states he sent only three divisions. Following this example, the current chief of staff chose to go against the nearest enemy, France, and to send only a few corps against the Russians. After a few border skirmishes the Russians came at us with a large force much earlier than expected. Three weeks after the war declaration the Russians entered East Prussia with a force twice as large as the German one. One army, under Paval Rennenkampf, came from the east; the other, under Yakov Zhilinski, from the south.[5] They were separated by the Masurian Lakes, in the middle of which is our Fort Lötzen. Facing this twofold pressure, the German army began to withdraw to its line of defense, the Vistula River. But suddenly, after a command change that appointed General von Hindenburg with General Ludendorff as chief of staff, the whole German force fell on the southern army of Zhilinski. Strength on both sides was roughly equal, with the Russians perhaps a bit larger. The principle of the lightly manned line had already been used against the French, and it was used even more effectively against the Russians, who were poorly trained and led. It was reported to me that the former chief of staff, Count Schlieffen, had put forth the battle of Cannae, as described in my *History of the Art of War*, as the archetypical battle that a modern commander could fight.[6] In contrast to the densely packed Romans, Hannibal made his line very thin, extended his flanks, and using his superior cavalry, surrounded the Romans on all sides. In this way he won not only a victory but a victory in which his enemies were virtually annihilated. Hindenburg's victory at Tannenberg is an example of this strategy.

The center of the German forces was made up only of reserves, and they stood fast while line troops surrounded the Russians. As at Cannae this enormous battle destroyed fifty thousand and took ninety thousand prisoners. It was a greater victory than Sedan insofar as at Sedan the Germans had a very large numerical superiority, so they could press against the French without great danger.[7] And it was a greater victory than that of the Carthaginians over the Romans, because the second Russian army under Rennenkampf was nearby.

As Zhilinski was being destroyed, the Rennenkampf army was only two or three days' march to the rear of the German army. Had Rennenkampf any idea of what was happening, and attacked the northernmost German army, it would have been lost. With truly Napoleonic wisdom General von Hindenburg changed destiny. But he knew the Russians, because the psychology of the opponent is an important part of the art of command. The Prussian officer corps not only exercises and maneuvers; it studies. From the exemplary work of Colonel von Tettau on the Manchurian war we know how fault-prone and lackadaisical are the Russian commanders.[8] Hindenburg also knew about the large but erroneous reputation of Rennenkampf. Zhilinski should have stayed in telegraphic communication with Grand Duke Nikolai as well as with Rennenkampf. Perhaps Zhilinski saw the danger too late. To secure victory in the south, Hindenburg had put only a thin screen between himself and Rennenkampf and reduced the fortress at Königsberg to reserves. After the Zhiliniski army was out of action, Hindenburg turned around and, with reinforced armies, hit the Rennenkampf army in the rear. With heavy losses it would have been surrounded if it had not taken flight at the last moment. The army of Rennenkampf was nine and a half corps. According to our reckoning, Zhilinski's army was five corps, and altogether these fourteen and a half corps made up a third of the whole Russian field army.[9]

Equally important are the events on the Austrian-Russian front. At first it appeared the Austrians had sent half their field army against the Serbians, to crush them permanently and then turn against the Russians. There was a certain similarity between this strategy and the German strategy of facing France and Russia. But whether the Austrians ever had that in mind or not, they soon saw that there was insufficient time to do both. They made a massive incursion into Serbia, then withdrew many of those forces, repelling Serbian attacks. After initial successes in Galicia the overwhelming superiority of the Russians finally pushed them back, and bulletins indicated heavy casualties. That posed the question, If the Russians six weeks after the opening of the war could develop such great superiority over the Austrians, what next? The Austrians, with a smaller area and a tighter railroad system, could inflict heavy damage on the Russians, whose huge masses of men were available but only very far behind the lines. At first many Austrian troops were engaged against Serbia, where they remained fighting, and only came to the Galician campaign area late. Before they arrived, the incoming Russians had become seemingly unstoppable and caused great anxiety. The Russians in Galicia arrived faster than anyone believed they could have, and even the reserves seemed combat ready. At the same time as Rennenkampf was trying to reinforce his army at the last moment to save himself, in Galicia the Russians threw in sixteen new divisions against the Austrian left flank in a massive offensive.[10]

If the chances of a German military decision have decreased a bit, economic factors look much more favorable than they did at first. Neither raw materials for industry nor food will be in short supply for the summer of 1915. The closing down of the world market is not so complete as expected by our opponents, and the occupation of Belgium and northern France has opened up new sources of supply. When England cut off the flow of supplies to us, they also cut it off to the occupied lands, their allies. We are undoubtedly correct in taking over the food supply in occupied areas as if it was a captured fortress. As the shortages grow, we will feed ourselves first while food and supplies for Britain and her allies shrink.

As important as the food question is, that of exports for the industrial sector is even more significant, and in this area England is as badly hurt as Germany. If Germany has lost nearly all its export market, it still has a huge inland market and some of the export sector has converted to war production. England, even if its harbors are not blockaded, has a much more difficult task than Germany in restoring its world markets. Since England is so much more highly industrialized than Germany, exports play for England a much larger role than its domestic market, and its reduced agricultural sector cannot pick up the slack. If we recall how splendidly German financial power funded the great war loans, now we can hope England's goal of economically starving us will not come about.

As long as both sides expect victory, there will be no peace making in sight. But the neutrals are already beginning to talk, and we ourselves are saying we need a peace that gives us complete security from such attacks as these in the future. It is very important to make clear exactly what is meant here.

Complete security that an overwhelmingly superior enemy will not use a favorable opportunity to renew the fight would come only by subjugating an enemy, thus forcibly preventing it from renewing the war. The Romans used this strategy as the basis of their world empire. Fortunately that is no longer possible. A second method is to create great provincial dependencies, to build occupation fortresses and squeeze the enemy economically. Napoleon took this course in Prussia after 1807. He seized half our lands, occupied the Oder River forts, limited the size of our army, and levied contributions so large that we could not pay them back even over many years. It did not work. Material oppression served only to awaken German moral strength. God protect the German Empire from embarking on Napoleonic conquests after its expected victory. An unending series of wars would result.

Conditions for peace will be created only by using political moderation to disarm the mistrust aroused by armed force. Stated in different words, our goal must be to restore the balance of power on land and to create a balance of power at sea. We must avoid the mistake Napoleon made in simultaneously trying to defeat England and achieve continental hegemony. In attempting to do both, Napoleon lost everything.

# The Strategic Situation in December

*1914*

---

Delbrück directly compares the developing war situation up to early December 1914 with the eighteenth-century warfare of Frederick the Great and Prussia during the Seven Years' War. Using French and Italian sources, he presents the world war as a novel form of combat unheard-of since before Napoleon—impregnable positions and wars of position and attrition—and and calls for a different form of strategy than Germany had followed up to that time.

---

Again and again, when our opponents have won a battle, they say that the final victory will be theirs because of innate necessity. They, including their black populations, have 782 million people against 116 million people in our alliance. This mathematics lesson is not simply a theoretical exercise; it is one reason for the practical form that both alliances have taken.

Why did Belgium finally choose the side of our opponents? Belgium saw that in a great European war her geographic position would be swallowed up. Small states, if not fully protected, lean toward the greatest power, and not only Belgium but others saw the Dual Alliance as the weaker side. In the most recent Italian parliamentary debates Senator Barzelotti said that the hope of an alliance victory depended on the heroism with which Germany fought. It could be, he said, that neither party would win a complete victory. In other words, Barzelotti, celebrating the energy of Italian neutrality, sees our position as analogous to that of Frederick the Great, when the world could not believe he would fight against so many superior enemies. And that is how the English and French see it too.

From an American who visited here eight days ago from

Paris, I heard that the Parisians are of the same mind as we: faith in ultimate victory and happiness over the success of the seventy-five-millimeter French field gun. That was before the most recent success of Hindenburg. Since then the French have been depressed. The declaration of Minister Viviani in the French Chamber of Deputies that the war should be "fought with no holds barred until the recapture of Alsace-Lorraine" has a mournful, slightly negative undertone.[1] In England this tone has not gone as far. Victory in the Falkland Islands raised morale.[2] Great success came in Egypt, and the Turkish attack was pushed back, but after bombardment of the English coast English journalists worried that England had sent too many troops to France.[3] So great was their anxiety that the old cry for coastal protection from an invasion by the German fleet has been replaced by a new fear that the zeppelins and airplanes will appear over London. But these pressures on the nerves are not enough to bring about a movement toward peace, and the war party is hopeful that recruiting, on which everything depends, will fill up the barracks.

In October I reported that the German army had been pushed back from the Seine and Aisne; both armies had halted, with no one able to move forward; and each sought to extend its attack against the flanks. In the past three months this situation has not changed. True, Antwerp has fallen, but it appears that decisive victory has eluded us. The enormous human power of both opponents is too large. If the German army in front of Antwerp was too weak to besiege the fortress fully, now come new forces from England, India, and French Africa, stretching out the French front to the North Sea and barring the way. The superiority of our opponents is so large, from Arras to Armentières, Ypern to Dixmuiden and Nieuport, that they are full of hope to defeat us and retrieve Belgium. It is incorrect to portray our heavy casualties in attacks against the northern flank as unsuccessful. The other half of the story is that the attacks of our opponents are also unsuccessful, and casualties on both sides are probably about the same.[4]

We now have a strategic situation that has been unknown since the days of Frederick the Great: the impregnable position.

Forts capitulate after a certain length of time, but well-prepared and defended field positions appear unconquerable. For Napoleon and Moltke there were no impregnable positions. If the center could not be broken through, they could go around one or the other flank. Is it true that French positions from Switzerland to the North Sea cannot be overcome even as they cannot successfully attack us?

As Frederick the Great wrote after the conclusion of the peace of Hubertusberg in his *History of the Seven Years' War*:

> It is quite probable that the Austrian generals cannot succeed with the methods of Marshal Daun and that we will see in the next war the same methods as used in this one. A general is incorrect when he attacks the enemy in a mountain position or in rough terrain. When one makes war against another of equal power, one can obtain advantages by cunning, without putting oneself in great danger. Many small victories can result in a big victory. Generally an attack against a protected position is a hard piece of work. One is easily beaten and thrown back. If one is victorious, it is with a loss of fifteen or twenty thousand men. That leaves a great breach in the army. Recruits can replace the lost quantity but cannot replace the lost quality. Meanwhile, as the army is renewed, the land is depopulated, the troops degenerate, and if the war lasts long, one finds oneself finally leading poorly drilled, poorly disciplined farmers, with whom one hardly dares to appear before the enemy.

Even more emphatically the king described in 1768 in his *Military Testament* how he would lead the next war:

> I would occupy so much land that my food supplies are taken care of and favorable terrain is provided for campaigns at the expense of the enemy. I would quickly reinforce my defensive lines, before the enemy appeared. I would reconnoiter the land as well as one can before a war breaks out. I would obtain excellent maps of all terrain and determine which forts serve our enemies and which ones could be be-

sieged. In these ways I would enhance my knowledge of the land and gain an idea of the attackable and unattackable positions. I would secure my camps and use detachments to strike the enemy, so that even if his corps were not destroyed, they would be brought into disorder. It is much easier to crush fifteen thousand men than to attack eighty thousand, and yet both are risks. To multiply small successes means general savings. We have lots of time. We attack fortified positions only in extreme necessity. Why? Because the advantage is on the side of the defenders. When a clever general takes a position, he puts himself on a hill with three thousand feet in front cleared for his batteries. He may begin the action with his cavalry but not if they will be wastefully destroyed. He should not attack an occupied position with infantry or artillery.[5]

On the basis of this and other essays I concluded that there is a fundamental difference between the strategy of Frederick the Great and his predecessors Prince Eugene, Marlborough, and Gustavus Adolphus on the one hand and Napoleon and Moltke on the other hand. At first this conclusion was hotly disputed. I spoke about it once with Field Marshal Count Blumenthal, who agreed with me and pointed out that the strategy of Frederick the Great could return again.[6] Has it?

Frederick's system, like that of Prince Eugene, Marlborough, and Gustavus Adolphus, was double-poled: it used two methods to achieve its goals, according to changing circumstances and the insights and wisdom of the commander. Here they used the bold blow of battle to destroy the enemy; there they used marches, maneuvers, and besieging magazines and forts to exhaust the enemy. The longer the Seven Years' War continued, the further the king moved away from the pole of battle and closer to the pole of attrition. Even victorious battles were insufficient in relation to the enormous casualties suffered. As today, with improved weapons and other technology, at that time it was the greatly improved artillery that made attack so dangerous.

Characteristic for Frederick's experiences is the campaign of

1758. Without attacking the Austrian main army, the king first sought to besiege the fortress of Olmütz. Then both armies maneuvered around and stood facing each other for six weeks in Bohemia, near Königgrätz, with neither one having enough strength to risk an attack. Meanwhile the Russians had arrived, seizing East Prussia. Frederick turned and fought them at Zorndorf. But the victory was not enough to bring peace. The Russians remained in his kingdom and attacked Kolberg.

There are clear similarities to the present war: a standoff in one campaign area, battles with little outcome such as in Hügelland-Moravia-Bohemia, and the seeking for a great decision on the Russian front. But there are also many differences. We do not know yet if the fighting on the western front has only paused, to be followed by a breakthrough and complete destruction of the French. The victory of Hindenburg over the Russians is much greater than Frederick's victory at Zorndorf. The power relationships of today are much more favorable than those of Frederick's day. Frederick lost not only East Prussia and Cleve but a great part of his central provinces, including Berlin twice, and yet he finally emerged victorious. Frederick also lost many battles, for example, Kolin, Kunersdorf, Hochkirch, and Maxen. We have had much success: the initial march to the Seine, the attack against Ypres, and the march of Hindenburg to the Vistula. Our own country is affected by the enemies only at its frontiers. We have not yet lost any battles. Our ally is doing less well. Austria-Hungary has retreated from Galicia after heavy casualties and now must fight for more space, and they are again fighting over Serbia, which they had thought to overrun.

Through brilliant strategies Field Marshal von Hindenburg has gained the upper hand in the eastern campaign areas outside Serbia. At first Grand Duke Nikolai led this attack. From Warsaw to Berlin he moved directly against the powerful German flank positions on the lower Vistula, the fortresses at Thorn, Graudenz, Danzig, and finally Netze-Warte-Küstrin. This position, which can be lightly defended but quickly reinforced or evacuated, was the main protection for Berlin. The Russians thought to use only a few corps there, with the main attack to the south. In case they were able to overwhelm Hindenburg's troops, they could move into Silesia and from there attack either Berlin or Vienna. The Russians were close to the Silesian and Polish borders when suddenly the news came that the Hindenburg armies, with the help of the excellent Prussian railroad, had attacked from Thorn outward in a great flank attack. This blow hit the right flank of the Russian corps as they began their approach march against Thorn, a very difficult maneuver for so large an army. Part of the Prussians showed up in the rear of the Russian army between Lodz and Warsaw. It was not as great a victory as Tannenberg, in which an entire army surrendered, but the number of Germans in relation to the number of Russians was much smaller. The Russians called up their reserves from Warsaw and sought to hit the Prussians in the rear. To avoid encirclement the Prussians had to move out. If no Russian army was destroyed, its march toward the German border was halted, and meanwhile Hindenburg had reinforced his troops so that the Russians had to move back to a fortified position thirty miles from Warsaw. The fighting is still going on, and we do not know the outcome yet. The main thing is that the Russian offensive power has been weakened and perhaps definitively broken.[7]

Here is a parallel to the actions of 1758 in the Seven Years' War. What did Daun do when Frederick attacked the Russians at Neumark? He carried out a whole series of small marches against Prince Henry's army corps and tried to figure out the best place to attack. Before he did, Frederick had returned from Zorndorf, and if Frederick had not made the mistake of leaving unprotected camps at Hochkirch, Daun would have failed.[8] A mistake such as Hochkirch will not be made by the current German commanders. In the west we have strong and secure defensive positions. Joffre, after the transfer of some German corps from west to east, took a long time to decide what to do. Finally, perhaps pressured by the Russians, he began an attack, which has been repulsed with heavy casualties. The offensive power of the French appears to be weakening. What the Allied armies can do against us that we cannot do against them is yet to be shown.

# The War in April and May

*1915*

---

The battle of Gorlice causes Delbrück to review the whole war. He finds huge differences between east front and west front. In the east, railroads, artillery, vast open stretches, and armies of varying quality create flexible battle situations not seen on the west front since the summer of 1914. He points to heavily defended lines and German air superiority for reconnaissance in the west.

---

The battle of Gorlice (2–6 May) has created a new war situation from which the whole strategic picture may be reviewed. The first battles of this war demonstrated how extraordinarily difficult it is to succeed in a frontal attack. Next the armies sought to attack the flanks and extended them out so far that they came to the end: no more flanking possibilities existed. Finally tactical decisions ended when frontal fortifications were perfected. Since September 1914 the troops on the western front have remained nearly in the same positions. In some places there are thousand-foot stretches that in reality cannot be fought over anymore. Each side watches the other, and individual soldiers from time to time try to throw grenades or fire bombs. But behind them in the trenches life is made as comfortable as possible. Vegetables are grown, chickens fattened, exercises and athletics are done. Nearby, where the terrain is more favorable or there is an angle in the trenches, the bloody war goes on, with high energy and heavy casualties. The role of the attacker falls to the Entente. Our job is already done, namely, to protect what we have taken in northern France and not to use up so many troops on this front that it takes away from our efforts in the east. In only a few places, where the relationships are very favorable, German troops have attacked, and the result has been more important in terms of morale—to suggest to the French that at any moment German forces can take the offensive—rather than in any direct strategic advantage.

That is what happened in front of Soissons and again at Ypres (23 April), where the French had an extending corner that could be attacked on a flank. It was different with our opponents. In many outflanking moves and in a whole row of repeated actions in different locations, they tried to break through with increasingly enormous losses. Losses that are so large that even when they obtained some small local success such as at Neuve-Chapelle, they created nothing positive but only an overwhelming feeling of failure. Thus it was in the winter battle in Champagne, 16 February to 9 March. There two weak divisions of Rhinelanders, supported by little more than one brigade of Guards, turned back six complete army corps.[1] That is more than a five-to-one minority. The French supported their attack with masses of heavy artillery, and more than one hundred thousand shells fell.

Nearly as typical is the fighting on the east and south sides of Verdun, where we put a dent in the enemy trench lines by seizing the forest near St. Mihiel on the Meuse River. The French could attack this salient from three sides. Since the beginning of April they have tried over and over to seize it, but we have held it, and every captured trench is immediately counterattacked and retaken before the enemy can turn the shooting charts around to the other side. As reports confirm, the land is very hilly and covered with trees, so that our artillery was protected: the enemy airplanes could not tell where it was. Enemy heavy artillery, other than field artillery, was cleared out as soon as it was discovered. Otherwise the success of St. Mihiel would have been impossible.

If we look at these experiences theoretically, we conclude that an attack of unprotected troops against protected, dug-in positions will not succeed. If one uses artillery preparation to soften up the trenches, then one calls down on oneself an unusual amount of fire. If one line is broken through, behind it there are a second and a third line, and one is in a sack. As the offensive moves forward, it is attacked on both flanks.

How have the Austrian-German armies broken through the Russian front behind the Dunajec, Narev, and Bug rivers? Here the impossible becomes possible; here is something new.

The situation in the eastern campaign area in April was that in Poland as far as Grodno and Kovno the opponents watched each other, while in the Carpathian Mountains they fought intense battles. In January a few German corps were sent to support the Austrians but found it impossible because of winter conditions in the mountains. Only in Bukovina did we have success, with all the eastern approaches to the Carpathians freed and the Dniester River crossed. To counter this effort, at the end of April the Russians assembled troops in Odessa to operate against Constantinople and from there move into Bukovina. But in the Carpathian Mountains after the fall of Przemysl on 25 March a free-standing German-Austrian siege army arrived, pushing over the Kamm River and into a position not far from there at the opening into the Hungarian plain. Nearby our new reinforcements had seized one or two mountain passes. In the old days that would have been easy. It was figured that when a position was overrun with overwhelming superiority, all the other passes around it would also fall. For example, in 1866 direct defense of a mountain was considered dangerous and unwise. But with the enormous numbers of today, all the passes can be made so strong that overwhelming them is difficult and lengthy.

The east front now goes through Poland from north to south, between Cracow and Przemysl, and then turns east near the city of Gorlice and goes into the Carpathian Mountains to the border of Romania. The Austrian chief of staff, General von Hötzendorf, defined the southern part of the Russian west front as the breakthrough area, from the city of Gorlice northward to the Biala River and to the city of Tarnow and on to the Dunajec, ending fifteen miles farther in the Vistula River. This part of the Dunajec is occupied by the Russians, but it does not really belong to the battle line, as it is full of swamps that are very dangerous to cross. The attackable front, therefore, stretching from Gorlice to Tarnow, is roughly thirty miles wide.[2] A major difference between the east front and the west front is the much larger size. The very rugged offensive of the French in Champagne was only five miles wide, and as soon as it moved forward, it was attacked on the flanks.

The reason General von Hötzendorf chose the Biala line for attack lay less in its topography and more in the fact that two railroad lines run exactly parallel to this front, the northern above Cracow, the southern near Neu-Sandec. Both lines make rapid reinforcement possible. Only in the last twenty-four hours did the largest part of the German forces arrive there. The Guard Corps that fought so long in France was first sent to Alsace and then suddenly to Neu-Sandec and Gorlice in Galicia, where it moved immediately into its assigned position next to the Hanoverians and the Bavarians. No where else can such large forces be moved so quickly into action.

It is the same for artillery. No fewer than fifteen hundred guns stood ready, mostly heavy howitzers and mortars. In the days before the battle they were used only when airplanes could pick out enemy batteries. Newly formed batteries are instructed by those already in place to stay concealed as much as possible and move only at night. Russian pilots, few in number, do not see them.

On this basis the surprise attack was planned. What happened can be read in our official reports, and it makes magnificent reading.

On 30 April it was reported that the German army from Tilsit and Memel had attacked in Kurland and moved sixty or seventy-five miles from our frontier. The action must have begun around 24 April. By 26 April Grand Duke Nikolai had arrived in Warsaw to reinforce it with troops from the north. At least he sent an army corps from Galicia. In any event reinforcements did not arrive there until at least 1 May, as our general staff report said; in the whole of Russian Poland a lively artillery duel took place, and from Schaulen forward the Germans moved in the direction of Mitau. Long columns picked out by Russian pilots in Poland were reported in Russian newspapers as Russian prisoners instead of German troops.

On the morning of 2 May we may suppose the Russians thought less of their section of the front than of that at Biala and in Dunajec. Looking toward Kurland, they must have asked if Hindenburg indeed was going to march to Riga. They laughed at the heavy artillery battle in Poland. They hoped for good news from the Carpathians and Bukovina. None other than General Dmitriev, the Bulgarian commander of the third Russian army on the Biala, looked confidently at the strength of the front lines and appeared ready for any event. He was not ready for a surprise. Suddenly, at six in the morning, fifteen hundred guns opened up a four-hour-long fire at his trenches, batteries, and reserve positions. At the stroke of ten the barrage ceased and the troops attacked across the whole front in deep storming columns. How could they be resisted? In many places the enemy front was broken through, and reserves brought forward were turned back before they got there. The second and third lines were hit with artillery fire or occupied. It was too late to bring up more troops. Even so, where should they go, with the lines overrun? Instead Russian troops fled to the rear in masses. German attackers were strong enough to overrun outposts in the flanks and rear. From position to position the Russians retreated. Many places held out longer, such as the city of Tarnow, captured on the fourth day, and positions on the lower Dunajec. To counterattack against this superiority was unthinkable, and those who tried became prisoners.

The main goal of strategy is to be stronger at the decisive point. By this method the Russian position at Gorlice has been captured. The overrunning was due to painstaking preparation and rapidity of execution. The Austrian von Hötzendorf, the German von Falkenhayn, who led other German army corps without notice and remains unnoticed here also, and General von Mackensen prepared the Austrian-German army for its attack and saw to it that everything went well.

Offensive field battles that are the result of long, careful preparation are rare in military history. Mainly field battles take place when two armies come on each other unexpectedly or one army overtakes another during a march. Victories in such battles are, for example, Hohenfriedberg and Wagram and perhaps also Hochkirch. At Hohenfriedberg, Frederick had been waiting for Daun in Silesia, expecting him to come over the Riesen Mountains. Every route was thoroughly reconnoitered, especially the bridges, and the troops and commanders were fully prepared to fight. As soon as it was clear which routes the Austrians were taking, Prussian troops were set in motion; they made a night march and attacked the Austrians at four in the morning, when they had not yet accustomed themselves to their new encampment site. By eight that morning the battle was finished and the Austrians were fleeing over the mountains. Napoleon won the battle of Wagram by slipping one hundred thousand men unnoticed into Aspern to attack with heavy guns and a well-prepared and secure crossing of the Danube River.

With the breakout and destruction of the whole Russian position from Gorlice to the Vistula River, our victory was still incomplete. Immediately afterward German troops not only attacked the beaten army, taking prisoners, matériel, and space, but used one Carpathian route after another to attack it in the rear. We have heard that the Russians stayed deep in these passes, as they themselves wanted to attack out of them. Every step forward they paid for with rivers of blood, but retreating wore them completely out. They had either to make their way in the midst of the swirling masses of the beaten, fleeing army of Dmitriev or to put themselves directly in the path of the incoming Germans. The spirit of Belle Alliance has been awakened. At that time Gneisenau did not let up chasing the enemy during the entire night after the battle but pushed forward and finally stormed Paris. As he could not take Paris from the north, the army, half its former size and unsupported by allies, immediately surrounded the city, attacked it from the south, and forced its capitulation. Now the united Austrians and Germans have moved up to the fortress at Przemysl, and the news is that it is as good as fallen. New and difficult fighting continues against Russian reinforcements sent by the grand duke from Warsaw and from Bukovina. We have seen that the army of Odessa, thrown into difficult battles with inferior numbers, has withdrawn to the Pruth River.

Could not this same method be used against the English and French and a breakthrough be made in the west front? No, for the situation is different in three fundamental respects. First, the lines are much more heavily defended than those of the Russians, including much more artillery. In Galicia if few guns were captured in relation to men, it was not because we did not try to get them but because the Russians did not have them. Second, both sides have more and better pilots than the Russians, and they quickly spot any large concentrations of troops. Finally there are so many railroad lines behind the front that reserves can be brought up very quickly. In France airplanes and railroads are roughly equal on both sides.

In summary the Russians must have lost 250,000 men more than we and the Austrians did in the April–May battles.[3] Even more important, they have lost all the guns and weapons belonging to these men, weakening their overall forces even more. Now let the Italians come on!

# The War in August

*1915*

---

Delbrück compares German and Russian soldiers, finding great differences. In comparing strength-to-casualty ratios, he concludes that differences in military infrastructure have a significant impact on both armies.

---

Looking at the eastern campaign as a whole, one has the impression that until late new year 1915 the Russian army and the German army fought evenly and had roughly equal forces. What advantages the German army had in quality and execution the Russians had in sheer numbers. When the Germans not only threw the Russians out of Prussia but seized a large part of Poland, it was credited to the leadership of Hindenburg. But even brilliant leadership can be blunted when faced with overwhelming numerical superiority. The Russians were led, if not with genius, at least with consistency, and it looked as if the eastern war would become a war of position as in the west. As the Russians took Przemysl and moved deeper and deeper into the Carpathians, it appeared they possessed the advantage.[1]

The Italians finally joined the enemy side, and the Austrians seemed about to break. But before that came about, a great change took place. The Germans and Austrians together won a great battle in Galicia (2–5 May), and the Russians were pushed back. Now this effort has gone further. Irresistibly the Austrian and German troops have pushed the Russians before them. No fortress, no prepared position has halted this move. But it is not the leadership that is doing this; it is the overwhelming superiority of the troops. In comparing German and Russian soldiers, the superiority of ours is noteworthy. Why?

One of the crucial factors in correct judgment of military actions up to now has been almost completely overlooked. That is the strength-to-casualty ratios. This relationship has contributed to our advantage, in that the overwhelming numerical superiority of the Russians has melted away. First of all the Russian losses have been much larger than ours, especially in prisoners captured and wounded. Second, because of their deficient military organization, their losses have not been replaced. There are men enough but no officers, no education, no training, no organization. For these same cultural reasons, before the war Russia did not build the needed infrastructure, that is, the many support units such as supply, transportation, and especially heavy artillery. The German army built up all these before the war, and they have become stronger during the war itself. That gives us an objective superiority over the Russians and leads to unique capabilities, for example, in the aftermath of the breakthrough at Dunajec, to handle more than two hundred thousand prisoners.[2]

In other words, we have the means so that our commanders can carry out the most far-ranging strategic ideas. The Russian army, from the shores of the Gulf of Riga to the banks of the River San, do not. They depend for supplies and subsistence on fortresses. The Russians lost Przemyśl not because it was overrun by force but because its garrison became hungry.

Russian commanders, as far as we can see, are doing what they can to repair this situation. As the German attacks from the north, west, and south moved forward, they gave up their Narev line and concentrated everything in the south against the Mackensen army.[3] Even the Russian Guard Corps, sent back to St. Petersburg after the defeat in the Masurians to quell unrest in the capital and to refit itself, was sent to this battlefield. The outcome must have given the Russian commanders something to think about. It freed the way for the Germans to advance to Riga, the capital of Latvia, and opened the way to St. Petersburg. The Russians had to retreat from Kurland.

Such moments are of very great moral importance. Friend and foe must realize how weak the Russian army is. But a victory over Mackensen would bring them back, and Nicholas is strategist enough to understand the possibilities of giving the necessary orders and saving himself.[4]

# America
# between Germany and England

*1916*

---

Here Delbrück sums up his arguments against unrestricted submarine warfare. It will probably bring the United States into the war against Germany, he asserts, which will mean another huge army to fight as well as enormous economic resources for the Entente powers. For promulgating this view he was called to the censor's office, given a stiff reprimand, and forced thereafter to vet all *Prussian Yearbook* articles before publication.

---

More important than the war itself is an urgent political question that has arisen this month and demands the attention of all diplomats. It is the relationship of Germany to the United States.[1] From the beginning of the war public opinion in America has been overwhelmingly against us. The Americans not only wish for our destruction but find it nearly impossible that 150 million can in the long run prevail against 750 million. Our victories and successes have jolted their views a little but not really changed them. And we may be assured that President Wilson shares the views of the majority of his countrymen. They have demonstrated their convictions by supplying munitions and war matériel to our opponents.

An accident of technological development has created a new problem in international law. The normally complicated laws of the sea have no provision for the submarine. A warship of the old kind, sighting a merchant ship, could approach fairly close without danger to itself. A submarine is fitted with a torpedo, a very effective offensive weapon, but defensively it is so weak that a lightly armed merchant ship can destroy it with a single cannon shot.

The natural consequence is that every enemy merchant ship, as soon as it is understood to be armed, is torpedoed and destroyed without warning. This practice endangers not only the combatants, who want to destroy each other, but also the neutrals, who want only to trade. Enemy merchant ships often carry neutral goods or people. Beyond that, ships sometimes fly false flags so as not to be hindered. If German submarines look on all American or Norwegian flagged ships as neutral and not dangerous, then English or French ships on the high seas will fly American or Norwegian flags. If the Germans board, to see if the ship legitimately flies the neutral flag, they risk coming up against an armed English ship and being destroyed. So it was with Captain Weddigen, whose submarine was destroyed.[2] So it was with the *Baralong*, which fooled the Germans with an American flag, then murdered the entire crew.[3]

The submarine is not the only place where the old sea law is flawed.

The Paris Convention of 1856 provides that, to be legal, a blockade must be effective. Because of the submarine and torpedo boat, that is no longer possible. To blockade Hamburg and Bremen, the English fleet must cruise near Helgoland. By applying the old law of the sea, the English government has in fact blockaded the neutral lands of Holland, Denmark, Norway, and Sweden no less than Germany. A whole list of goods—silk, food, oil, and rubber—is declared absolute contraband. The natural law that two neutrals, such as America and Denmark, may trade between themselves undisturbed is not considered by the English.

One state exists on the earth whose power allows a different outlook. That is the United States. It is able to take a different position regarding the progress of technology and the law of nations. It proposed to Germany an exemption from the submarine war against merchant ships, if England would follow the London Declaration of 1909. Germany directly challenged the United

States on this proposal by its note of 16 February 1915, and America replied on 22 February 1915 that submarine warfare against merchant ships should be forbidden. Germany accepted this proposal but England did not.

Before the negotiations went further, the misfortune of the *Lusitania* took place, in which more than one thousand persons, among them roughly one hundred Americans, drowned, and now President Wilson has changed his position. He declared that the questions of submarine warfare and the noneffective blockade and contraband have nothing to do with each other.

The torpedoing of the *Arabic, Hesperion, Ancona,* and *Persia* raised new questions. The English and the Anglophile American press mocked President Wilson, saying he wanted to embrace the Germans. Public opinion in the United States, led by Roosevelt, was infuriated by his weak policies. They finally demanded that Wilson declare the German torpedoing of the *Lusitania* illegal, a demand Germany rejected as dishonorable. At the same time, Germany intercepted a coded message from the ship *Woodfield* containing secret information that England was not only systematically arming its merchant ships but also firing on every submarine that came close as soon as the captain believed an attack might be forthcoming. With this development, the possibility is nearly gone that a submarine could allow an attacked ship to put its men over the side into lifeboats. A German submarine must presume that every English ship is armed and that the submarine will be shot at if it attempts closer inspection. Ships flying neutral flags have to be suspected of being British ships in disguise. The German government has given instructions to all neutrals that armed merchant ships will be treated as warships.

If Canada, with its 9 million inhabitants, gives England a helping hand, that provides around 250,000 men. But the United States, with 110 million, could provide a land army of enormous power. Whereas up to now only a few American factories have worked for the Entente, a large number of factories could be enlisted for the war effort, and because of the adaptability of American factories, that could be done quickly. In addition, there is the financial strength of America. It has already served the Entente, but not very much: American loans are only half what they might be. The longer the war goes on, the more it becomes a finance war. The money England needs to win is almost gone. In Russia and Italy the treasuries are about empty. If America puts her enormous financial power behind the Entente, our enemies will set to work with new courage, and even the neutrals will be unfavorably influenced. Participation of America against us will have a big morale impact in Romania, Greece, and other countries.

In reality I do not believe in the danger of an American war. The issue is not important enough. Under the American constitution the president alone cannot declare war, and those elements in America that are friendly to Germany, less friendly to England, or at least mainly positive toward Germany are so strong that a majority vote for war against Germany in the Congress would not be easy.

I will not lie: it is very difficult to judge correctly the danger of war. Accidental events that cause Americans to fear for their lives could suddenly raise passions so much that all rational thinking is overcome and the people plunge themselves into war fever. Many Americans look anxiously at German "militarism" and the possibility of a German victory. At the very least, they want the war to end in a draw.

In spite of his mistrust of us, President Wilson has a strong national and personal interest in doing something favorable for us. Whereas certain circles depend on war supplies sent to the Entente, others would be hurt by the breaking off of trade with Germany, especially cotton growers. Wilson's politics will be determined by his desire to be reelected in this coming November election.

What is our most favorable course of action? What will give us the best chance? Cutting back on the submarine war or loosening the blockade by pressure on neutrals, so that we can get cotton, oil, fat, and rubber directly or indirectly? Certainly the one is as difficult as the other. If the English increase their blockade as much as they can, and the neutrals press on as much as they can, the worst is that we would become uncomfortable. We are certain that this does not mean defeat and that we can carry on through it. But it is important not only that we know it but that the English know it. To starve us out is their last best hope, and it cannot be done. But it will make a great difference for our economic life whether England understands this a few months earlier or a few months later. The Americans will in no way decide the war, but whether the war will end soon or only after a long time may depend on them.

Can we bring the war to an end with unrestricted submarine warfare? It is very difficult to know how to approach this question. According to English newspapers, Germany has built a new submarine of the dimensions of a small cruiser, whose capacity is very great. The main point is the reduction of ship space needed to supply England with food and raw materials. The whole German trade fleet is out of world trade, and a very large part of the English merchant fleet, perhaps 40 percent, is also destroyed by the war. If a good part of this fleet is destroyed, it would appear that not only England but also her allies will die. Already England cannot supply her ally Italy with coal.

Nevertheless success is in no way certain and in any case not yet achieved. The English fleet is very large and well organized. Off- and onloading can be speeded up. The English are building new ships and buying old ones in the world market. To the old fear of war with America is added another that, without any declarations of war, a great part of the German merchant fleet, now lying useless in harbors, will become valuable objects of plunder. We hear that the Portuguese government has tied up German ships in the harbors of Lisbon. Soon enough they will serve England.

The decision that our government must make is a difficult one. There are two choices. Do we try to bring the neutrals to our side under American leadership, cutting off English policy and, in that case, allowing us to win the war? But will America go that far? The Americans' own interests suggest lengthening the war, but against that is their antipathy to us. The opposite is to seek to destroy England by unrestricted submarine war. But the question is, How much will that increase American antagonisms against us? Whatever way, we are confronted with a foreign power whose decision cannot be predicted.

Throughout world history wise statesmen have tried to deal with such difficult questions by compromise.

# The War in March

1916

---

This reading is mainly about Verdun, but it manages to deal with actions on several other war fronts as well, taking up casualty figures, the Russian "fifth" season, and the chaos in the Entente high command. Again one is reminded of the responsibility Delbrück had, as a major media figure, to cheerlead his countrymen even though he did not agree with the war leadership, a responsibility he admitted after the war.

---

As we closed the preceding month's journal, the great attack on Verdun had begun. The main motive behind our attack appears to be that this location is an exposed salient of the French front. If the attack moves forward, not only is the defender pushed back into an especially bad position, but the attacker seizes the initiative. The advantage of the attack against an exposed angle is that it is not a fully developed assault but instead secures advantages without significant strategic risk.

A French military critic, Senator Humbert, identified the German seizure of the railroad connections as a decisive moment.[1] Three lines lead directly to the German front from the north and east. Using these lines the Germans could bring heavy guns, munitions, cannons, and grenades directly into firing position. An English journal, the *Nation*, said the tactic of the Germans was to hammer again and again at the French front, to exhaust the French in this terrible nerve-shattering battle, so that their defenses would break. That, says the *Nation*, is a thoroughly viable tactic and raises the question whether France can sustain the casualties that Verdun's defense will bring. As the first overwhelming success of the attack resulted in only a small move forward, our enemies breathed a sigh of relief, as if the Germans had failed to reach their objective. If the *Nation* is right, however, the goal of the German command is not a powerful breakthrough to seize Verdun but the wearing down and destruction of a great part of the enemy army. The attack on Verdun is in no way comparable with a breakthrough against the French front. Larger and larger French casualties and finally the moral collapse of the French can be seen as equal to a great field battle.

Earlier one could call a battle the highest example of the power of two competing armies. The "battle of Verdun," as the newspapers call it, gives us an entirely different image.[2] How it may end we do not know. But we can say with complete certainty that the advantage is ours. The attackers choose the points of attack and concentrate their power, whereas the defender, uncertain where he may expect the next blow, must apportion strength equally along the line. The uniqueness of the modern artillery battle, which precedes everything else, is that the batteries are so placed that they cannot be discovered by the enemy and can inflict much greater damage on the defender than on the attacker. For the same reasons the munitions supply is much more important for the attacker than the defender. If the fortifications are not very strong, modern portable guns cannot be withstood. Thus the casualties of the defenders are always much larger than those of the attackers, because the attackers are careful to use infantry only when a part of the enemy fortification is completely destroyed and success ensured.[3] The battle of Verdun is a strategic action that we can describe by saying, "The means is the end."

Naturally the French knew Verdun was an extruding angle that was vulnerable. They made it as strong as they could and readied themselves for an attack. They may even have thought to mount an attack from there. That we have chosen such a strongly defended spot to attack not only increases the importance of a decision but takes away from the French a good deal of their operational freedom. Why is it important that under this bombardment they might give up a heavily defended small city? Even the size of their defensive measures, the thick structure of their defense lines behind it, tells why. Such entranceways to weakness and collapse need to be protected. They have joined this battle, and now they must see it through. The longer it goes on, the larger becomes the distinction between its casualties and its value. The German army command has no reason to give up extraordinary casualties to win a decision.[4] It can wage the battle from one day to the next. But the French are so heavily committed to Verdun that their initiative may have to await the power of help from somewhere else.

That is, they expect help from their allies the English. With their colonies there are 60 million English and only 40 million French. Of the 60 million, 130,000 have become casualties. Of the 40 million, 800,000 have become casualties.[5] Now it appears indeed that it is England's turn. But up to now we have not heard anything about an English offensive in Flanders. Such an offensive may be in preparation. We are already hearing about a New Year's offensive. But perhaps it is like the helping expedition to the Serbs. Before the English could arrive in Salonika and begin to fight, the Serbs were already destroyed. Or have the English lost their courage for an attack against the German trenches?

The Russians and Italians are more willing to fight, but after a brief, casualty-filled attack, the Italians have again sunk back and the very heavy attack of the Russians has not had any strategic impact. On the eastern front the so-called Russian fifth season has begun: the time between winter and the New Year, four to six weeks, in which the melting weather makes travel impossible. Here and there the Russians have fought tactical forays but with no strategic consequences, because the inability to move makes any follow-up impossible. At the end of April or beginning of May this period will end. It is also possible that the Russians have undertaken these actions for political purposes. But an attack undertaken for political not military reasons is condemned from the beginning. Do the Russians push their men into German fire with heavy losses only to convince the French of their goodwill? General von Falkenhayn can operate in the west, however, knowing that for a period of weeks there will be little activity in the east. Is the Allied war council, now meeting in Paris, thinking of a helping action in the east?

The *Temps* of 18 March talks of a secret plan.[6] There are important men on the war council, but within it there is much conflict. It takes no genius to understand that it is impossible to create a consensus for a single, decisive military concentration from public opinion, the parties, the press, and the parliament.

# The War in February and March

*1917*

---

Delbrück describes "Operation Alberich," the voluntary withdrawal of German forces in France to a position that became known to the French as the Siegfried Line and to the Germans as the Hindenburg Line. Against this line the new French commander Robert Nivelle threw his forces in April and May 1917, resulting in huge casualties, a hundred-regiment mutiny in the French army, and Nivelle's dismissal.

---

If there is a fundamental rule that all the actions in a campaign should be united, a principle difficult to carry out in practice, we have had a movement in the last few weeks on the northwest front that is completely new. So much in this war is new, even though we try to find a historical counterpart to it. The closest analogies are to the wars of Frederick the Great with their impregnable wings, formidable artillery, unassailable field positions, and rare tactical decisions and consequently their similarities to today's war of position and attrition. Now something has happened with no previous parallel. It is our voluntary retreat from the front that we have defended for two and a half years with extreme steadfastness. A voluntary retreat, to improve a position or for better supplies or better attack positions, is rare in military history.

Since New Year 1915 many new methods have been tried to overwhelm the front, to outflank and go around it, to break through it. First the French tried to break through in a single place, then with an attack against a very broad front of 18 to 25 miles, finally with a great double attack on both flanks. Then General Brusilov tried with a powerful attack across an even broader front of 180 miles. For five months the English and

French on the Somme hoped to break our power and crash through our lines with a great numerical superiority. In the new year it appeared that they had prepared another example of their offensive, using a new technical means, gas grenades. Whatever was tried, failed.

An attack against a well-prepared modern position needs a very long period of preparation. The enemy trenches and artillery positions must be searched out by espionage and airplanes, artillery positions rebuilt and guns repositioned. Ship and rail facilities must be built to bring up the artillery and the enormous masses of ammunition. There must be highly developed, well-supported structures so that reserve forces can be moved in immediately behind the front, brought up, and then moved back. There must be numerous observation posts for the artillery observers and commanders and a thick network of telephone lines keeping forward and rear positions in touch with each other. Even when there has been a success—the lines pierced, troop units overrun and captured—ultimately the attack has failed because the reserves, especially the heavy artillery and its ammunition, cannot be brought up quickly enough and in sufficient quantity.

The method and power of the modern breakthrough tactics depend on technical preparation, and to that category belongs the new Hindenburg method of voluntary withdrawal.[1] This new defensive tactic means that land is freely given up and casualties usually suffered at the start of every attack completely avoided.

But the enemy who moves into this evacuated territory finds that the land it has seized is a wasteland. Its own shells have so destroyed it, it is cratered like the moon. Underground explosions and collapsed trenches completed its destruction. The roads are broken, the bridges destroyed, the trees felled, the houses burned, the wells fouled. It takes a great deal of work to bring such an area back for troop occupation. Here and there the enemy press has sought to portray these moves into deserted cities and villages as military successes, but these triumphal voices are soon stilled. Wise critics soon noted that it will be a long time before these stretches are ready for occupation, and meanwhile the Germans have withdrawn to even stronger positions. Will an unstoppable counterattack follow across this wasted land before the Entente rights itself? Or will all this bring a complete change in the war of position and a going over into a war of movement? Quite systematically the English and French military writers are examining all these possible outcomes. It is a symptom of the genius of Hindenburg's strategy that our enemies are clueless about what they may now expect.

# The War in May and June
*1917*

Delbrück compares tactical combat in 1914 and three years later. He finds major differences. He brings up the strength-to-casualty ratio, takes up defensive-offensive strategies, and finishes by dealing with English coal and food supplies and the Russian Revolution.

Great battles have been fought on four fronts during May and June, but there is not a great deal to say about them from the standpoint of strategic considerations.[1] They have demonstrated nothing new and only repeated past events. The English and French have continued their offensive, the Italians have tried for the tenth time to break through against the Austrians at Isonzo, and General Sarrail has mounted a strong attack against the Bulgarians and Germans in Macedonia. But the outcome of all this is the same. Here and there momentary, single success but, finally, paralysis. The fronts of the Central Powers are strong and unbroken in all campaign areas.

From the standpoint of tactics and technology there is a great deal new out there, but results come slowly. A new invention or a new method works only gradually. If some success is achieved, they go back and ask themselves how greater success can be had. In comparing the form and method in the war from the fall of 1914 to the new year 1915 with the form and method of the last three months, it appears we are in an entirely new world. For example, instead of one line of simple, shallow trenches and battery positions using trees, hills, and houses for cover, we have deep built structures, several trench lines, and the whole system hooked together one behind the other. In front of the main position is a forward position; behind the main position is a reserve position.

In these ways the defense is made even stronger, but it is also released from its foundations so that it can more easily go over into an offense. The war of position is beginning to change into a war of movement. The main means of defense has become the counteroffense: to destroy as many men and take as few casualties as possible. Meanwhile the defenders attack again and inflict large casualties, or if that does not work, shell the newly lost positions with heavy bombardment.

On the other hand, the attack that begins on a more or less broad front with its artillery preparation and then seeks to storm ahead has now developed a new twist. Without any or with a very small artillery preparation, it picks a favorable point with great numerical superiority, breaks through, and then attacks in the rear. In other words, instead of destroying the whole enemy defense, it makes a sharp stab in the back. To help this attack, all the new technology is employed: gas fogs, bombs that erupt from underground, flying bombs from above, and finally the tanks, which recall the old chariot, just as terrible and also as little valued.[2] According to the leading military authorities, these inventions, so long in preparation, are a long way from full practical employment.

All these things jump out at us from the war reports but seem to have no definitive impact on the war as measured by a key indicator, the strength-to-casualty ratio. Although this exact ratio is unknown and must remain so, only by counting casualties do we have a sure measuring rule for combat effectiveness.[3]

Why were all these battles fought? What was the underlying reason that enemy commanders suffered these enormous casualties? If they indeed hoped and expected that our front, whether in France, on the Isonzo, or in Macedonia, would be broken through and a great field battle won, then the answer is very simple. The old rule of strategy says that the defense is by nature superior to the attack. Defense is the stronger form of war, but with completely negative outcomes. The attack has the positive outcome. The attacker chooses his position with careful planning and is confident that sooner or later he will break through and win, whereas the defender, even when he repulses many attacks, has not achieved anything positive.

In world history successful defensive battles are extremely rare. The great victories of Marathon, Austerlitz, and Belle Alliance were won as defensive-offensive battles, in which the defender went over to the attack at the proper time. I wonder if military historians will call our coming victory a victory of pure defense in a war of position. It is even more noteworthy that before the war in Germany theories of strategy taught the superiority of the offensive: it was always to be preferred.

In its new year's offensive it is possible that the Entente has introduced some new and different battle principles, for example, the staggered offensive. The English began it on 9 April in Artois. The French started fighting on 16 April sixty miles away in Champagne, Sarrail attacked in Macedonia on 4 May, and Cadorna assaulted the Isonzo on 16 May. Then the English attacked again on 7 June in Flanders and the Italians on 10 June on the Tirolean border in Suganatel. The Entente press always talks of the united front. Is this it?

Now, when all these actions have failed, the enemy press reports that the war will go on until the fall of 1917 or New Year 1918, and then with help from the overwhelming numbers of the Americans, they will win. Unless, of course, Germany, her food and raw materials exhausted, surrenders before then. If that is so, why did they give up all the bloody sacrifices during this new year? How is it possible to hope for success after the failure of the Russian offensive power in the Mediterranean? How is it that the Germans and Austrians now advance at their discretion on the eastern front?

One possibility is that the economy of the Entente is used up: until the Americans arrive, it can do no more. Instead, after the great attempts to attack, it must try peace negotiations.

Another possibility is the Russian situation. In spite of the fact that the revolutionary Russian government has called for an end to the war and the fighting power of the Russian army is now doubtful, the goal of the Entente is for the Russians to hold out as long as they can, destroying as many German and Austrian forces as possible in the process. If nothing happens but the casualties are very large, at least it is better than having done nothing. With the right press treatment the Russians can portray themselves as having a great success, while German power can be described as weakened and headed for collapse.

As the essential offensive means on our side we have the submarine. Its technical success is splendid and much greater than expected. We can as of yet draw no conclusions as to the economic impact of its large number of successful sinkings. The idea that the Americans will send ships to help the English is wrong, because the Panama Canal is not large enough for ocean-going ships. On the other hand the expectation that neutral ships can travel outside the blockaded area has proved false. The price of some foods in England is very high and will be increased, as with us, by profiteering, especially for meat and rice. English coal supplies are low: 11,696,000 tons in the first quarter of 1915 compared with 9,417,000 tons in the first quarter of 1917. But it appears that France and Italy have partially made up for this drop.

Keeping in mind these material factors, the whole western press is busy assuring its peoples that they must hold out until the Americans come and that will bring the victory. It is said that Canada, with only 9 million people, has sent 519,000 men to Europe. The United States with its 100 million must send a million-man army. On our side we play this possibility down and emphasize that America will send an army but that first it must be transported across the ocean. Help from America cannot be underestimated. If we expect no masses of troops, it is certain that America will provide greatly increased quantities of weapons, munitions, and all other war matériel used by the Entente, plus even more technical support. For example, it is to be expected that the importance of airplanes will increase and good American pilots will be added. Finally the morale foundations, the consciousness of a great reserve of power among the western peoples, may not be underestimated.[4]

But our success in the east is so great that it brings everything into balance again.

# The War from July to November

*1917*

---

Delbrück analyzes what came to be known as the Caporetto campaign. He calls it the twelfth battle of the Isonzo and deals with it in terms of geography and infrastructure, undergirding his discussion with Clausewitz's theories on mountain warfare.

---

Great battles have been fought this summer and fall on the west front without strategic thought or success being effected. The occupation of Riga and attack on the islands in the Gulf of Riga are events of importance and interesting for the combined use of army and fleet.[1] But now in Italy has come about something of a unique kind executed in a grand style. The eleventh time the Italians attacked the Austrian front at Isonzo, they failed.[2] Since May 1915 they have attacked over and over again, gaining a few dozen square miles. More than a hundred thousand casualties have resulted. General Luigi Cadorna prepared for the twelfth attack with great exertion, and French minister Clemenceau said the victory would be complete this time. Then suddenly a German army with the Austrians at its side attacked the Italian front. And with very few losses they broke through and routed the whole Italian position. How did this happen? Absolute qualitative superiority of the troops? Superior leadership? Special strategic relationship? New unique technology? It may have been all these things together.

The special strategic situation lay in the fact that the Austrian positions from the Adriatic Sea to Lake Garda were aligned in a three-quarter circle, as if they were on the outside of an umbrella. Cadorna had stated over and over, as the Italians tried here and there to attack, that the difficult topography of the Italian front meant a great deal. In the spring of 1916 the Austrians tried to lead a great attack. From the Tirol to the area of Seven Gemeinden and Asiago-Arsiero they went forward, and their success seemed to confront the Italian army with imminent destruction. The Italians were saved by the onset of the Brusilov offensive. Austria pulled its troops back from Italy to fight in Galicia.[3]

For many weeks it has been known that a new offensive was being prepared with the help of a number of German divisions. The enemy press busied itself discussing all the various possibilities. Fortunately our leadership was lucky: Cadorna did not know of the attack point until the very last moment. How wrong are those who maintain that surprise has no place in modern strategy! It is nearly a decisive moment when the enemy intelligence service finds out, especially troop movements. It was natural for the Italians to await the attack at the place where they expected it and where the first successes had been made. But the place this time was very different from where the Italians waited. It appears that Cadorna expected the attack where he himself would have placed it, that is, on the Isonzo. The place where the German army under General von Below inserted itself into the Austrian-Hungarian lines was a little north of the old battlefield of Isonzo, with its southern point roughly twenty-seven miles from the Adriatic Sea. This point is not so dangerous for the opponents as the position at Asiago-Arsiero, but because of the umbrella-like position of the Italian armies, every breakthrough goes directly into a compressed section of the enemy rear.[4]

The attack began at seven in the morning on 24 October, quite like Gorlice. In contrast to the method used by the English and French against us, there was only a very brief artillery preparation and then immediately the storm of the infantry. In contrast to Gorlice, this attack made use of unheard-of amounts of fog covering the battlefield. By suddenness and intensity the German troops broke through before the Italian reserves could be put into action. The first day it appears Cadorna was uncertain where the main attack was being made, as the Austrians also made a movement on the high ground of Bainsizza south of Boerz. As the Germans and Austrians moved forward, taking one hilltop after another, up came the Italian reserve divisions. But they were ineffective in the mountains, and as they arrived, they were overwhelmed. Many were taken prisoner and marched away. By the second day there were 10,000 prisoners; by the fourth day, 27 October, there were 60,000; and then, as German troops neared Cividale, in the open came 100,000. The mountain region cut across in this way by our troops is eighteen miles wide in a straight line. How small that seems, eighteen miles in five days, and yet what enormous work capacity that means: to overcome mountains and valleys for eighteen miles, every step defended. What triumphant reports the English and French generals would send home if they were able in a week-long battle to advance five miles on the west front!

With entry into the flatland they moved forward swiftly. The German troops surrounded the Italian positions right and left and took them in the flank and rear. Nothing is so effective as a rapid attack against the rear. Cadorna felt himself so safe that he had disarmed the great fortress Cremona, which crossed the southern railroad. It was taken by the Austrians without difficulty. More than half the Italians' heavy artillery and most of their ammunition, readied for the twelfth offensive, fell into our hands. Smaller and larger units were caught up in the offensive and taken prisoner, finally totaling close to 300,000.[5] Finally the army of General von Hötzendorf was successful in Tirol on the old battlefield Asiago. In this place the Italians had foreseen an attack and with fortified positions and mountain forts made it, as they believed, an invincible barricade. But one fort after another has fallen; one mountain after the other is overcome. Where this battle will end is unclear. It remains to be seen if the French and English have sent reinforcements or will send them to give the Italians a morale lift.

Favorable geography, the element of surprise, superior leadership, superior operational and tactical execution, and the morale deficiency of the Italian army explain the ease and greatness of the Austrian-German victory. The *English Morning Post*, which usually tells fables, maintains that many Italian troops never fought because they did not want to fight: it says that "Leninism" affected not only the Russian army but also the Italian army and that naturally German agents infected the Italian soldiers with pacifistic spirits. In reality we will not know for a while if the Italian soldier has indeed lost his will to fight.

To fully understand these events, we must ask the question, Why did this breakthrough succeed when Cadorna's breakthrough attempts failed? Experience teaches us that a breakthrough, if it is well prepared and well executed, will almost always achieve an initial success. We have seen that happen on our own west front. The decision on the Italian front came after the initial success and the overwhelming of enemy reserves, and it came because the reserves in the mountains could not be brought up and deployed fast enough. After that failure the German-Austrian victory was so great that it could not be reversed. If that is so, why had Cadorna not done it before?

Understanding is to be sought in the nature of mountain warfare. Clausewitz taught that mountains were favorable for the defense in single small battles but unfavorable for great defensive battles, because the attacker can choose any place to attack, the defender must defend single narrow passages, and reinforcements cannot be brought up from unattacked locations.

The Austrians used so much power to put up a stiff resistance in the mountains that Cadorna could move forward only slowly. His rear lines of supply were so stretched out that finally he had to turn back. What was he to do when he had seized a piece of Tirol or when he had crossed into Pustertal, or when he arrived at Villach or even Klagenfurt? Such actions would bring him fame but would not bring a decision in the war. The only place where a great victory would bring success was on the Isonzo, which opened the way to the seizure of Trieste and perhaps Fiume. That would have given the Italians hegemony over the Adriatic Sea, which was their goal.

The Clausewitzian view that mountains are favorable for an

attacker who sought a great decision was proved right for General von Below. He had already accomplished a great deal when he broke through the Italian front and pushed the enemy with its reserves from the Isonzo back against Tolmino-Flitsch. Perhaps Below had nothing more in mind. But eighteen miles in front of him lay the open plain, where he may have hoped to bring his victory to completion. Cadorna believed that if there was any fruit to be picked, it was on the Isonzo. I do not know if we may fault him there. The apparent mistake chalked up to his command was that he thought the German breakthrough would stop in the mountains. If he had fought a delaying battle in the mountains, bringing his reserves against the Germans, as he had done beyond the mountains, he would have had a sufficient superiority to parry the German attack. But the decision to leave the mountains without further fighting was certainly important. Here, as so often in military history, criticism after the event comes easily.

# The Military Collapse
## 1918

---

Delbrück ties German military defeat directly to German politics, specifically the lack of political leadership caused by the
subordination of politics to the military point of view, military
interests, and military personalities. Three months earlier this
piece would have been censored and Delbrück perhaps jailed
for sedition. Now, three weeks before the armistice, the letter
of allowable public statement has not changed but the spirit has
totally altered, and this bold statement was published unhindered.

---

The same day I completed the previous volume, the most terrible fate we feared overcame us. Our southeast front in the Balkans broke completely open. The Bulgarians were defeated,
their king abdicated, and the army of the Entente that had
so long defended Salonika was on the march to the Danube
River. In Syria the English not only fought but destroyed the
Turkish army and took Damascus. In Constantinople the Ger-
man-allied Turkish government of Enver Talaat is gone. It will
not be long before the English fleet has free access to the Black
Sea. Austria-Hungary is in full dissolution. On the west front
our hope that the enemy offensive would not pass through our
Siegfried Line is unfulfilled. Under heavy losses of prisoners
and matériel, our army retreats from one place to another. The
superiority of our combined enemies not only in men but also
in matériel, airplanes, tanks, and munitions far exceeds expectations and calculations.

When we remember how strong we looked to the world this
past spring, and our battlefield successes from 21 March
through June, our sudden reverse is hard to believe. It began

on 19 July and from there followed blow after blow. Yet we were saved from the worst. Many days it looked as if the front was completely broken and large parts of the army cut off. That affected the caution of the leadership and the courage of the troops. Later news was better and prospects improved. But the military defeats had a big impact on our politics.

We must give up the self-assured position not to negotiate during a time of battlefield defeats. It would have been better to have begun negotiations as we were victoriously moving forward. But that unfortunately did not happen, so now there is nothing to do but begin negotiations under unfavorable conditions.

Throughout the war I have maintained that the German constitutional system is not only valid historically and nationally but objectively better than the western parliamentary systems. Western parliamentary systems, however, have one great advantage. That is in the training and education of political leaders. This advantage loomed very large during the war, whereas in Germany the lack of political leaders became evident to an almost incredible degree. The fissure in our political education between officials and officers on the one hand and popular speakers, journalists, and parliamentarians on the other hand resulted in a complete drying up of leadership. In Germany we have only technical specialists but no one trained for political leadership. When a high position had to be filled, we always confronted a dilemma, and during the war this dilemma became a disaster and led to our destiny. After Bethmann-Hollweg, German politics was left without any leadership. Michaelis needs no comment. But Count Hertling was also a complete failure.[1] Wherever one looked, there was nowhere any hint of creative political leadership.

A year ago the change of persons did not have a great deal of meaning. Now the change of persons—Prince Max von Baden as chancellor—is also a change of system. It must be clear that the catastrophe that has now overwhelmed us is, in its origins, a consequence of our constitutional system, and deep-seated change is unavoidable.

Above all, we must subordinate military authority to civilian political control. The decision that carried us to our fate
was a one-sided military decision: the declaration of unrestricted submarine warfare on 1 February 1917. Bethmann-
Hollweg as imperial chancellor did not oppose it; indeed, he
acquiesced in it because he could not stop it. He tried to resign
and would have been better off if he had, but he stayed on to
avoid worse. If he had been in a superior position, he would
have been able to hinder or prevent this unfortunate decision.
The pure military questions must be decided by the military,
but this decision was not a pure military one; it had unavoidable political complications, as generally all great strategic decisions have. If this is "militarism"—when such decisions are
made only or mainly from the military point of view—then
the charge of our opponents, that we are ruled by militarism, is
correct. This must be ended, especially as the military does not
speak for a large part of public opinion.

# Part 4

# Postwar, 1918–1929

# Armistice, Revolution, Defeat, Republic

## 1918

Poetic and sad, Delbrück describes the collapse of his country by framing it within two centuries of Prussian-German history and the Greek tragedy of Pericles.

How greatly have I erred! As bad as the situation seemed four weeks ago, I did not give up hope that the front, if weakening, would hold and that the enemies would sign an armistice protecting our borders. That, domestically, long-simmering democracy would develop without a complete break with the past and under management of existing political forms. These hopes are gone. Our pride is broken. I have always had confidence that our military prowess allowed us political moderation. Has this moderation saved us from the catastrophe that is now upon us? So much is clear, that I have underestimated our inner decay and the convulsions of our once strong political structure.

I believed victory would be won by a successfully executed defense.[1] Four weeks ago I never doubted in this victory by defense, leading to a more or less favorable armistice. Now has come to pass what I doubted. The brave army that four long years withstood the entire world, defeating its enemies in numerous battles, is beaten and has signed an armistice that may be compared to a capitulation. The army is in moral disarray. Alsace-Lorraine and Strasbourg are lost to Germany. The kaiser has abdicated and fled abroad. The Reichstag, like the emperor, has disappeared and is nearly forgotten. The two social democratic parties, allied with the men of the mutinied regiments, have proclaimed a provisional republic and set up a temporary government whose longevity is uncertain. In the east our position is weak. Truthfully such an outcome I never dreamed of in my darkest hours and worst fears.

Anyone who holds moderate views during a war is always in a quandary. It is clear and simple to say, full of enthusiasm, Victory, nothing but victory. When we have defeated the enemy, let us dictate peace. Our situation in the world war demanded a different attitude. Whoever said we should only destroy the enemy led to our doom. But whoever said we could not do it threatened our confidence and thereby weakened our will to victory. I can now reveal that I have published many confident statements that I did not feel in my heart. A few times I have misleadingly passed on confidential reports from the army and navy. A publicist is like a general who must inspire confidence not only in words but in demeanor and appearance, even when he himself stands before an unavoidable defeat. In warning of the need for political moderation I voiced my own inner convictions, at the same time not completely overlooking the possibility of an unfavorable outcome. I gave a favorable tone to the figures on the impact of the submarine war on the English economy. Whoever looks back can see that these figures could also have been interpreted as unfavorable.[2] In another place I reiterated a point made by Napoleon, that in single battles, bravery, discipline, and the ability of the commander could overcome numerical superiority, but that it seldom worked in a whole war. I wanted to push further with these analogies, but the censor prevented it. The reports of the English and American governments that monthly ship construction was one hundred thousand tons more than monthly ship destruction was passed along with the remark only that it was incorrect. Here is what I wanted to print in August 1918:

> On 11 July 1918 American secretary of war Baker sent a report to President Wilson that described troop ships. It was printed in the London *Times*. The main figures were as follows. To France were sent in June 1917, 12,000 men;

in July, 13,000; in August, 18,000; September, 33,000; October, 38,000; November, 23,000; December, 43,000; January 1918, 47,000; February, 48,000; March, 84,000; April, 117,000; May, 247,000; June, 276,000. Altogether, 1,019,115 men. Lost at sea were 291 men. The original goals, said the Baker report, were not only reached but exceeded: they were six months ahead of schedule.

When that was published, the English press was angry that the Germans could obtain a view of American defense mobilization and in that way figure out what was happening to them. They were correct. We understand now how Foch's great offensive of 18 July between the Marne and the Aisne was made. The powerful German attack from March through June broke the English-French front so much that Foch had to use all his reserves to bring the lines to a halt. There was nothing left for an offensive. The arrival of the Americans, untrained but fresh and physically able, brought new power. We may say that of the million Americans who now stand in France, more than 600,000 were front-line troops, built up from the ship landings in May and June, whereas earlier, American troops had been used in rear area supply and work details. This powerful reinforcement, which will undoubtedly continue, explains the numerical superiority with which the Entente attained the advantage over German leadership.

Both these passages were deleted by the censor. I remonstrated that these numbers had already been published in the *Times* and that the German people were owed an explanation for the retreat then taking place. I was told, The high command has expressly forbidden the publication of these figures from the standpoint that the Baker report was only an American bluff to mislead us. If the figures were genuine, the censor said, they would not have been published.

Was it really necessary to withhold such facts from the German people to keep morale up? Did the high command not know by July that it had to contend with an enormous American army? The defeat had already begun on 18 July with the shattering of our attack near Riems and the successful advance of the French north of the Marne. Now I have been told that General Ludendorff was at that moment very uncertain.[3] Nevertheless for nine weeks he and State Secretary von Hintze did nothing to secure our political position.[4] Finally, on 29 September, Ludendorff admitted our destruction by his request for an armistice.

Foreign and domestic politics worked together to produce this disastrous outcome. In October I read letters from brave young officers at the front who held the home front guilty for the military defeat. They said replacements coming from home and letters sent from home poisoned and destroyed troop morale. If democratic feelings had not gone so far, they said, if morale at home had been better, the front would not have broken. That might seem correct from the standpoint of the company commander. But in relationship to strategy it was contradicted by realities. Everything told us that the morale of the army on 21 March, as it began the offensive, was as splendid as it had been during the stormy attack in August 1914. Even so we failed to capture Arras, Amiens, or Ypres. Unlucky accidents broke the attack and halted success. The superiority of the enemy, marked by the arrival of the Americans, was much greater than we thought, and not only the superiority of men but also of tanks, airplanes, artillery, and munitions. Because of this superiority our losses were so great that finally our power failed, and only then did our morale break. It may be that some of this came from the home front, but what good could the best morale do against losses of half a million, against an ever larger enemy and its inexhaustible supply of war matériel? No. The troops could not fool themselves. They knew battlefield success was no longer possible, and finally their morale broke. This is the same army that for four long years fought with unparalleled bravery, endurance, and honor.

The campaign and the war were lost not because morale had

sunk, but instead, morale sank after the troops began to feel that the war was no longer winnable. It is nothing more than the well-known art of the demagogue when Count Reventlow in the *German Daily News* now writes that our men were made tired of victory by pure democratic ideas, so they could no longer bring forth bravery.[5]

I can say now that at the end of June 1917 as Bethmann-Hollweg left, Prince Max von Baden should have taken over the leadership of foreign policy. How different it might have been than the unclear games Secretary of State von Hintze played. When the prince took over on 1 October 1918, he discovered General Ludendorff's report of the imminent collapse of the army and the demand for an immediate armistice. Had the old regime put forth this request, the bankruptcy of its position would have been completely clear. The prince did not believe General Ludendorff was correct. He believed the situation was better than it was reported to be, that the troops could stand up fairly well against the attacks of the enemy. He believed there was no possibility that the demands of the high command would be fulfilled. He could only seek to use the advantages he was known for. He was a man of peace, and he hoped his request for an armistice would be taken not as an indication of weakness but as a consequence of a change of government and an expression of the humane feelings of the new men in charge. There was nothing else for him to do. But the enemy was not fooled. It took advantage of its military superiority, and then came the most terrible events. Before the negotiations with the enemy could be concluded, the Social Democratic Party ended the regime and at that moment made Germany defenseless.

It is the military Pan-German leadership that has gotten Germany into this misfortune. The Social Democratic Party completed it by not waiting for the end of negotiations but, at that moment of catastrophe and of the weakening of the final German power, allowing necessities to dictate. The responsibility of the Social Democrats in 1918 is no less than the responsibility of their opponents beforehand for the war fever, the annexation policy, and the submarine war. The military power of

Germany today is so nonexistent that not only do we have no resistance to make against the Entente if it tries to carry out an invasion of Germany, but even our east border is insecure against Poland, which has no army.

I will put away all feelings of pain, shame, and despair and try to give a clear overall picture of how this came about.

The Prussian-German army was created out of the old mercenary army of Frederick the Great melded with the noble officer corps, raised out of the ashes of 1806 and fused with the idea of general conscription. The enormous power that this army developed in 1813, 1866, 1870, and the world war derived from the fusion of these two elements. From the old army came the concepts of discipline and honor. From general conscription came the idealism of national defense and the levy en masse. As effectively as these elements worked together, a certain tension always remained between them. The officer corps was filled with middle-class elements, but the sharp distinction between it and the soldiers was maintained. The methods of military discipline were a hard, often brutal experience for sons of a free people and endured only with difficulty. But as long as the army remained victorious, this system was inviolable. Men endured the occasional malpractice so as not to endanger the whole organization. The middle-class parties overlooked the complaints concerning the mishandling of soldiers made by the Social Democrats in the Reichstag, and only with the Zabern affair were large segments of public opinion made aware that this militarism, if very infrequent, had occurred.[6] So we can say that the German people in August 1914 went to war with domestic unity and secure war system. Within this unity, however, there existed a polar tension, and the break finally came at the place where Scharnhorst had first united the professional army and the army of the people. It was a revolt of the men, the armed people, against the professional soldiers, the officer corps.

This conflict came to a head in the navy. As it was realized that the armistice would bring a turning over of German warships to England, the idea spread among the sailors that the officers had decided, rather than submit and surrender with their ships, to risk one last battle against England and seek a watery grave. In all naval history the hero is that captain who goes down with his ship, striking his flag and sacrificing himself. The sailors suspected that they would be sacrificed for the idea of military honor and the oath to the flag. They were no longer bound to these ideals. As early as 1917 Admiral Capelle reported in the Reichstag that a dangerous attitude was noted among the sailors at Wilhelmshaven and suppressed only with difficulty.[7] Undoubtedly a systematic preparation of the sailors in revolutionary ideas had taken place, and the orders to take the fleet out to sea ignited the ammunition.

For a few days it seemed that the fire had been put out. But soon it was clear that this was not a local matter but something found as well in the land army spread throughout Germany. In all corners and ends it broke out. Officers no longer had their men under their command.

What did the soldiers want? Had they all suddenly become republicans? Even the Social Democrats were republicans only in theory. Their leader, Bebel, had declared over and over that a republic was not part of his program: he wanted only a sufficiently limited monarchy.[8] Before a few weeks ago the number of Germans whose politics included a republic was very small. Agitation, in combination with the Bolshevik regime in Russia, appeared more than it was. It was much more the flow of events than the will of the people that turned victory into revolution and Germany into a republic.

The Entente leaders held the conviction that world peace would not be secured until the officer corps–supported emperor was removed from power. President Wilson spread the word that peace would be made when Germany had changed its autocratic regime into a more democratic one. This requirement was impossible to fulfill. But the continuing demands of the armistice awakened in wide circles in Germany, not only among the Social Democrats but also among the conservatives, the idea that Germany would make a better peace if the emperor abdicated. The crown prince aroused no feelings of

sympathy, so they went further and declared that he should re-
nounce the throne also. They wanted to smooth the transition
to the new form of the state in a legal way and prepared a regency for the oldest son of the crown prince, twelve-year-old
Prince Wilhelm. The regent would have been the oldest
brother of the crown prince or, if he renounced it, the next in
line.

I fought against these ideas as quite impractical. An oath of
the army in the name of a boy seemed to me morally impossible, a smoke-and-mirrors trick out of which nothing good
could come. The only form that could make a full transition to
legal change was if the kaiser had been declared unsuitable for
office and a deputy named, with Chancellor Prince Max at the
same time declaring that there would be a national assembly to
decide the future form of the state. Then the abdication would
have worked and the national assembly could have decided.[9]
This method was the one used by the grand duke of Baden to
turn over his power.

It was impossible to come to a timely decision, as the kaiser
immediately left Potsdam for the front and headquarters. He
could not have done anything worse at that moment. The
chancellor called him back, but his advice was not listened to.

Thus was created a completely impossible situation. The
question of what to do with the kaiser was openly discussed in
the newspapers. The troops did not want to fight anymore. A
useful legal solution was not in sight. Mutiny turned to revolution.

Everything was decided by the unanimous defection of the
troops. In Berlin no battle took place as far as one could see.[10]
Eight persons, sacrifices to the revolution, were buried with
great ceremony, but it appeared they had died accidentally.
The royal stable, the library, and the cathedral were occupied
by officers and defended, but after long goodbyes the defenders left without a word. At the German State Library it
was said that a locksmith from the revolutionary night watch-
men tried to play a part. In other places shots were believed
heard, the same sort of suggestion as the guerrilla fighters

rumored to have played so fateful a role in Belgium. Real resistance was impossible and did not happen. The reality that there was no other solution gave the revolutionary party the upper hand.

The military mutineers, who had nothing to do with the Social Democrats, fell in with them because at that moment the only way through for a positive program was the republic. Hopelessness at the front forced peace; to bring peace meant the abdication of the kaiser; abdication meant revolution; and revolution at that moment meant Germany's complete powerlessness and the undermining of the collapsing regime. The idea that the abdication of the kaiser would bring us better peace terms immediately turned out to be an illusion. Germany was dependent on the grace of our opponents. They had not forgiven us, and they will not forgive us.

The ancient notion of hubris warns us today about the fates the gods have sent down on us. Have the German people followed false prophets? Who is guilty? Who is responsible, the false prophets or the people who believed them?

The closest historical analogy to the world war is the Persian Wars, the fall of Athens and tearing to pieces of the Hellenistic states. How powerful, proud, and confident Athens was as she entered these wars under the leadership of Pericles.

# Seventieth Birthday Reminiscence

*1918*

---

This reading is Delbrück's response to his seventieth birthday, which came on the day World War I ended. It was remembered by his colleagues, students, and family in a subdued celebration at which these words were spoken.

---

My life, my work, and my ideas were born and given form during the historical epoch that now lies behind us, closed. I came from a bureaucratic and learned family. On my mother's side a Berlin family. As a child I knew an old man who, as a boy, had seen Frederick the Great. My earliest political memory is going on board a French warship in Kiel that had fought against the Russians in the Crimean War.[1] I remember well the story of my father about the Indian Mutiny.[2] As I was unhappy that he could not tell me about more battles, he suggested I read in my history books about the Seven Years' War, for there also war was fought for a long time without any battles. During the Italian war of 1859, as a ten-year-old, I took the position that the Italians were fighting for freedom and nationality but that our archenemy the French would try to prevent this.[3] From my family and my education came a strong idea of the state, the ideal of freedom, Prussia, German nationalism, and humanism. The "conflict time" filled me with passionate hatred against the constitution-breaker Bismarck, who was preventing the unification desired by the German people. I went to war and was a reserve officer. After 1870, when I returned from the war, I adjusted myself to Bismarckian politics. I lived for five years in the palace of the crown prince, the late Kaiser Frederick III. I belonged to the press. I was an academic teacher. Although for a time a member of the Prussian Landtag as well as the Reichstag, I never played or aspired to play a parliamentary role. I felt that this activity was not for me: it was beyond the boundaries of my knowledge. I remained a learned man in politics, not a professional politician. Parliamentary life and experience enriched my scientific views, as scientific views helped my political judgments, but I was no politician and the longer I stayed in politics the more this became true. But it broadened my horizons. There was no sphere of life in Berlin that I did not know something about.

Goethe in his seventieth year wrote, "I must again organize my life amid ethical debris and wreckage through daily actions in which the productive power of our nature demands restoration and creativity."[4] Are we really forced to regard as ethical debris and wreckage everything from Frederick the Great to 4 August 1914? On his ninetieth birthday Ranke declared that he had decided to write his world history during the German victory of 1870. This victory was a victory of conservative ideas over revolutionary ones, and it assured him that what had been built in the past would not be destroyed. If the revolution had fully succeeded, it would have destroyed interest in the past and the sense of objective recovery of the truth.

What Ranke foresaw has now happened.

Shall now our political ideals, our science, and our feeling of unity with past humans be cut up, cut off, and destroyed? As England created and developed democratic ways, at the head of the movement along with the philosopher Mill stood the historian Grote.[5] But he became so unhappy with these democratic ways that once in the evening of his life he said, "I have outlived my beliefs." Now I understand the whole enormous tragedy of these words.

The future lies dark before us. We are incapable of putting forth a conception of what will happen in tomorrow's Germany. But it is impossible that the heroism of these four war years will remain unfruitful and that the creative power of this people of eighty million will be extinguished.

# Ludendorff's Self-Portrait

*1922*

---

Delbrück gave many accounts of World War I: in the *Prussian Yearbook*, to the Reichstag Committee of Investigation, and in a series of articles and pamphlets published widely in Germany.[1] This reading is his most famous statement, published as a hundred-page booklet. It went through ten editions the first year.

---

All military critics fault the German operations plan of 1914 because it stretched out the German army to take in two-thirds of Alsace and extend to the Swiss border.[2] In Schlieffen's plan it was only to go as far south as Strasbourg. The only military writer who defends this modification, called by Field Marshal Hindenburg a "watering down," is Ludendorff. He has good reason to: he himself was chief of the operations section of the general staff, 1908–13, when this change was made. The year after his appointment to the section, the change was made. Other general staff officers say he is the author. Ludendorff protests and says that Moltke's strategic adviser was General von Stein, later war minister.

How is the authorship of the change divided among the three? Clearly Ludendorff took part, and the tone of his justification is that of self-defense. Only incidentally does he mention that once during a general staff ride he objected. When I first began work on this problem, one knew only the fact of the displacement of the advance line to the Swiss border but not the reason why. In 1921 I suggested that the general staff hoped to attain a greater victory or that it was necessary because of the enormous increase in the Russian army since Schlieffen's day. Then there appeared a letter from Ludendorff in the *South Ger-*

*man Monthly* which clarified the relationship. He said they wanted to protect Baden, overrun the French in the southeast, and achieve a nice partial success at the start of the war.

If Clausewitz taught anything, it was that in war there is only one success and that is the final success. The beginning success is nothing; the final success is everything. A beginning success that reduces the chances for the final success is a loss. Insofar as Ludendorff praises the beginning success as such, he not only places himself in contradiction to the unanimous judgment of the military critiques but also falls into a fundamental error of strategic thinking. General von Moltke told the Reichstag delegate Matthias Erzberger in January 1915 he thought it a mistake from the beginning to send the mass of the German army against the west.[3] One must first go east, break up the Russian steamroller, and be satisfied with protecting the western borders. Why he, the responsible chief, did not carry through with his views he did not say. He was certainly not opposed by the kaiser, especially if he had his operations department behind him. The resistance must have been located in the operations department, and in his new book Ludendorff declares, "It was a natural idea to attack at the beginning of the war in the west and to defend in the east. Every decision-seeking operation in the east demanded a very long time based on the relationship of its campaign areas. During this time we could not hold off the French at the western borders: the industrial provinces would fall, at least partly, into enemy hands. If we were able later to push the enemy back across the border, the result of the destruction of war industries might be decisive in the long run. The idea to conduct the war in this way would not work."

The error of this argument lies in the words "decision-seeking." A decision against Russia was to be attained only after a very long time or not at all. It is possible that a plan for an offensive in the east had once been fully considered. In 1904–5, disorganized by the war against Japan, the Russian army was very weak, and Germany could hope to protect its eastern borders with a few army corps while defeating the French.[4] This relationship changed fundamentally thereafter. With astonishing power and French money the Russians restored their army and increased its strength. As we know today, the French and Russian general staffs agreed that on the day of mobilization all power would be set forward to attack Germany.[5] They came to this conclusion after lengthy deliberations and negotiations: each feared to be exposed by itself to the powerful German attack.

One German plan was to thrust immediately at the very large Russian army and hope with our operative superiority to bring about a destructive loss, and then, having dispatched the Russians, turn against the French with a large force. The French, meanwhile, might have with difficulty overpowered our positions between Metz and Strasbourg or taken on themselves the odium of crossing the Belgian border.

Alongside this proposal there was a second possibility: instead of using the new troop strength brought about by the army reforms to march against the right flank at Mézières or Maubeuge, as Schlieffen planned before 1906, to stretch the attack out to the sea. That would have given us quite a powerful chance.

They chose a third way, however: to lengthen the attack to the left flank and extend it to the Swiss border. By this means the Schlieffen Plan lost its soul, whose essence was a strengthening of the right wing of the army and a withholding of the left. Now our whole army strength was pretty evenly divided across the whole front.[6] The plan, to obtain a victory in Lothringen and then to move the troops behind the front from the left wing to the right, was too complex actually to carry out. Ludendorff maintains that the plan was correct and only the execution failed. But the plan is universally condemned by military critics.

But more important is the offensive of 1918.[7] It began so hopefully and ended so catastrophically. What did Ludendorff want from this offensive? Was it reasonable? Had he a clear purpose in mind and did he follow it consistently?

As a result of Russia's dropping out of the war and the enormous losses incurred by the French and English in their repeated, vain attacks against the German lines, German army leaders in January 1918 for the first time had a small numerical superiority. With it Ludendorff wanted to force a decision. He wanted to break through the enemy front, seize the reserves lying there, expand the breakthrough, cut the enemy lines, and tie both ends together, squeezing against the middle and surrounding those in between. A strategy in the grand style. Napoleonic in the highest sense of the term.

In 1918 there were two opposing views among the English on the continuation of the war. One, advocated by the chief of the general staff Robertson, was that they should fight on as before, even if the losses were very great.[8] The numerical superiority of the Entente must finally bring success. "When all the Germans were dead, there would still be some Englishmen and Frenchmen alive and they would be the victors." Robertson's strategy was based on the idea of enlisting always more troops. The other view, advocated by Lloyd George, who was advised by General Wilson, was to remain on the defensive in France in 1918 but to lead a defensive blow against Turkey in Syria.[9] If Turkey's Syrian base could be broken, that would be a blow to the whole central alliance. At the same time, one could be confident about maintaining the defensive in France. Lloyd George reasoned that if the English and French, in spite of double superiority of numbers, failed to break through the German lines with repeated, continued attacks, Ludendorff with fewer troops could scarcely do any better. Then when the Americans arrived in 1919, the Entente would open an offensive in France and finish the war.

For a successful defense, Lloyd George wanted to create a unitary leadership. He believed one reason they had failed to be successful for so many years was that there was no unity of command among the different armies. He did not want a real high command; the opposition and the jealousy of each of the different nationalities was too great. But one could create a supreme war council at Versailles under the chairmanship of General Foch and give this council command over the reserves of all the Entente armies. Up until then they had followed an offensive strategy and each army had attacked on its own. But if they went into a defensive, Lloyd George feared they were in danger that the enemy might develop a very great superiority at a single point and overwhelm the Entente one by one, because the reserves of a single country, whether English or French, would be insufficient.

The defensive could be safeguarded only by a general reserve, controlled by one commander whose view was not limited by the borders of his own front or the dangers to its own troops. But the supreme war council, which would have disposition over these reserves, was also in reality a limited high command. Members of this council were to be the Frenchman Foch, the Italian Cadorna, and the American Bliss.[10] For the English member, Lloyd George did not choose Robertson but instead selected General Wilson.

Robertson, associated with the distinguished military critic Colonel Repington, charged a military-political plot.[11] In order to condemn it, Repington published in the *Morning Post* of 11 February 1918 the essentials of the new war plan, the creation of a unitary reserve, and a supreme command. Repington agreed with the views of Robertson that one should not seek the decisive blow in a secondary campaign field such as Syria but had to attack on the main campaign field in France. They hoped that the House of Commons would be carried away by their explanation and would overthrow Lloyd George and General Wilson. That the Germans would find out about all this was of no concern to Repington. Lloyd George brought charges against Repington but wisely only mentioned the Syrian venture incidentally, so as not to make Germany aware how important it was for England. Repington was convicted and fined, and the House of Commons supported Lloyd George, who maintained himself in office and fired Robertson.

Here is a striking comparison with Germany, with the same dramatis personae, the same series of events, but a different outcome. In England the intrigues of the generals were put down and the more correct strategy of attrition was adhered to.

In Germany the opposite occurred. The generals won out and the strategy of annihilation was pursued.

On 21 March, Ludendorff, with forty or fifty divisions, broke the front open through a stretch twelve miles wide on both sides of St. Quentin. He believed he had overwhelmed the opponent. But according to English sources, the English had pretty correctly known the location and the goal of the German attack. It took place at the southern part of the English front, where it joined with the French. The powerful mass of German troops stood near a part of the Byng army but squarely in front of the Gough army, in all fourteen divisions abreast.[12] At the main point of the attack General Hutier's twenty-three German divisions faced only three to four English divisions.[13]

This stretch of the front, which the English had only recently taken over from the French, was particularly weak. Every division had four miles to defend. Haig wanted to reinforce the northern part of his front to protect the important English channel ports.[14] The southern part of the English front was to be supported by the French, something they could do only slowly and unenthusiastically, because the French wanted above all to protect Paris. The English defended themselves to the last man, and the whole army of Gough was destroyed, as it was really an entire week before any help came to them. The Germans advanced to the door of Amiens and nearly took this road and rail center, the English and French were split, and the great victory Ludendorff had dreamed of was won. Clemenceau informed President Poincaré that he must be prepared to move the French government to Bordeaux.[15]

The scattering of reserve divisions in equal portions just behind the front, instead of assembling them farther to the rear, and the completely unsuitable agreement between Haig and Pétain on bringing up reserves made any rapid reinforcement impossible.[16] The attack point of Ludendorff brought him practically the decisive advantage.

In spite of all this effort, the Germans did not achieve their goal, the occupation of Amiens. At the last moment Foch brought up French divisions, whose resistance paralyzed the attack. We must say that at the beginning of this attack Ludendorff was favored by an almost unparalleled run of luck. One easily avoidable, incalculable mistake of the enemy command may be charged up to fate for both sides. A German victory was indeed nearly achieved. It escaped us, because the Ludendorff plan itself suffered under a fundamental error, which in no way was to be made up for. "The munitions supply was not abundant enough and also there were problems of food supplies," wrote Ludendorff himself. "The restoration of the roads and railroads took too much time in spite of all anticipated prior preparation."[17]

These specific difficulties were the same consistent, recurrent, and severe problems that had dominated all previous campaigns of the Entente. Even after winning momentarily great advantages, it had been impossible for the Entente to break through the German lines. The German attack of 1918 miscarried for the same reasons: not so much because of enemy resistance but because of inherent German weaknesses. There was a great scarcity of horses. The food supply was poor. Gasoline for automobiles was scarce. The infrastructure to support a rapidly moving attack did not exist.[18]

The result is that Lloyd George, the civilian, better evaluated the military experiences of the first four years of the war than General Ludendorff, the soldier. Lloyd George cold-bloodedly maintained that the Entente could not go through the enemy lines any more than the enemy could go through Entente lines. But Ludendorff, instead of comprehending the hopelessness of his undertakings after the failure before Amiens, tried again and again, now here, now there, sacrificial full assaults that always came to a stop after an initial success. What happened in reality was that the first successful assault resulted from a situation of divided Entente reserves and the incompetence of Entente leadership. But in alarm over our advance, finally the opposition of Haig and Pétain was struck dumb and yielded to the unitary leadership of Foch. From then on, any possibility of German victory was gone. One must not therefore delude oneself that the second and third assaults, in Flanders and on the Chemin des Damen, were great successes. The offensive, with its generally well known advantages over the defensive, this time yielded only an initial success. But it is the final success that is decisive, and it was determined by the existing power relationships. It failed finally in front of Amiens not because of enemy resistance but because of weaknesses and exhaustion within the German army.

Ludendorff's great offensive of 1918 was from the start without hope and condemned to failure. General von Kuhl defended it, with the comment that Falkenhayn's strategy of attrition in 1915 and 1916 had not brought the end of the war nearer.[19] That is incorrect. Falkenhayn's successes, together with the submarine war, had brought a negotiated peace very near in the summer of 1917. There was at least the possibility of such a peace, if Ludendorff had not forced Chancellor Bethmann-Hollweg out and his successors had not refused to follow his methods. The attempt at a Napoleonic strategy of annihilation was completely false. They could think of a decision only in the Frederician sense, an offensive with limited goals, to use an expression of Clausewitz. These limited aims should not have been used on the western front but instead employed on another campaign area of the world war: Italy.

The Austrian general Krauss had reported how great were our chances for an attack against the Italian army headquartered in Venice.[20] In October 1917 the diversionary offensive of the Austrians, a mere thrust, was a mistake. They should have used instead a campaign of annihilation with all their power. The Italian army stood as in a sack and could have been cut off and destroyed by a simultaneous attack from the Isonzo front and from the Tirolean front.[21] The attack at Tolmino threw the Italian army almost completely overboard. In the new year 1918 we could have sent this offensive further, according to Krauss.

Naturally there was no decision to be fought in Italy which would have brought the Entente alliance to its knees. Such a campaign was impossible. It would have been valid only if considered in the light of where best to achieve the greatest success with an offensive of limited goals. If Ludendorff had thought clearly about the strength relationships of men and machines, he would have seen that a Napoleonic victory in the west was nothing more than a fantastic dream. Then he must have come to the conclusion that a partial success, which made the enemy willing to begin negotiations, was most easily and most certainly to be achieved against the Italian army. There he could have not only captured land but had good expectations of destroying the Italian army. If one may not expect to overwhelm the enemy main force in a battle, said Frederick the Great in his military testament, then one must seek to destroy a detachment. In his new book Ludendorff strongly recommends the works of Frederick, but he himself apparently did not read them or he would not have so recklessly repeated the error that under all circumstances a decisive battle must be fought. What for Frederick the Great was an enemy detachment in relation to the main force, so was the Italian front in its relationship to the west front in the world war. In the highest Entente war councils they worried about an attack against Italy and complained about the unfavorable railroad connections that made a rapid reinforcement of the Italians so difficult.

Now if we had joined a large part of our troops with the Austrians against the Italians, would the Entente have renewed its assaults on the west front? Ludendorff depicts how terrible were our defensive battles, how great the casualties we had taken, and how much more briskly our troops went over into the attack. Quite right, but not decisive. Up to that time the western powers had generally attacked our front with dreadful losses. We know that General Robertson in fact desired that. But on 11 February 1918 Colonel Repington had advised the whole world in an article that the braggart Lloyd George, because of cowardice and a fear that his Entente allies would be fainthearted, shied away from a fight to the finish in France and wanted instead to seek the decision in Syria. I published the essentials of his article at that time.[22] Through the indiscretion, we might even say treason, of Repington, from that day on we knew that a great offensive in the west was at least very improbable. By that time our preparations for the great western offensive were already in full swing, but until the beginning of the attack, on 21 March, five weeks passed. It would have been possible to discard this plan and mount a great offensive in Italy.

What had given Ludendorff all the luck of war up to that time? The exposure of the enemy plan, dissension among Entente commanders, the erroneous disposition of the reserves, and the disagreement over their employment by Haig and Pétain. But in the long run, as Moltke the elder said, only the able have luck.

As he saw that the first great attack did not achieve complete success either at the Cambrai bend or in the capture of Amiens, then, says Ludendorff, he asked the government to use the success that had already been achieved and that made France tremble, for diplomatic purposes.[23] Nothing happened. Had Ludendorff possessed the moral courage and self-control to understand the consequences of his partial successes, then he, like Napoleon or Frederick in similar situations, should have clearly asked for a declaration over the independence of Belgium. It is not true, as Ludendorff in his lack of historical understanding and his faulty psychology says, that a peace offering is always a sign of weakness.

In support of carrying out the plan in France and not in Italy, one could allege that if the great operation did not succeed, a partial success could be attained. Quite right, but even a partial success would remain purposeless unless it was decided at the start to use it diplomatically. Ludendorff was only semi-conscious of this. He tells us that the German supreme command in May suggested a halfway declaration on Belgium.[24] It was on 8 May after the occupation of Kemmel that again they were favored with luck: a breakthrough against the Portuguese divisions, portrayed as a great German victory. How could it help that Ludendorff suggested a partial declaration on Belgium but not its complete renunciation?

After the failure of the attack at Reims, 18 July, Foch now

made the long-contemplated flank attack and brought about the defeat of 8 August. How could an observant army leadership not see the results of this attack? Work power failed. But in Russia we had six hundred thousand men, among them many no longer fit for combat but at least fit for work. Not only the hands but also the spirit that directed the hands had failed when they were most needed.

On 1 June 1918 Crown Prince Rupprecht had written to the chancellor that Ludendorff believed that a victory over the enemy was no longer to be expected. Ludendorff hoped, however, for a deus ex machina, namely, the sudden domestic breaking up of one of the western powers in the manner of the catastrophe of the Russian Empire. Is that strategy or is it the dream of a man without feelings of responsibility? Is it strategy to have no more plans and to hope for the unexpected?

The darkest point in Ludendorff's life is the demand for a sudden complete armistice. Here again Ludendorff did not know what to do. If the enemy would not give us honorable terms, then we would fight on. If we could fight on, why must we ask for an armistice without delay? At that point Ludendorff declared he did not have a breakdown of nerves. I am able to say something on this question. In Colonel Bauer's book one finds that Bauer was not in Berlin from 29 September to 22 October. But he came to Berlin at the beginning of October and here told various gentlemen, who told me, that Ludendorff would have to leave his position as his nerves had completely gone.[25]

To justify the failure of the great offensive and to account for the final collapse, the accusation was put forth that the Social Democrats had undermined the sinews of the attack and deprived Germany of an almost completed victory. In his blind irritation Ludendorff wanted to make even Bethmann responsible for the retreat. Apparently he forgot that Bethmann had left the chancellorship a year before.

There are two things to differentiate here. One is the accusation that the front-line troops themselves did not give a suitable performance. The second is the revolution that made us unable to fight on and forced us to give up all conditions for an armistice.

Until the summer of 1918 the west front was as good as immune from Bolshevik undermining. For this conclusion we have the testimony of Colonel Nicolai from the army leadership, commanders who had their hands on the pulse of army morale.[26] The deputy chief of staff of the Second Army expressly declared that the number of followers of social democracy was very small.

The attack began. Why in July the change?

This change did not take place. It is correct that the independent socialists and communists tried to poison the morale of the troops by appealing to reinforcements arriving from the home front. It is also correct that the front troops were weakened by thousands of deserters in the rear areas and even by those few who went over to the enemy. Nevertheless, with the exception of a very few, the army fought on flawlessly until the collapse and kept itself in order even during the retreat following the armistice.[27]

The weakening of the fighting power was a result of the terrible losses, enormous exhaustion, poor supplies, and insufficient successes. The decisive stroke was not the denial to fight on the German side, however, but the powerful increase in fighting power on the Entente side. The English sent 160,000 or, according to another source, 350,000 replacements across the Channel. Beginning in June a half million Americans were sent into the front lines, and more and more tanks arrived.

What could we do against this increase and why fight on? Ludendorff had wanted to fight a great victory that would bring us peace. We have seen that he himself expected no more victories.

When the commander himself realizes that, what about the men who are sent into the hail of bullets? No troops in the world will fight on when the fight is hopeless.

If then in August and September a certain lessening of the

fighting will and weakening of the front through desertion took place, why and how did this situation, in no way hopeless, end in complete collapse, mutiny, and revolution?

The collapse was not the result of the revolution, but instead the revolution was the result of the collapse. Serious mutinies had already taken place in the French army in 1917, but the troops returned to discipline because the hope of final victory still remained. In Germany the bonds of duty and loyalty broke when the soldiers lost hope, as the fall and collapse of Bulgaria and Austria-Hungary isolated Germany, as Ludendorff's sudden armistice demand gave knowledge to all the world that for Germany the war was lost.

The German high command had gambled away the war intentionally and criminally; then it had done everything in its power to hinder the start of peace negotiations, asking for them only when it was too late.

If one condemns the treason of the mutinied army, one must not forget that the first mutiny was that of the commander, Ludendorff, who left the service of the kaiser because he could not abide the kaiser's politics.[28] Ludendorff changed the defensive war into a war of conquest. He did not understand the strategic requirements of the war and, by his resistance to the king and government, brought on the revolution that finally buried the German Empire. Just as two great men, Bismarck and Moltke, built the German Empire, so two others, Tirpitz and Ludendorff, destroyed it.

# The Peace of Versailles

*1929*

This reading is Delbrück's last speech, completed a few days before his death, 14 July 1929. It commemorates the tenth anniversary of 23 June 1919, the day representatives of the German government signed the Treaty of Versailles. It was scheduled to be delivered at Berlin University in the celebration of the day of German universities.

---

It is the day of Germany's deepest humiliation. Ten years ago Germany signed the Treaty of Versailles. *Germany in Its Deepest Humiliation* was the title of the book whose author, the book dealer Palm, was shot by Napoleon in 1806. After this humiliation followed a rebellion, then the long dead period of the German Confederation, revolutionary convulsions, and finally the new national state, then the catastrophe of the world war, and finally the disgrace of the Treaty of Versailles. Proud Germany was not only defeated and struck dumb but dishonored and condemned to perpetual economic slavery. We do not know if the German people can bring themselves back to their historically strong position. It is a new epoch of world history, in which the relationships of peoples to one another be maintained not only through war and power but also through moral influences. If that is not so and the world is totally ruled by war and chaos, then the shape of the future will be so changed that comparisons with earlier epochs will be of little value.

Is it appropriate to say *anything* on such a fateful day? Would not the most appropriate response to these circumstances be silence? I once experienced what a powerful impact complete silence can have. In 1888 I was a member of the Reichstag. On 9 March the Reichstag met on the occasion of the death of Kaiser

Wilhelm I. His son, Kaiser Frederick, was in San Remo, Italy. To announce the succession, Chancellor Prince Bismarck had first to put himself in touch with the successor and ask what name he would use. The hour of the sitting came and the Reichstag assembled, but President von Wedel remained in his chair in stonelike quiet, without opening the session, without moving, without saying a word, and by his silence held the entire Reichstag in his spell. No one spoke, no one moved. A full hour passed until Bismarck entered and announced the news of the death, which everyone knew. But more than his words, so deep were the feelings that the previous silence had consecrated the moment.

It was natural that this memory was awakened as I asked myself, What can be said publicly on this day, without damaging German honor?

Silence is a valid response to misfortune, but today is an occasion to speak, to mourn, to give what consolation can be given. Mourning cannot remain without accusation, and accusation must be directed not only at our enemies but also at ourselves. Such a catastrophe does not come without responsibility. The prophets of old did not mourn the fate of their people without accepting responsibility. Our sin was that before and during the war the soul of our people was contaminated.

After we were beaten and made defenseless, our enemies not only damaged our democratic foundations and doomed us to unending economic slavery but also shamed our national honor and marked us as criminals. In the peace treaty, they forced us to sign a war guilt article. It said that Germany and its allies caused the war to gain world hegemony and thereby committed the greatest crime against humanity of any civilized nation. With this sentence our enemies assumed the arrogance of the victors.

The condemning judgments against Germany are false and unjustified. They are based on erroneous documents. To refute such statements is not easy, and only very slowly can the truth be known. The opening of the Russian archives through the revolution was helpful, and it has not only been German researchers but also English, American, and French scholars who have systematically combed through the sources to illuminate the web of Versailles lies. There is scarcely an honest person left who accepts the Versailles thesis. But the battle is not thereby ended. If one no longer defends the idea that the war was let loose for the purposes of German world hegemony, there are other theories that still credit the Central Powers with guilt for the war.

The Austro-Hungarian state, they say, was about to break up naturally. Its ten nationalities were fighting against one another, waiting for the death of Franz Joseph, after which each people would go its separate way. Russia had no cause to unleash an enormous general war, but Austria, fighting for its existence, would be renewed by a victorious war. Without it Austria was condemned to death. The outbreak of the world war, according to this view, lay in the domestic relationships of the Hapsburg states and was grounded in despair.

The fundamental mistake of this interpretation is that the Austrian successors are not national states but without exception mixed nationalities, just as the old Austria was. The minorities in these states are suppressed with great brutality by the ruling nationalities, as happened in old Austria. The nationalities living in the middle and lower Danube River from the Sudetenland to the Adriatic Sea are itinerant and mixed; they do not form a pure national state.

The idea that the Pan-Slavists did not cause the world war, because they did not need it, is also fundamentally false. Only a powerful blow, an enormous catastrophe, could destroy the Hapsburg dual monarchy. By removing Archduke Franz Ferdinand, Serbia could destroy Austria from within. Austria finally decided to move against Serbia as an act of despair. Despair of the attacked, of the invaded, of the violated, to protect not only their honor but also their lives.

In this situation the German kaiser and government tried to avoid the catastrophe or at least to seek a compromise between Austria and Russia. A compromise was impossible, because Russia, as soon as she saw that Austria was in earnest and that her Serbian friends would be alienated, terminated negotiations and mobilized.

The assassination, which brought on the catastrophe, was the work of fanatical Serbian nationalists who eleven years earlier had killed King Alexander and his wife and pitched Serbia out of the Austrian orbit and into that of Russia.[1] The guilt of the Serbian government was that it, in spite of being informed beforehand, neither gave notice nor tried to stop the assassination, and after it had occurred, the government used it for its cause. To the Austrian government it made no difference if the Serbian government itself had inspired the deed or if the government was too weak to punish this wound against law and morality.

A government is responsible not only for what it does directly but also for the actions of its agents. If the laws of civilized states are broken, it remains to rectify them. The Serbian state was responsible.

German policymakers were convinced of this responsibility. Germany consulted its allies and wanted to negotiate between Austria and Russia. To negotiate, Germany could not be too closely associated with Austria but had to have a free hand. It assumed that the czar, in his empathy for the prince's assassination, would be ready for an understanding. German diplomats worked faultlessly to this end, but when the Russians were not ready to enter into any compromise, the effort failed. The fact that the kaiser without consulting the chancellor had assured the Austrian ambassador of German help in the event of war was perhaps a formal mistake.

After maintaining for more than ten years that Austria, by its mobilization, provoked Russian mobilization, finally France and England admitted that Russian partial mobilization began before, not after, Austrian mobilization, while continuing to maintain that Austria had decreed full general mobilization before it knew of full Russian general mobilization. Quite correct: that is the way it was.[2]

But in peacetime the Russian army was three times as large as the Austro-Hungarian. Half the Austrian army was mobilized against Serbia, not against the Russian border. Then occurred the Russian partial mobilization, four-sevenths of the whole Russian army. Because of this move Franz Joseph mobilized the other half of his army. To save his state, could he do anything less? Already the Russian partial mobilization confronted him with a powerful superiority, and one day later came the Russian full mobilization.

Finally the German mobilization followed. Some liked to believe that we were pitched into the war by our alliance with Austria. Recent research, however, has concluded that it was not the threats against Austria, as bad as they were, but certain knowledge that the Russians had mobilized on the German east border which brought the German mobilization order.[3] The German government cannot be reproached for its mobilization.

If one does not accept the Versailles guilt thesis, there are other accusations against the Central Powers. Without exception, they are all unfounded. Not in the sense that every single point of German policy and diplomacy was correctly carried out, or that there was not much controversy, or that mistakes were not made, or that here and there the opposite of what was desired eventually happened. But nowhere in all this is there anything that can prove that Germany or Austria wanted to cause a general war.

After the German, Russian, and English prewar documents had been made public, the French government also decided to open its archives. The French document publication comes from a commission with forty-four members, including all the currently living ambassadors who were responsible for these decisions. What can we expect from such a volume?

The demand was put forth that a neutral judge choose documents on the war guilt question. Pierre Rénouvin, the president of the French commission, said it was possible that in the publication of the archives the interests of truth might be subordinated to national interest, and there would be no guarantee the commission would not suppress documents painful to its own government.

If Germany and Austria do not consider themselves guilty of causing the war, what then? The English minister Lloyd George, who during the war was irreconcilable, changed a few years afterward and concluded that the Versailles war guilt clause was invalid. He now believes that all the powers slid into war together. In other words, accidents and mistakes pitched the world into this catastrophe.

If the Central Powers were not guilty, who was? We cannot be satisfied with the formulation that Germany is not alone guilty. Germany, as far as willing the world war, was completely innocent. But there were powers that meddled in German politics and that wanted and willed a war, because without the war they would not have reached their goals, which were the return of Alsace-Lorraine and hegemony over Constantinople. Poincaré himself said in 1920, "In my youthful dreams I saw one purpose for my generation. To bring back the lost provinces." Using the French president as a witness, we may say that he remained true to his dreams.

It is very difficult for those French parents who lost a son, those wives who lost a husband, or those children who lost a father in the world war to understand that France in 1914 was not overwhelmed by evil enemies but that the leading French statesmen themselves did everything they could to bring on the war.

Germany had nothing, no goal, no desires that could be reached only by war. According to the Entente ultimatum of June 1919, German war policy was nothing but a crime against humanity and against culture: the greatest crime of world history.[4] For generations and centuries France had been the preeminent power on the European continent. She lost this position in 1870 and regained it in the world war. Germany, which in 1870 had the same number of people as France, grew so much that by 1914 she had 67 million, whereas France had only 39 million. To stop Germany's forward movement, France introduced general conscription, which for us existed only on paper, and by the year 1913 militarism had progressed so far that all young men without exception had to serve three years of active duty. In terms of education, that was an unacceptable absence. After an absence of three years a scientific, artistic, or technical career is in most cases no longer recoverable. France had either to shorten the three-year service law or seek to get out of the world crisis in a very short time. They sought the war, but the sacrifices it cost were terrible for the world. If this result had been foreseen, they might have restrained their national ambition. But they did not. They believed not only in victory but in a quick victory.

Until the fall of 1912 they operated cautiously, and Poincaré restrained the Russians. Then came the change. The Turks lost to an ally of the Balkan alliance, namely, the Bulgarians, and the Russians saw it was no longer necessary to keep part of their army ready to fight the Turks, but instead they could throw their entire strength against the Central Powers. That gave them confidence in the certainty of victory.

From the Russian foreign minister, S. D. Sazonov, even if he entered into the decision with a certain fear, came the observation that the whole war would be over in six weeks. The Russians were certain that Italy would withdraw from the Triple Alliance and thus Russia-France-England had an overwhelming superiority. The German kaiser and his military advisers went into the war with anxiety. France and Russia entered the war with more than five million men, but Germany and Austria had not quite three and a half million. It is of the highest importance to the origins of the world war to understand and keep before our eyes this power relationship. The unsurpassed work capacity of the German army has obscured this truth for many Germans. In the face of the overwhelming enemy superiority, our generals saw our only salvation in speed. As soon as the Russians mobilized, we had to attack, and that created the appearance that we had let it loose, as if the war were not to be avoided.

# Notes

## Abbreviations

BA-KO    Bundesarchiv, Koblenz
DSB    Deutsche Staatsbibliothek, Berlin
LDM    Lina Thiersch Delbrück, "Hans Delbrücks Leben, für seine Kinder aufgezeichnet" (deposited in BA-KO)
PJ    *Preussisher Jahrbücher (Prussian Yearbook)*

## Preface

1. Gordon Craig, "Delbrück, the Military Historian," in *Makers of Modern Strategy*, ed. Edward Mead Earle (Princeton: Princeton University Press, 1943), 270–87.

2. Hans Delbrück, *Geschichte der Kriegskunst im Rahmen der politischen Geschichte*, 4 vols. (Berlin: Walter de Gruyter, 1962–66).

3. The Preussische Staatsbibliothek was later renamed the Deutsche Staatsbibliothek. A catalog of the Delbrück materials in the DSB is contained in Horst Wolf, *Der Nachlass Hans Delbrück* (Berlin: Deutsche Staatsbibliothek, 1980).

4. Arden Bucholz, *Hans Delbrück and the German Military Establishment: War Images in Conflict* (Iowa City: University of Iowa Press, 1985), 41; see Franz Mehring, "Eine Geschichte der Kriegskunst," *Die Neue Zeit*, 16 October 1908.

5. Alfred Vagts, *History of Militarism* (New York: W. W. Norton, 1937).

6. Arden Bucholz, *Moltke, Schlieffen, and Prussian War Planning* (Oxford: Berg, 1991).

7. Arden Bucholz, "Hans Delbrück and Modern Military History" (lecture presented at the annual meeting of the American Military Institute, Duke University, March 1991); published under the same title in *The Historian* 55 (spring 1993): 517–26; see also Bucholz,

"Hans Delbrück," in *Research Guide to European Historical Biography, 1450 to the Present,* ed. James Moncure, 10 vols. (Washington DC: Beacham, 1993), 5:2777–87.

8. Friedrich Carl Scheibe, "Marne und Gorlice: Zur Kriegsdeutung Hans Delbrück," in *Militärgeschichtliche Mitteilungen* 53, no. 2 (1994): 355–76, is a rare exception. In two recent German publications on topics and areas in which Delbrück was a highly visible participant, he is not mentioned: Wolfgang J. Mommsen and Elisabeth Müller-Luckner, eds., *Kultur and Krieg; Die Rolle der Intellektuellen, Künstler und Schriftsteller im Ersten Weltkrieg* (Munich: R. Oldenbourg Verlag, 1996) and Notker Hammerstein, ed., *Deutsche-Geschichtswissenschaft um 1900* (Wiesbaden: Franz Steiner, 1988).

## Note on Translation

1. H. T. Lowe-Porter, "Translator's Note," in *Buddenbrooks,* by Thomas Mann (New York: Alfred A. Knopf, 1938).

2. John Biguenet and Rainer Schulte, eds., *The Craft of Translation* (Chicago: University of Chicago Press, 1989), xi.

## Introduction: Delbrück's Life and Work

1. This history is based on my work, *Hans Delbrück and the German Military Establishment: War Images in Conflict* (Iowa City: University of Iowa Press, 1985); materials from the Delbrück papers in the Deutsche Staatsbibliothek, Berlin, (DSB) and Bundesarchiv, Koblenz (BA-KO); and Lina Thiersch Delbrück, "Hans Delbrücks Leben, für seine Kinder aufgezeichnet" (LDM) a fourteen-chapter, several-hundred-page manuscript written by Delbrück's wife after he died and deposited in the Bundesarchiv, Koblenz. This last work is a running account of Delbrück's life, monthly and sometimes daily, including his publications, notes on persons he visited, letters he received and sent, and activities he engaged in. In every case this document has been checked, verified, and in some cases corrected. I also consulted Lina Delbrück, "Hans Delbrück in Briefen" a 134-page compilation of Delbrück's letters to his mother and father and his parents' letters about him. The original is in the Delbrück Nachlass, DSB.

2. LDM, 1:110.

3. LDM, 1:100.

4. LDM, 1:61.

5. LDM, 1:127.

6. LDM, 1:62.

7. Margaret Festieg, *The Origins and Development of Scholarly Historical Periodicals* (Tuscaloosa: University of Alabama Press, 1986), 4–6, 20–38; Georg Iggers, *The German Conception of History* (Middletown CT: Wesleyan University Press, 1968), 116.

8. LDM, 1:66.

9. "Hans Delbrück in Briefen," 4.

10. LDM, 1:68.

11. LDM, 1:136.

12. LDM, 1:96

13. LDM, 2:164; Elizabeth Hull, *The Entourage of Kaiser Wilhelm II* (Cambridge: Cambridge University Press, 1982), 412.

14. Arden Bucholz, *Moltke, Schlieffen, and Prussian War Planning* (Oxford: Berg, 1991), 135.

15. It is interesting to speculate on the origins of this invitation. One of Hans's uncles, Friedrich Delbrück (1768–1830), a theologian and progressive educator, had been the most important tutor for both Crown Prince Friedrich Wilhelm (later Prussian King Friedrich Wilhelm IV) and Prince Wilhelm (later King and Kaiser Wilhelm I) from 1800 to 1810. The two oldest royal princes became very attached to their tutor, who fled with them to Königsberg and Memel after Prussia was defeated by Napoleon, 1806–7. David E. Barclay, *Frederick William IV and the Prussian Monarchy, 1840–1861* (Oxford: Clarendon, 1995), 26–27.

16. An interesting clue to Delbrück's social circles at this time is suggested by his relationship to Hermann Grimm (1828–1901). Grimm, a philosopher, art critic, and literary historian known for biographies of Michelangelo and Raphael, six volumes of essays, and a famous set of lectures on the life of Goethe, maintained an apartment on the Mathaikirchstrasse in Berlin that was a famous meeting place for literary people and intellectuals. In addition, he was the husband of Gisela von Arnim, daughter of Bettina von Arnim, one of the important figures of German romanticism. Grimm is also known for his correspondence with Ralph Waldo Emerson, whom Grimm introduced to the German reading public in a series of essays, and his friendships with George Bancroft and Andrew Dickson White,

American diplomats in Berlin and two of the founding fathers of the nineteenth-century American historical tradition. Frederick W. Holls, ed., *Corrrespondence between Ralph Waldo Emerson and Herman Grimm* (Boston: Houghton Mifflin, 1903), 3–13; Ruth Michaelis-Jena, *The Brothers Grimm* (New York: Praeger, 1970); Murray B. Peppard, *Paths through the Forest: A Biography of the Brothers Grimm* (New York: Holt, Rinehart and Winston, 1917).

17. LDM, 1:107.

18. Erich Eyck, *Bismarck and the German Empire* (New York: W. W. Norton, 1964), 5–67; LDM, 2:196.

19. LDM, 1:111.

20. Hans Delbrück, *History of the Art of War*, trans. Walter J. Renfroe Jr., 4 vols. (Lincoln: University of Nebraska Press, 1990), 1:13.

21. Dahne Bennett, *Vicky: Princess Royal of England and German Empress* (New York: St. Martin's Press, 1971), 81.

22. Thomas Kohut, *Wilhelm II and the Germans* (New York: Oxford University Press, 1991), esp. 22–29.

23. "He was the Emperor's tutor, knows the inside of things, edits the Pr. Jahrbücher, having quarrelled with Treitschke and is a professing liberal, but imperialistic, and colonially expansive. He talks perfect English, and lectures on universal history, from the military point of view." Lord Acton to Lord Bryce, 18 January 1898, Oxford University, Bodleian Library, Lord Bryce Papers, MS Bryce 1, folio 100. I am grateful to Professor John F. Kutolowski for this citation.

24. See Hans Delbrück, "Persönliche Erinnerungen an den Kaiser Friedrich und sein Haus," *PJ*, August 1888; rpt. in Hans Delbrück, *Erinnerungen, Aufsätze, und Reden* (Berlin: Georg Stilke, 1902), 64–86.

25. Other officers were Generals Walter von Gottberg, Hugo von Winterfeld, Albert von Mischke, and Frederick von Unruh; Colonels Gustav von Dresky and Hans von Geissler; and Major Boie. Delbrück, *Art of War*, 1:14. He had coffee with Chancellor Otto von Bismarck, who occasionally visited the Neues Palais to consult with the crown prince: they were both struggling with Kaiser Wilhelm I.

26. Agnes von Zahn-Harnack, *Adolf von Harnack* (Berlin: Hans Bott, 1936), 354.

27. LDM, 1:121.

28. LDM, 1:122; Arthur J. May, *The Hapsburg Monarchy, 1867–1914* (New York: W. W. Norton, 1951), 150.

29. On the crown prince's court, see John C. G. Röhl, *Wilhelm II: Die Jugend des Kaisers, 1859–1888* (Munich: C. H. Beck, 1993). Hed-

wig von Brühl was one of Crown Princess Victoria's ladies-in-waiting. Hannah Pakula, *An Uncommon Woman: The Empress Frederick, Daughter of Queen Victoria, Wife of the Crown Prince of Prussia, Mother of Kaiser Wilhelm* (New York: Simon & Schuster, 1995), 444.

30. Fransecky's Seventh Division had played a pivotal role in the battle of Königgrätz; Gordon Craig, *The Battle of Königgrätz* (Philadelphia: Lippincott, 1964), 104.

31. LDM, 2:173–74.

32. LDM, 2:179.

33. See Hans Delbrück, "Persönliche Erinnerungen an den Kaiser Friedrich und sein Haus" and "Kaiserin Friedrich," *PJ*, October 1890; rpt. in Delbrück, *Erinnerungen, Aufsätze, und Reden*, 606–25. LDM, 2:191.

34. Bucholz, *Hans Delbrück*, 26–30.

35. LDM, 2:185. Delbrück was elected to the Prussian Landtag, 1881–85, and to the German Reichstag, 1884–90.

36. LDM, 2:194.

37. LDM, 2:222.

38. LDM, 2:227.

39. The most recent biography in English, Robert Southard's *Droysen and the Prussian School of History* (Lexington: University Press of Kentucky, 1995), does not deal with military matters.

40. Hans Delbrück, "Etwas Kriegsgeschichtliches," *PJ*, November 1887, 610. See reading 3.

41. Theodore Dodge, *Caesar* (Boston: Houghton Mifflin, 1892), 376, 750, 768. J. F. C. Fuller commented that Caesar's apotheosis took shape after the Renaissance and thereafter became an idée fixe in the historical imagination. *Julius Caesar* (New Brunswick: Rutgers University Press, 1965), 12.

42. Bucholz, *Hans Delbrück*, 34.

43. Bucholz, *Prussian War Planning*, 23–24.

44. Bucholz, *Prussian War Planning*, 49.

45. Mary Douglas, *How Institutions Think* (London: Routledge & Kegan Paul, 1987).

46. Bucholz, *Prussian War Planning*, vii.

47. One wonders if the age of the generals making these decisions played a part. In the German army before 1914, generals were generally fifty-five to eighty years old. Helmuth von Moltke the elder, for example, would have remained completely unknown if he had died at age sixty-three, the year before the Danish war; he remained chief

of the general staff until he was eighty-eight years old. When these old-timers looked back to their own "worst case" combat scenarios, if they had any, they may have retreated to the lowest common denominator. In other words, in a "kill or be killed" situation they were reluctant to try something new, whether tactical formations or new weapons, but instead backed themselves up to the old and familiar.

48. Delbrück reviewed Bloch in "Zukunftskrieg und Zukunftsfriede," *PJ*, May 1899; rpt. in *Erinnerungen, Aufsätze, und Reden*, 3d ed. (Berlin: Herman Walter, 1905), 498–525. He concluded that, although Bloch's arguments suggested a future war would end up like Frederick the Great's eighteenth-century warfare—fought with the strategy of attrition in which the two sides destroyed each other with no clear outcome—nonetheless history contained ambivalent evidence for looking ahead.

49. At the time, however, Delbrück had more combat experience than many of the officers who opposed him.

50. Martin Bernal, *Black Athena: The Afroasiatic Roots of Classical Civilization* (New Brunswick: Rutgers University Press, 1987), 302.

51. Iggers, *German Conception of History*, 61.

52. Iggers, *German Conception of History*, 79.

53. Leo Tolstoy, *War and Peace*, trans. Ann Dunnigan (New York: Signet Classics, 1968), 330–31.

54. "Hans Delbrück in Briefen," 6.

55. Tolstoy, *War and Peace*, 331–32.

56. Hans Delbrück, *Die Perserkriege und die Burgunderkriege: Zwei combinierte kriegsgeschichtliche Studien* (Berlin: Georg Reimer, 1887), 20 (my translation).

57. Francine Du Plessix Gray, "Forty-Eight Years, No Secrets," *New Yorker*, July 1994, 76–81.

58. Bucholz, *Hans Delbrück*, chaps. 1–2.

59. His papers contain several hundred pages of notes for these lectures. Delbrück Nachlass, DSB, part 5, files 72–85.

60. LDM, 2:231.

61. His uncle, Ludwig Delbrück, principal of this bank, was administrator of Kaiser Wilhelm II's personal fortune of roughly 140 million marks. Röhl, *Kaiser and the Court*, 75.

62. The historiography on the coming of World War I has been gigantic since that war ended and shows no signs of slackening. Recent works include M. B. Hayne, *The French Foreign Office and the Origins of the First World War* (Oxford: Clarendon Press, 1993), and David

Herrmann, *The Arming of Europe and the Making of the First World War* (Princeton: Princeton University Press, 1996). My own views are stated in "Armies, Railroads, and Information: The Birth of Industrial Mass War," in *Changing Large Technical Systems*, ed. Jane Summerton (Boulder CO: Westview Press, 1994), 53–70.

63. Hans Delbrück, "Der russisch-japanische Krieg," *PJ*, February 1904; rpt. in *Vor und nach dem Weltkrieg* (Berlin: Otto Stollberg, 1926), 35–49.

64. Bucholz, *Prussian War Planning*, chap. 4; see also D. C. B. Lieven, *Russia and the Origins of the First World War* (New York: St. Martin's Press, 1983); John Kieger, *France and the Origins of the First World War* (New York: St. Martin's Press, 1983).

65. Hans Delbrück, "Schwüle in der internationalen Politik" *PJ*, July 1908; rpt. in *Vor und nach dem Weltkrieg*, 205–13; "Kriegsgefahr," *PJ*, 26 July 1908, rpt. in *Vor und nach dem Weltkrieg*, 259–275.

66. Bucholz, *Prussian War Planning*, chap. 6; see also Samuel R. Williamson Jr., *Austria-Hungary and the Origins of the First World War* (New York: St. Martin's Press, 1991); Lieven, *Russia and the Origins of the First World War*; Volker Berghahn, *Germany and the Approach of War in 1914*, 2d ed. (New York: St. Martin's Press, 1993).

67. Hans Delbrück, "Der Abschluss des Morokko-Congo-Handels und die Reichstagswahlen. Verstärkte Rüstungen: Flotte oder Armee?" *PJ*, December 1911, rpt. in *Vor und nach dem Weltkrieg*, 352–61.

68. Bucholz, *Prussian War Planning*, 260. See also Zara Steiner, *Britain and the Origins of the First World War* (New York: St. Martin's Press, 1977); Keiger, *France and the Origins of the First World War*; Berghahn, *Germany and the Approach of War in 1914*.

69. Bucholz, *Prussian War Planning*, 261.

70. Hans Delbrück, "Die Alldeutschen," *PJ*, December 1913; rpt. in *Vor und nach dem Weltkrieg*, 397–403.

71. Bucholz, *Prussian War Planning*, 277.

72. Bucholz, "Armies, Railroads, and Information," 65–66.

73. LDM, 11 (1914–15): 43.

74. LDM, 11 (1914–15): 105–15. Our knowledge of the precise timing of the implementation of all preparatory actions—partial, half, and full mobilizations—during the July 1914 crisis is still vague and, to an uncomfortable degree, unknown. Equally important, the results of these mobilization actions within the slowly uncoiling coun-

teractive war systems of'each of the five great-power participants have been forgotten.

75. LDM, 11 (1914–15): 56.

76. LDM, 11 (1914–15): 57.

77. Hans Delbrück, "Das Zahlen-Übergewicht unserer Gegner und die Politik Belgiens. Die Strategische Lage," *PJ*, December 1914; rpt. in Hans Delbrück, *Krieg und Politik*, 3 vols. (Berlin: Georg Stilke, 1917–19), 1:70–80.

78. Hans Delbrück, "Amerika zwischen Deutschland und England," *PJ*, February 1916; rpt. in *Krieg und Politik*, 1:202–16.

79. Bucholz, *Hans Delbrück*, chap. 4.

80. LDM, 11 (1914–15): 86.

81. LDM, 12 (1916–17): 59. This comment was made in August 1916. He was in the Stilllachhaus sanitarium in Oberstdorf, Bavaria, and his doctors had just told him that he must give up all political activity, including reading newspapers.

82. See Holger Afflerbach, *Falkenhayn: Politiches Denken und Handeln im Kaiserreich* (Munich: R. Oldenbourg, 1994).

83. LDM, 11 (1914–15): 162.

84. LDM, 12 (1916–17): 6. They apparently got on very well. One topic of discussion was military history. Falkenhayn said that from the standpoint of the high command, the German battle in the Masurian Lakes in September 1914, in spite of capturing the Tenth Russian Corps at Augustow, was in reality almost a failure because the Germans, stopped by a snow and ice storm, were unable to break through the Russian front completely. Curiously, in his description of this battle Norman Stone makes no mention of weather. See Norman Stone, *The Eastern Front, 1914–1916* (New York: Charles Scribner, 1975), 68–70.

85. See Afflerbach, *Falkenhayn*, 437–57.

86. LDM, 12 (1916–17): 114.

87. Bucholz, *Hans Delbrück*, 97–99.

88. LDM, 12 (1916–17): 168. A folder in the Delbrück Nachlass, DSB, is filled with the things Delbrück collected on this trip: dinner orders of service, photographs at various sites, and letters to and from commanders whose troops he visited.

89. LDM, 12 (1916–17): 189.

90. LDM, 12 (1916–17): 189. Delbrück constantly sent articles from the *PJ* to members of the kaiser's official and household staff. They responded with notes thanking him, usually adding comments about

the article. Delbrück edited a book of German-Polish stories he sent to General von Beseler.

91. Hans Delbrück, "Das Beispiel Napoleons," *PJ*, March 1917; rpt. in *Krieg und Politik*, 2:153, 139.

92. LDM, 12 (1916–17): 171–72.

93. Bucholz, *Hans Delbrück*, 104; LDM, 12 (1916–17): 188.

94. It should be remembered that Valentini's memoirs are blank for the years 1910–18. See Rudolf von Valentini, *Lebens Erinnerungen* (Berlin: E. S. Mittler, 1921); see also Isabel Hull, *The Entourage of Kaiser Wilhelm II* (Cambridge: Cambridge University Press, 1982), 242–43.

95. Bucholz, *Hans Delbrück*, 105.

96. LDM, 13 (1918): 34, 35.

97. LDM, 13 (1918): 45, 48.

98. LDM, 13 (1918): 52.

99. LDM, 13 (1918): 82.

100. LDM, 13 (1918): 76.

101. LDM, 12 (1916–17): rpt. in *Krieg und Politik*, 1:175.

102. "Die Freude darüber verfliegt mir immer wider nur zu bald, da dahinter immer fürchterlicher die Sorge auftaucht, dass gerade die Grösse des Sieges uns in die Bahn des Verderbens locken wird." LDM, 13 (1918): 77.

103. LDM, 13 (1918): 80.

104. LDM, 13 (1918): 124.

105. Bucholz, *Hans Delbrück*, chaps. 5, 6.

106. For this period the Delbrück papers in the BA-KO are a rich source. There is also the account of his daughter, Helene Hobe, who worked as her father's secretary for five years right after the war before she married and moved to Spain. Helene Hobe, "Einige Erinnerungen an meinen Vater Hans Delbrück," six-page typescript, May 1974. Copy in both Delbrück Nachlässe, Berlin and Koblenz.

107. Arden Bucholz, "Germany and the Death Paradigm," *Central European History* 24, no 2. (1991): 187–94.

108. Later, as Delbrück was about to leave for the peace conference, Conger visited him again. Fritz Epstein, "Zwischen Compiègne und Versailles: Geheime amerikanische Militärdiplomatie in der Periode des Waffenstillstandes 1918/19: Die Rolle des Obersten Arthur L. Conger," *Vierteljahrshefte für Zeitgeschichte* 3 (1955): 418–37; see Donald Smythe, *Pershing: General of the Armies* (Bloomington: Indiana University Press, 1986), 30. In 1910 the army had sent

Conger to Germany to study military history and the German military. In 1916 he was studying at Harvard and still preoccupied with the German military. See Arthur L. Conger, "Moltke's Plans of Campaign," *Military Historian and Economist* 1 (January 1916): 297–306.

109. LDM, 14 (1919): 245.

110. LDM, 14 (1919): 248, 251.

111. LDM, 14 (1919): 341.

112. Bucholz, *Hans Delbrück*, 139–42.

113. In September 1919 Delbrück sold the journal for twenty-eight thousand marks. The changeover to the new editor, Dr. Schotte, came 1 December 1919.

114. It is interesting to note that, in one of Max Delbrück's last formal statements on general human affairs, his commencement address to the graduating class of 1978 at Cal Tech, his father's philosophy of history is clearly in evidence. "Can you separate the historian from the history he describes?" he asks. Max Delbrück, "The Arrow of Time—Beginning and End," *Engineering & Science* 42 (September–October 1978): 5–9.

115. Arden Bucholz, "Hans Delbrück and Modern Military History," *The Historian* 55 (Spring 1993): 526.

116. Bucholz, *Hans Delbrück*, 148, 154.

117. Bucholz, *Hans Delbrück*, 152.

118. Felix Gilbert, letter to author, 23 October 1986.

119. See, for example, Department of the Army, Pamphlet 20-261a, *The German Campaign in Russia: Planning and Operations, 1940–1942*, for the use of military history and war gaming before the Russian invasion (Washington DC: Department of the Army, 1955).

120. Emil Daniels and Paul Rühlmann, eds., *Am Webstuhle der Zeit* (Berlin: Reimar Hobbing, 1928); Ferdinand J. Schmidt, Konrad Molinski, and Siegfried Mette, eds., *Hans Delbrück, der Historiker un der Politiker* (Berlin: Otto Stollberg, 1928).

121. Bucholz, *Hans Delbrück*, 1.

122. Theodore Ropp, *War in the Modern World* (New York: Colliers, 1961), 1.

123. Michael Howard, "The Use and Abuse of Military History," *Journal of the Royal United Services Institute* 107 (February 1962): 5.

124. Paul Kennedy, "The Fall and Rise of Military History," *Yale Journal of World Affairs* 1 (Fall 1989): 12–19.

125. Kennedy, "Fall and Rise of Military History," 16.

126. Walter J. Renfroe Jr. for Greenwood Publications, Westport CT, 1975–83.

127. Archer Jones, *The Art of War in Western Civilization* (New York: Oxford University Press, 1986).

128. Four volumes, University of Nebraska Press, 1990.

129. Bucholz, *Hans Delbrück*, 33.

130. See Bucholz, "Hans Delbrück and Modern Military History," 523.

## Reading 1. Letters from the Franco-Prussian War

1. The Eifel is the area around the Moselle River between Koblenz and Trier, made up of low mountains along the river with vineyards and fields. It appears that Delbrück's unit got into part of the Moselle wine country, around Bernkastel, before turning southeast toward Saarbrücken.

2. German law provided that whether for peacetime maneuvers or wartime operations, civilians were legally required to quarter troops in their homes. From 1871 to about 1908 the German army gradually built up a group of about twenty-five maneuver grounds, one for each army corps. By about 1910, when the grounds were completed, it was there that summer exercises were held, with most troops under tent, although the commanders and some officers often stayed in homes nearby. In any event, the quartering law remained right through to 1918.

3. He is referring to the battle of Spichern. Of roughly forty-two thousand German forces, 12 percent were killed or wounded. French historian Guillaume Auguste Bonal wrote that French general Frossard, undefeated, thought he had been defeated, and so he was. Prussian General von Zastrow was half-defeated but refused to be and so was not. That was the secret of the Prussian victory. Michael Howard, *The Franco-Prussian War* (New York: Collier, 1961), 98. Although this battle was mythologized as a great victory at the time—streets were named after it all across Germany—military historians generally regard it as a disaster from start to finish. Arden Bucholz, *Moltke, Schlieffen, and Prussian War Planning* (Oxford: Berg, 1991), 79–81.

4. Casualties at Gravelotte were very high, especially for German forces. The First Army lost 4,219, the Prussian Guard more than

8,000. Total losses were 20,163 for the Germans, 12,273 for the French. Howard, *Franco-Prussian War*, 181.

5. Prince Frederick Charles, commander of the Prussian Second Army.

6. This event occurred at night in the Mance ravine area near Point du Jour, where the German Seventh and Eighth Corps, decimated by French fire, retreated. As they fled they were fired on by their own troops, the German Second Corps, advancing in the dark. Chaos and death ensued until a cease-fire was sounded at 9:30 P.M. Howard, *Franco-Prussian War*, 179–80.

7. Thousands of corpses lay decomposing under a light covering of soil. Heavy rains repeatedly washed it off, causing health and morale problems for those soldiers bivouacked nearby. Howard, *Franco-Prussian War*, 259.

8. Major General Ferdinand Maltzin, commander of the division of which the Twenty-eighth Rhenish Infantry was a part.

9. As Alfred Vagts once wrote me about his own experiences in World War I, German soldiers were formally addressed by their officers as "children," even after 1914.

10. These figures indicate a casualty rate of more than 32 percent, very high even for the Franco-Prussian War. Undoubtedly some were wounded, captured, or had just wandered away and were lost during the fighting. See Bucholz, *Prussian War Planning*, 79–81.

11. Delbrück was referring to the fighting of the Greeks in the Persian Wars described by Herodotus and to the Roman Empire under such commanders as Julius Caesar.

12. Peter von Henning, who died in October from wounds received at Sedan.

13. Delbrück was essentially correct: after 7:30 P.M. the French retreated when they were about to be outflanked.

## Reading 2. Prince Frederick Charles

Hans Delbrück, "Prinz Friedrich Karl," *PJ*, November 1885; rpt. in *Historische und politische Aufsätze* (Berlin: Walther & Apolant, 1887), 306–14.

1. Gordon Craig, *The Battle of Königgrätz* (Philadelphia: Lippincott, 1964), esp. 31.

2. Michael Howard, *The Franco-Prussian War* (New York: Collier, 1961), 60.

3. This statement is reminiscent of a famous comparison made by Clausewitz using nearly the same materials. Clausewitz wrote, "Action in war is like a movement in a resistant element. Just as the simplest and most natural of movements, walking, cannot easily be performed in water, so in war it is difficult for normal efforts to achieve even moderate efforts. Friction, as we choose to call it, is the force that makes the apparently easy so difficult." Peter Paret, "Clausewitz," in *Makers of Modern Strategy from Machiavelli to the Nuclear Age*, ed. Peter Paret (Princeton: Princeton University Press, 1986), 203.

4. The first four are battles fought by Frederick the Great; the last four are from the Franco-Prussian War.

5. Wilhelm Rüstow, a Prussian lieutenant of democratic leanings, was the most impressive military historian Delbrück read before he became one himself. Rüstow fought under Garibaldi, ended his military career in the Swiss army, and thereafter became a historian. His work included *Geschichte des griechischen Kriegswesens von der ältesten Zeit bis auf Pyrrhos*, with Heinrich Köchly (Aarau: Verlags-Comptior, 1852); *Griechische Kriegsschriftsteller*, 3 vols. (Leipzig: Engelmann, 1853–55); *Geschichte der Infanterie*, 2 vols. (Zurich: Ferdinand Forstemann, 1857); and *Heerwesen und Kriegsführung C. Julius Caesars*, 2d ed. (Nordhausen: Foerstemann, 1862). In the first volume of the *History of the Art of War* Delbrück pays tribute to Rüstow's work on ancient warfare for its overall framework combining political, economic, and social factors.

6. Field Marshal Ludwig August von Benedek, Austrian commander in chief.

7. Carl von Clausewitz (1780–1831), author of *Vom Kriege*, the classic study of war, best read today in the translation of Michael Howard and Peter Paret, *On War*, rev. ed. (Princeton: Princeton University Press, 1984). See Paret, "Clausewitz."

8. General Antoine Henri Jomini (1779–1869), served in the French army of Napoleon. His *Précis de l'art de la guerre*, 2 vols. (Paris: Editions Richelieu, 1838), translated as *Summary of the Art of War* (Philadelphia: Lippincott, 1863), claimed that all successful soldiers had followed certain principles of war. Jomini is said to be the most influential writer on war in the first half of the nineteenth century. See John Shy, "Jomini," in *Makers of Modern Strategy*, ed. Paret, 143–85; but see Edward Hagerman's comments in *The American Civil War*

*and the Origins of Modern Warfare* (Bloomington: Indiana University Press, 1988) 4–5. Wilhelm von Willisen was a German war theorist of the same period. Both carried forward the eighteenth-century rationalist-mathematical limited approach to war, in contrast to the more romantic notions of Clausewitz about war as culminating in the force and violence of battle.

9. This battle occurred in early January 1871. Bad weather, irregular terrain, and overwhelming German force coupled with broken morale finally overwhelmed French forces. See Howard, *Franco-Prussian War*, 398–403.

10. In fact it was more complicated than that. Both armies were exhausted, but the French more so. See Howard, *Franco-Prussian War*, 398–403.

11. These men are all important figures in the Prussian army, 1795–1830. See Gordon Craig, *The Politics of the Prussian Army* (New York: Oxford University Press, 1955).

12. General Karl Friedrich von Steinmetz fought as a lieutenant in 1814, won a Pour le Mérite in Denmark in 1864, was the most successful commander of all against Austria in 1866, and was finally relieved as commander of the First Army against France in 1870 for insubordination. He ended as governor of Posen. See Hans von Krosigk, *General-Feldmarshall von Steinmetz* (Berlin: E. S. Mittler, 1900).

13. This approach has been called variously "Auftragstaktik" and "directive command." Higher commanders laid out general orders but allowed subordinate commanders to apply their own wisdom, intelligence, and ability in choosing the precise methods used to execute these orders. See the excellent article by Martin Samuels, "Directive Command and the German General Staff," *War in History* 2, no. 1 (1995): 22–42.

14. Friedrich Wilhelm von Seydlitz was a famous cavalry commander under Frederick the Great. G. L. von Blücher became a field marshal fighting for Prussia against Napoleon's armies. Both were known as forceful characters.

### Reading 3. A Little Military History

Hans Delbrück, "Etwas Kriegsgeschichtliches," *PJ*, November 1887, 607–33.

1. *Aus meinem Leben: Aufzeichnungen aus den Jahren 1848–1871* (Berlin: E. S. Mittler, 1907).

2. Hohenlohe's books under review are *Militärische Briefe: Über Kavallerie, Über Infanterie, Über Feld-Artillerie*; *Strategische Briefe*; and *Gespräche über Reiterei*, published by E. S. Mittler, Berlin, 1886–87.

3. Theodor Mommsen, *Romanische Geschichte* (Berlin: Weidmann, 1883); Max Duncker, *Griechische Geschichte*, 5 vols. (Leipzig: Duncker & Humblot, 1888); Karl von Noorden, *Prinz Eugene und Marlborough* (Leipzig: Duncker & Humblot, 1885); Johann Gustav Droysen, *Das Leben des Feldmarshall Grafen York von Wartenburg*, 2 vols. (Berlin: Walther & Apoland, 1851); Heinrich von Sybel, *Friedrich der Grosse* (Düsseldorf: Buddeus, 1862).

4. See Michael Howard, *The Franco-Prussian War* (New York: Collier, 1961), 5–6.

5. Battle in the Franco-Prussian War, between Gravelotte and St. Privat, 18 August 1870, in which Delbrück participated.

6. At the victory parade in Berlin, 4 May 1864, Hindersin led the troops accompanying wagons loaded with Danish war trophies for the first few minutes, then turned them over to King Wilhelm I at the Brandenburg Gate for the rest of the ceremonies and celebration. Theodor Fontane, *Der Schleswig-Holsteinische Krieg* (Berlin: Königlichen Ober-Hofbuchdruckerei R. von Decker, 1866), 261.

7. See Edward Hagerman, *The American Civil War and the Origins of Modern Warfare* (Bloomington: Indiana University Press, 1988), 22.

8. A conspicuous absence in military literature is a comprehensive work on artillery of this period. General works include Ian V. Hogg, *A History of Artillery* (London: Hamlyn, 1974); William Manchester, *The Arms of Krupp, 1587–1968* (Boston: Little Brown, 1968); Clive Trebilcock, *The Vickers Brothers: Armaments and Enterprise, 1854–1914* (London: Europa, 1977); J. D. Scott, *Vickers: A History* (London: Weidenfeld & Nicolson, 1962); Shelford Bidwell and Dominick Graham, *Fire Power: British Army Weapons and Theories of War, 1904–1945* (Boston: Allen & Unwin, 1985). The best work on Prussian-German guns may be Dennis Showalter, "Prussia, Technology, and War: Artillery from 1815 to 1914," in *Men, Machines, and War*, ed. Ronald Haycock and Keith Neilson (Waterloo, Ontario: Wilfrid Laurier University Press, 1985), 115–51. The most recent work on World War I, David T. Zabecki, *Steel Wind: Colonel Georg Bruchmüller and the Birth of Modern Artillery* (Westport CT: Praeger, 1994), notes the general

lack of interest in artillery by soldiers of other branches, a lack apparently shared by military historians.

9. General goals included a certain number of shots within a target area.

10. See Archer Jones, *The Art of War in Western Civilization* (New York: Oxford University Press, 1986), 401. Michael Howard wrote that the effectiveness of Prussian artillery was the greatest tactical surprise of the Franco-Prussian War. Howard, *Franco-Prussian War*, 6.

## Reading 4. Moltke

From three essays all entitled "Moltke": *PJ*, November 1890, May 1891, and October 1900; rpt. in *Erinnerungen, Aufsätze, und Reden* (Berlin: Georg Stilke, 1902), 546–75.

1. Gerhard Johann David von Scharnhorst, Prussian army reformer and early chief of the general staff during the Napoleonic Wars.

2. Franz von Lenbach, a contemporary of Delbrück and Berlin court painter known for his heroic figures.

3. Catholic priest and historian Ignaz Döllinger educated Lord Acton. See W. H. McNeill, "Lord Acton," in *Mythistory and Other Essays* (Chicago: University of Chicago Press, 1986), 109–24.

4. Christian August von Haugwitz, in partial charge of Prussian foreign relations.

5. Themistocles was a Greek commander at the battle of Salamis, 480 B.C., against the Persians; Epaminondas was a Greek general and leader of the Theban army in 369 B.C.; Scipio was a Roman general who fought in the Second Punic Wars, 218–201 B.C.; Prince Eugene of Savoy was a famous Austrian commander in the War of the Austrian Succession, 1701–14; the duke of Marlborough was an English general in the late seventeenth century, early eighteenth century.

6. The duke of Wellington, English general during the Napoleonic Wars.

7. Rössler was a Berlin intellectual who wrote and edited the *Prussian Yearbook* in the 1880s. He helped Delbrück accommodate himself to Bismarckian Germany.

8. In the Austro-Prussian War, 1866.

9. In the Franco-Prussian War, 1870.

10. The standard biography is still Eberhard Kessel, *Moltke* (Stuttgart: K. F. Koehler, 1957). Cf. Arden Bucholz, *Moltke, Schlieffen, and Prussian War Planning* (Oxford: Berg, 1991), chaps. 1, 2.

11. The topographical section was one of the main sections of the general staff at the time. Its job was to map the kingdom of Prussia, for which no complete and accurate topographical cartography existed in 1828. Moltke had taught field drawing and published a book on it, *Military Drawing of the Land* (Berlin: E. S. Mittler, 1828), just before he joined the general staff. Moltke's plane table drawings, based on the triangulation system covering the kingdom, were made into finished sheets. His work on Lower Silesia, drawn in the field during the summers and completed as ordinance survey sheets during the winter, form part of the modern German Ordnance Survey Map 4870. See Bucholz, *Prussian War Planning*, 33.

12. Gerhard Ritter was correct when he wrote that Moltke's letters from Turkey are a brilliant example of German prose. And the illustrations, Moltke's pen-and-ink sketches, demonstrate his broad humanistic and artistic horizon—a creative talent of rare ability. Gerhard Ritter, *The Sword and the Scepter*, 4 vols. (Coral Gables: University of Miami Press, 1969–73), 1:188.

13. Humboldt (1759–1859), a chamberlain at the royal Prussian court, was one of the founders of modern science in Germany. About the time Moltke and he were in Rome with Prince Henry, Humboldt published *Kosmos*, one of the first books that gave a broad scientific view of the universe. One of Humboldt's protégés was Justus von Liebig, professor of chemistry, first synthesizer of plant chemistry, and Lina Thiersch Delbrück's maternal grandfather.

14. Count Albrecht von Roon, Prussian war minister, 1859–71.

15. Moltke led an intense investigation of the 1859 campaign. He sent observers to France and northern Italy to take note of the battlefields and of the demobilization of the armies, studied reports from military observers of the fighting itself, and lectured on the war, finally turning his lectures into an essay that was published in the *Military Weekly*, the house organ of the Prussian general staff. Bucholz, *Prussian War Planning*, 42–43.

16. Benedek had commanded troops in the campaign of 1848 and at Solferino in 1859.

17. Gordon Craig, *The Battle of Königgrätz* (Philadelphia: Lippincott, 1964), generally agrees; see 32–34.

18. Karl Gustav von Döring.

19. Berlin: E. S. Mittler, 1900. Sigismund von Schlichting (1828–1909), who led a company against Austria in 1866 and a battalion against France in 1870, finished active duty as commanding general of the Fourteenth Army Corps in Karlsruhe. He was the principal author of the infantry regulations of 1888, which institutionalized mission-type orders at the operational and tactical level of the Prussian army. In 1896 Schlichting was forced into retirement. In a series of books and articles he attacked the notion that Frederick the Great and Moltke had fought with the same strategy, thus taking Delbrück's side in the decades-long conflict over forms of historical strategy. In the Delbrück Nachlass in the DSB, Berlin, there are twenty-five letters from Schlichting, 1900–1908, commenting on his war experiences and war history. See Daniel J. Hughes, "Schlichting, Schlieffen, and the Prussian Theory of War in 1914," *Journal of Military History* 59 (April 1995): 257–78.

20. General Herwarth von Bittenfeld was commander of the Elbe Army, one of three Prussian armies in the Austro-Prussian War of 1866.

21. Craig, *Königgrätz*, 62–68, generally agrees, even to the casualty figures.

22. See Craig, *Königgrätz*, 67–69.

### Reading 5. The Russo-Japanese War

From "Der russisch-japanische Krieg," *PJ*, February 1904; rpt. in Delbrück, *Vor und nach dem Weltkrieg* (Berlin: Otto Stolberg, 1926), 35–49. The Russo-Japanese War began 8 February 1904.

1. See Bruce W. Menning, *Bayonets before Bullets: The Imperial Russian Army, 1861–1914* (Bloomington: Indiana University Press, 1992), chap. 5; D. C. B. Lieven, *Russia and the Origins of the First World War* (New York: St. Martin's Press, 1983).

2. Count V. N. Lambsdorff, Russian foreign minister from 1900 to 1907.

3. In the Russian journal *Nowoje Wremja*.

4. In the Franco-Prussian War, December 1870. Howard argues that the campaign failed because the plan was not thought out carefully and neither the railroad nor the supply systems to carry it out

existed. After the troops spent nearly a week on the trains, the food ran out and the hungry and cold soldiers were in no condition to fight. Michael Howard, *Franco-Prussian War* (New York: Collier, 1961), 407–15.

5. Delbrück's figure may be a bit high, but his point that it took a great deal of organization and infrastructure to fight a war so far from London is valid.

6. The Turkish army had been recently reorganized by German military missions and was superior in training, equipment, and leadership. After about thirty days the Greek army melted away, at which point the European great powers intervened. Ironically, the Greeks, defeated on the battlefield, ultimately received the island of Crete, which was what had started the war in the first place. See L. S. Stavrianos, *The Balkans since 1453* (New York: Holt, Rinehart & Winston, 1958), 469–71.

7. The *Kreuzzeitung* was considered one of the most conservative newspapers of that day in Germany, supposedly reflecting the views of the old landowners, army officers, and nobility. It is interesting that Delbrück takes his information wherever he can get it.

8. Russian railroad building to the east did not really begin until 1891, and the distances were so great that the link from Moscow to Vladivostok was not completed until 1905. But a good deal of the eastern line was built for nonmilitary needs. By 1911, there were more than 31,000 miles of railroad in European Russia and only 6,374 miles in Asian Russia. See J. N. Westwood, *A History of Russian Railways* (London: George Allen & Unwin, 1964).

## Reading 6. International Tension

Hans Delbrück, "Schwüle in der internationalen Politik," *PJ*, July 1908; rpt. in *Vor und nach dem Weltkrieg* (Berlin: Otto Stolberg, 1926), 205–13.

1. Arden Bucholz, *Moltke, Schlieffen, and Prussian War Planning* (Oxford: Berg, 1991), 256–59.

2. On 12 June 1908 English king Edward VII, accompanied by Charles Hardinge, and Russian czar Nicholas II, accompanied by Russian foreign minister A. P. Izvolski, met at Reval on the Gulf of Finland.

3. General John French, close associate of Winston Churchill in discussions within the British Committee of Imperial Defence.

4. Colmar Baron von der Goltz, German field marshal, author of widely read military studies, and adviser to the Ottoman Turkish armies in the 1890s.

5. This agreement, which concluded the 1905 first Moroccan crisis, was reached at a conference between France and Germany in Algeciras, Spain, in January 1906. The accord affirmed the tacit independence of Morocco under French military protection and opened up the country for European economic activity by establishing an international bank under French leadership.

6. The Young Turks were reformists who wanted to modernize the Ottoman Empire by establishing a constitutional government, strengthening the army, and instituting bureaucratic reforms. Erik Zürcher, *Turkey: A Modern History* (London: I. B. Tauris, 1993), 80–137.

7. See George F. Kennan, *The Fateful Alliance: France, Russia, and the Coming of the First World War* (New York: Pantheon, 1984).

8. P. A. Stolypin, chairman of the Russian Council of Ministers.

### Reading 7. Danger of War

Hans Delbrück, "Kriegsgefahr," *PJ*, December 1908; rpt. in *Vor und nach dem Weltkrieg* (Berlin: Otto Stolberg, 1926), 259–75.

1. By the Treaty of Compo Formio, October 1797.

2. Italian Foreign Minister Tommaso Tittoni. The 1878 Treaty of Berlin left Italy out, but the implication was that Italy could go ahead and expand into some parts of the Dalmatian coast, at the expense of Albania.

3. See D. C. B. Lieven, *Russia and the Origins of the First World War* (New York: St. Martin's Press, 1983), chap. 4.

4. See Bruce W. Menning, *Bayonets before Bullets: The Imperial Russian Army, 1861–1914* (Bloomington: Indiana University Press, 1992), 216–18.

5. Delbrück cited an article in the *Nineteenth Century*, an influential English monthly journal.

6. These figures include only active-duty or regular forces. Since, at war declaration, the bulk of these armies were made up of reserves,

the actual war-strength figure for the five European great powers by 1914 was twelve to thirteen million men.

## Reading 8. The Second Moroccan Crisis

Hans Delbrück, "Der Abschluss des Morokko-Congo-Handels und die Reichstagswahlen. Verstärkte Rüstungen: Flotte oder Armee?" *PJ*, December 1911; rpt. in *Vor und nach dem Weltkrieg* (Berlin: Otto Stolberg, 1926), 352–61.

1. The Franco-German Convention of November 1911 left France a free hand in Morocco but ceded to Germany three hundred thousand acres in French Congo, which connected the German Cameroons with the Congo and Ubangi rivers. The election referred to is probably the Reichstag election upcoming in 1912 in which the Social Democratic Party gained the largest number of deputies.

2. The idea that war is a vehicle of progress has been hotly debated. John U. Nef, *War and Human Progress* (New York: Harper & Row, 1951), is an older work dealing with the opposite viewpoint. It is by no means clear that Delbrück endorsed the general position outlined here.

3. The Navy League was one of several large national lobbying organizations created in Germany in the two decades before 1914. It had a national headquarters, membership rolls, publications, and local groups. Support came from many segments of society: the professoriat, officials and bureaucrats, big business. The league's purpose was to support the navy as an instrument of national policy, including the building of a big fleet. Delbrück backed these goals in the 1890s but gradually fell away after about 1905. Of the large literature see Eckart Kehr, *Battleship Building and Party Politics in Germany* (Chicago: University of Chicago Press, 1973); Jonathan Steinberg, *Yesterday's Deterrent: Tirpitz and the Birth of the German Battle Fleet* (New York: St. Martin's Press, 1965); Jeff Eley, *Reshaping the German Right* (New Haven: Yale University Press, 1980); Volkder Berghahn, *Der Tirpitz Plan* (Düsseldorf: Droste, 1971); and Wilhelm Deist and Hans Schottelius, eds., *Flottenrüstung und Flottenpropaganda* (Stuttgart: Klett Cotta, 1976).

4. Alfred von Tirpitz, one of the most successful naval builders of all time, lobbied for the series of naval bills passed by the Reichstag

from 1897 to 1912. These bills changed the German navy from a few patrol boats into a battle fleet that so frightened the English that they built their own dreadnoughts and turned away from Germany diplomatically. The astonishing thing is that the navy had no war plan in 1914, it was not integrated into the Reich war plans, and during World War I these battleships hardly fought and when they did, without consequence. Had the Germans not built a fleet or had they built submarines, the outcome might have been quite different. There is no good English- or German-language biography of Tirpitz and not much on his revolutionary fleet-building program. See Ivo Lambi, *The Navy and German Power Politics, 1862–1914* (Boston: Allen & Unwin, 1984); and Holger Herwig, *"Luxury" Fleet: The Imperial German Navy, 1888–1918* (London: Allen & Unwin, 1980).

5. See William H. McNeill, *The Pursuit of Power* (Chicago: University of Chicago Press, 1982), chaps. 7, 8.

6. From about 1897 to 1911 the naval budget saw huge increases while the army budget was increased only marginally. In 1911-12 this trend suddenly turned. In 1912 Erich Ludendorff, chief of the deployment section of the general staff, persuaded his superior, Helmuth von Moltke the younger, chief of the general staff, to ask for a size increase of 40 percent, or three hundred thousand men, in two years. The War Ministry and Military Cabinet opposed the plan, and Ludendorff was sent down to a regimental command; nevertheless the army bills of 1912 and 1913 enlarged the peacetime army by nearly 10 percent. In the cold war runup to World War I, which began in the 1890s, all five European great powers were involved in counteractive defense spending, alliances, and war plans. Stig Förster, *Der doppelte Militarismus* (Stuttgart: Franz Steiner, 1985); Arden Bucholz, *Moltke, Schlieffen, and Prussian War Planning* (Oxford: Berg, 1991), 259–64; Arden Bucholz, "Armies, Railroads, and Information: The Birth of Industrial Mass War," in *Changing Large Technical Systems*, ed. Jane Summerton (Boulder CO: Westview Press, 1994), 53–70.

7. One problem was that most taxes were reserved to the provincial states of the empire. Another was that there were no income or inheritance taxes. For a clear and complete discussion of imperial German tax problems, especially in the ten years before World War I, see Nicholas Stargardt, *The German Idea of Militarism: Radical and Socialist Critics, 1866–1914* (New York: Cambridge University Press, 1994), chap. 5.

## Reading 9. The Pan-Germans

Hans Delbrück, "Die Alldeutschen," *PJ* December 1913; rpt. in *Vor und nach dem Weltkrieg* (Berlin: Otto Stolberg, 1926), 397–403.
 1. These two Berlin daily newspapers had conservative leanings.
 2. On the Pan-Germans see Marilyn Coetze, *The Pan Germans* (New Haven: Yale University Press, 1993).

## Reading 10. Origins, Possibilities, and Goals

Hans Delbrück, "Die Ursachen des Krieges. Die Chancen. Das Ziel," *PJ*, August 1914; rpt. in *Krieg und Politik*, 3 vols. (Berlin: Georg Stilke, 1918), 1:28–45.
 1. Theobald von Bethmann-Hollweg (1856–1921) was a Prussian bureaucrat who became chancellor in 1909. The most telling story about his life is that when he went to the Reichstag on 4 August 1914 to obtain its support for war credits, he wore his reserve army major uniform. See Konrad Jarausch, *The Enigmatic Chancellor: Bethmann-Hollweg and the Hubris of Imperial Germany* (New Haven: Yale University Press, 1973), and the two Fritz Fischer volumes, *Germany's Aims in the First World War* (New York: W. W. Norton, 1967) and *War of Illusions* (New York: W. W. Norton, 1975).
 2. General Maitrot was the author of *Nos frontières du nord et de l'est*.
 3. Joffre was chief of the French general staff, 1911–16.

## Reading 11. August through September 1914

Hans Delbrück, "Die Kriegsereignisse von Ende August bis gegen Ende September. Der zukünftige Friede," *PJ*, September 1914; rpt. in *Vor und nach dem Weltkrieg* (Berlin: Otto Stolberg, 1926), 1:48–62.
 1. Delbrück's second estimate is close to the numbers generally recognized as valid. See C. R. M. F. Cruttwell, *A History of the Great War, 1914–1918*, 2d ed. (Oxford: Clarendon Press, 1936), 10; see also Arden Bucholz, *Moltke, Schlieffen, and Prussian War Planning* (Oxford: Berg, 1991), chap. 8.
 2. Alexander von Kluck, commander in chief of the First German Army.

3. General Max von Hausen, commander in chief of the Third Army; Karl von Bülow, commander in chief of the Second German Army.

4. Surprisingly this account generally follows the main lines of accounts written long afterward. Cf. Cyril Falls, *The Great War* (New York: Capricorn, 1959), 66–71; and Cruttwell, *Great War*, 22–35.

5. General Paval K. Rennenkampf was commander of the northernmost Russian army. In September 1914 Delbrück could not know that Yakov Zhilinski was commander in chief of the northwest front. His two subordinates, who lost these great opening-round battles, were Rennenkampf (Masurian Lakes) and Alexander V. Samsonov (Tannenberg). For an excellent treatment in English, see Dennis Showalter, *Tannenberg: Clash of Empires* (Hamden CT: Archon, 1991).

6. Absolutely correct. See Arden Bucholz, *Hans Delbrück and the German Military Establishment: War Images in Conflict* (Iowa City: University of Iowa Press, 1985), 63–64.

7. The turning-point battle of the Franco-Prussian War, fought in early September 1870.

8. Freiherr von Tettau, *Achtzehn Monate mit Russlands Heeren in der Manchschurei*, 2 vols. (Berlin: E. S. Mittler, 1907).

9. Recent estimates are roughly twenty-six divisions overall (a corps is about two divisions). Showalter, *Tannenberg*, 132.

10. Delbrück's account here is much less trustworthy than later ones. In addition to the huge differences in size between the two fronts, the flow of information from the east was probably much less reliable than that from the west front. See Showalter, *Tannenberg*; Norman Stone, *The Eastern Front, 1914–1917* (New York: Scribners, 1975), chap. 3.

### Reading 12. The Strategic Situation in December 1914

Hans Delbrück, "Das Zahlen-Übergewicht unserer Gegner und die Politik Belgiens. Die Strategische Lage," *PJ*, December 1914; rpt. in *Krieg und Politik*, 3 vols. (Berlin: Georg Stilke, 1918), 1:70–80.

1. René Viviani, French premier and foreign minister, 1914–16.

2. An English war fleet destroyed a German fleet off the Falkland Islands in early December 1914. See C. R. M. F. Cruttwell, *A History*

*of the Great War, 1914–1918*, 2d ed. (Oxford: Clarendon Press, 1936), 120–22.

3. In August a German minelayer penetrated to the Thames estuary before it was discovered and destroyed. Cruttwell, *Great War*, 65.

4. A recent work argues that the French, Belgians, and English suffered 250,000 casualties in the first month of the war, and the Germans somewhat less. Archer Jones, *The Art of War in the Western World* (New York: Oxford University Press, 1989), 439.

5. For an excellent recent discussion, see Dennis Showalter, *The Wars of Frederick the Great* (New York: Longman, 1996), chap. 7. Delbrück had argued for these familiar themes and the military had fought against them since the late 1870s. See Arden Bucholz, *Hans Delbrück and the German Military Establishment: War Images in Conflict* (Iowa City: University of Iowa Press, 1985).

6. Karl Leonard Blumenthal, Crown Prince Frederick's chief of staff in the Austro-Prussian War, 1866.

7. The account in Norman Stone, *The Eastern Front, 1914–1918* (New York: Scribners, 1975), chap. 5, shows how close Delbrück was able to stay, with incomplete and partially erroneous information, to the image of these events later constructed by historians using a variety of more complete and more reliable sources.

8. In the battle of Zorndorf, 25 August 1757, Prussia defeated but did not destroy an invading Russian army. At Hochkirch, fought 14 October 1758, Austria defeated Frederick the Great's army but did not drive it out of Silesia.

### Reading 13. April and May 1915

Hans Delbrück, "Die Kriegs-Ereignisse im April–Mai," *PJ*, May 1915; rpt. in *Krieg und Politik*, 3 vols. (Berlin: Georg Stilke, 1918), 1: 104–14.

1. Cruttwell says the French suffered 240,000 casualties and won only "a few hamlets and trenches." C. R. M. F. Cruttwell, *A History of the Great War, 1914–1918*, 2d ed. (Oxford: Clarendon Press, 1936), 148.

2. See Cruttwell, *Great War*, 174–75.

3. Here Delbrück does not give exact figures, which he perhaps did not have, but offers a comparison, using only Russian figures. He

may have been prevented from using the German-Austrian figures
by the censors.

### Reading 14. August 1915

Hans Delbrück, "Die Kriegsereignisse im August," *PJ*, August 1915;
rpt. in *Krieg und Politik*, 3 vols. (Berlin: Georg Stilke, 1918), 1:124–29.
    1. The Austrian garrison surrendered Przemysl on 22 March 1915.
Norman Stone, *The Eastern Front, 1914–1917* (New York: Scribners,
1975), 114.
    2. C. R. M. F. Cruttwell, *A History of the Great War, 1914–1918*, 2d
ed. (Oxford: Clarendon Press, 1936), 177–83; and Stone, *Eastern
Front*, 128–31, generally agree.
    3. General August von Mackensen (1849–1945), commander in
chief of the east front army.
    4. Grand Duke Nikolai, Russian commander in chief.

### Reading 15. America between Germany and England

Hans Delbrück, "Amerika zwischen Deutschland und England," *PJ*,
February 1916; rpt. in *Krieg und Politik*, 3 vols. (Berlin: Georg Stilke,
1918), 1:202–16.
    1. C. R. M. F. Cruttwell, *A History of the Great War, 1914–1918*, 2d
ed. (Oxford: Clarendon Press, 1936), 376–77; Arden Bucholz, *Hans
Delbrück and the German Military Establishment: War Images in Conflict*
(Iowa City: University of Iowa Press, 1985), 100–103.
    2. Commander Weddigen's U9 sank three armored cruisers off the
Dutch coast in August 1914. In March 1915 Weddigen's U12 was
caught by the British Fourth Battle Squadron off Pentland Firth, near
Scapt Flow, and fatally rammed by HMS *Dreadnought*. Cruttwell,
*Great War*, 67; Richard Hough, *The Great War at Sea, 1914–1918* (New
York: Oxford University Press, 1983), 175; Holger Herwig, *"Luxury
Fleet": The Imperial German Navy, 1888–1918* (London: George Allen
& Unwin, 1980), 162.
    3. *Baralong* was a British vessel disguised as a merchant ship but
armed with carefully concealed weapons. Known as a "Q-ship" and
manned by volunteers, it invited attack by venturing alone into dan-

gerous seas. On sighting a surfaced U-boat the Q-ship would put a lifeboat into the water. As the U-boat approached to examine it, twelve-pound guns and a Maxim machine gun would engage the submarine. Hough, *Great War at Sea*, 303–4.

## Reading 16. March 1916

Hans Delbrück, "Die Kriegsereignisse im März," *PJ*, March 1916; rpt. in *Krieg und Politik*, 3 vols. (Berlin: Georg Stilke, 1918), 1:221–26.

1. Just before the war, in early July 1914, French senator Charles Humbert presented a damning Senate report on the inferiority of French armaments in relation to Germany's. It was so strong that French president Raymond Poincaré feared it would hold up approval of the military budget. John F. V. Keiger, *France and the Origins of the First World War* (New York: St. Martin's Press, 1983), 149.

2. See C. R. M. F. Cruttwell, *A History of the Great War, 1914–1918*, 2d ed. (Oxford: Clarendon Press, 1936), chap. 15; Cyril Falls, *The Great War* (New York: Capricorn, 1959), chap. 11.

3. Underestimation of casualties was very important during World War I. Delbrück did not know until late in the war that casualties were much greater than reported or generally known. One wonders exactly when the huge casualties were known. Germany had more than two million dead, that is, an average of almost ten thousand men per week for the fifty-two months of the war. Ten thousand death notices or burials per week would have been noticed by someone and probably by many Germans at home. What percentage of dead were buried on the battlefield and what percentage were returned home, and when, for burial? When were those soldiers considered "lost in combat," that is, those men not definitely identified as killed, wounded, or taken prisoner, made known to their surviving families at home?

4. Censorship prevented Delbrück from knowing these casualty figures very fully. For example, until late in the war the German government generally made public roughly half the actual casualties the army had suffered in a given battle. It has been suggested that the casualties from the fighting at Ypres and Langemarck in October 1914 were so high they were not revealed for fifty years.

5. For the war as a whole it has been said that of 1,000 inhabitants,

France mobilized 168 and lost 34; the United Kingdom mobilized 125 and lost 16; Germany mobilized 154 and lost 30. But since France had a lower population than Germany, French deaths had a greater demographic impact than German. Jean-Jacques Becker, *The Great War and the French People* (Oxford: Berg, 1993), 6.

6. The *Temps* was a well-known Paris newspaper.


## Reading 17. February and March 1917

Hans Delbrück, "Der Krieg im Februar–März," *PJ*, March 1917; rpt. in *Krieg und Politik*, 3 vols. (Berlin: Georg Stilke, 1918), 2:163–67.

1. Cyril Falls, *The Great War* (New York: Capricorn, 1959), 276, calls it a "retreat"; C. R. M. F. Cruttwell, *A History of the Great War, 1914–1918*, 2d ed. (Oxford: Clarendon Press, 1936), 400, agrees with Delbrück that it was a "master stroke."


## Reading 18. May and June 1917

Hans Delbrück, "Der Krieg im Mai und Juni," *PJ*, June 1917; rpt. in *Krieg und Politik*, 3 vols. (Berlin: Georg Stilke, 1918), 2:240–46.

1. See C. R. M. F. Cruttwell, *A History of the Great War, 1914–1918*, 2d ed. (Oxford: Clarendon Press, 1936), 436–37; Falls, *The Great War* (New York: Capricorn, 1959), 268–69.

2. This comment, in a footnote in the original, suggests that Delbrück consulted with the military during the war.

3. Censorship and propaganda manipulated the flow of public information during the war on the German side. The attempts Delbrück made to obtain better information, for example, by using neutral or Entente sources, were not successful, and he often had run-ins with the censor. Arden Bucholz, *Hans Delbrück and the German Military Establishment: War Images in Conflict* (Iowa City: University of Iowa Press, 1985), 99, 106.

4. Delbrück was very careful in his public comments on unrestricted submarine warfare and its outcome, the American declaration of war against Germany. But privately he feared the worst. He wrote to friends that the outcome depended on whether President Wilson had been about to arrange a negotiated peace and whether

unrestricted submarine warfare had now stopped these negotiations or set them forward. Two days after Germany's declaration of total war at sea the United States broke off diplomatic relations; sixty-six days later the United States declared war. Bucholz, *Hans Delbrück*, 101.

## Reading 19. July to November 1917

Hans Delbrück, "Der Krieg von Juli bis November," *PJ*, November 1917; rpt. in *Krieg und Politik*, 3 vols. (Berlin: Georg Stilke, 1918), 2:354–62.

1. On the Baltic Sea. This early example of combined arms operations has received little historical attention. See Captain von Koblinski, "The Conquest of the Baltic Islands," *U.S. Naval Institute Proceedings* 58 (July 1932): 972–92; A. Harding Ganz, "Albion: The Baltic Islands Operation," *Military Affairs* 42, no. 2 (1978): 91–97.

2. See Cyril Falls, *The Great War* (New York: Capricorn, 1959), 307–10; C. R. M. F. Cruttwell, *A History of the Great War, 1914–1918*, 2d ed. (Oxford: Clarendon Press, 1936), 456–58.

3. During the fighting few other commentators were able to relate one front to another and in this way tie the whole war—west, east, and south—together.

4. This was the campaign in which Erwin Rommel, a lieutenant in a German mountain company, broke through and with a few German companies captured 150 officers, nine thousand men, and eighty-one guns, earning the Pour le Mérite, Germany's highest decoration for valor in combat. Desmond Young, *Rommel: The Desert Fox* (New York: William Morrow, 1978), 19–21.

5. Falls, *Great War*, 309, says 275,000; Crutwell, *Great War*, 462–67, uses 400,000; William L. Langer, ed., *Encyclopedia of World History* (Boston: Houghton Mifflin, 1963), 941, agrees with Delbrück's figures. This is the retreat so vividly described by Ernest Hemingway in *A Farewell to Arms* (New York: Harper & Row, 1929).

## Reading 20. The Military Collapse

Hans Delbrück, "Der militärische Umschlag. Prinz Max," *PJ*, October 1918; rpt. in *Krieg und Politik*, 3 vols. (Berlin: Georg Stilke, 1918),

3:181–88; see C. R. M. F. Cruttwell, *A History of the Great War, 1914–1918,* 2d ed. (Oxford: Clarendon Press, 1936), 543–76; Cyril Falls, *The Great War* (New York: Capricorn, 1959), 342–60.

1. Georg Michaelis, an unknown midlevel bureaucrat, was chancellor from July through 30 October 1917; next came Count Georg Hertling, Bavarian premier, who was chancellor through 4 October 1918, when Prince Max von Baden was appointed. He served through 10 November 1918, when he left office, turning the German government over to the leaders of the Reichstag majority parties.

### Reading 21. Armistice, Revolution, Defeat, Republic

Hans Delbrück, "Waffenstillstand, Revolution, Unterwerfung, Republic," *PJ*, November 1918; rpt. in *Krieg und Politik*, 3 vols. (Berlin: Georg Stilke, 1918), 3:203–24.

1. See Cyril Falls, *The Great War* (New York: Capricorn, 1959), 352–83; C. R. M. F. Cruttwell, *A History of the Great War, 1914–1918*, 2d ed. (Oxford: Clarendon Press, 1936), 543–69; Archer Jones, *The Art of War in Western Civilization* (New York: Oxford University Press, 1986), 475–80.

2. Reference to *PJ* 2 (June 1916): 245.

3. Ludendorff and his colleagues were in a state of shock following 8 August: they did not want to believe the offensive had failed and could not admit to anyone, even themselves, that such was the case. Arden Bucholz, *Hans Delbrück and the German Military Establishment: War Images in Conflict* (Iowa City: University of Iowa Press, 1985), 123–26, 135.

4. Paul von Hintze, former admiral and at that time secretary of state for foreign affairs.

5. Count Ernst von Reventlow, one of the leaders of the Fatherland Party, created to forward the "peace by victory" in the late fall of 1917.

6. At Zabern, in Alsace-Lorraine, in the autumn of 1913 a few arrogant army officers got into a dispute with civilians. The army and Kaiser Wilhelm II defended the officers, who had overreacted by declaring martial law, creating a cause célèbre and raising cries of militarism. See David Schoenbaum, *Zabern, 1913: Consensus Politics in Imperial Germany*, (London: Oxford University Press, 1982).

7. Eduard von Capelle, successor to Alfred von Tirpitz as secretary of state for the navy.

8. August Bebel, one of the leaders of the Social Democratic Party before 1914.

9. See Bucholz, *Hans Delbrück*, 121–29.

10. Delbrück plays down the violence in Berlin. Recent studies argue that from early November 1918 through March 1919 and even later a potentially revolutionary situation existed in and around the city. See Gordon Craig, *Germany, 1866–1945* (New York: Oxford University Press, 1978), chap. 11; Richard Bessel, *Germany after the First World War* (Oxford: Clarendon Press, 1993); Holger Herwig, *Modern Germany: Hammer or Anvil?* (Lexington MA: D.C. Heath, 1994), chap. 7; Dietrich Orlow, *A History of Modern Germany*, (Englewood Cliffs NJ: Prentice Hall, 1987), chap. 5.

## Reading 22. Seventieth Birthday Reminiscence

Hans Delbrück, "Danksagung," *PJ*, November 1918; rpt. in *Krieg und Politik*, 3 vols. (Berlin, Georg Stilke, 1918), 3:225–28.

1. England, France, and Turkey fought against Russia, 1853–54.

2. The great mutiny of 1857–58 against the British in India.

3. War of Italy and France against Austria.

4. Delbrück's daughter told me her father had been brought up on "Goethe, Goethe, and more Goethe."

5. John Stuart Mill (1806–73), English philosopher. George Grote (1794–1871), English historian. Franz Mehring, in a celebrated critique of Delbrück's work in 1908, said that Grote had used his knowledge of modern English politics to reconstruct the history of Athenian democracy in the same way Delbrück had used his knowledge of war to reconstruct military history. But Delbrück, Mehring said, was much more radical in applying the comparative method than Grote. Arden Bucholz, *Hans Delbrück and the German Military Establishment: War Images in Conflict* (Iowa City: University of Iowa Press, 1985), 41.

## Reading 23. Ludendorff's Self-Portrait

Hans Delbrück, *Ludendorffs Selbstporträt*, 10th ed. (Berlin: Verlag für Politik und Wirtschaft, 1922). Originally it was an eighty-page pamphlet reviewing nine books on World War I. Each edition took up the most recent historiographical controversies so that the book was a running literature review as well as a description of how Delbrück saw World War I.

1. Delbrück's testimony to the Reichstag committee was published in Deutschland, Nationalversammlung, *Das Werk des Untersuchungsausschusses*, 4th series, "Die Ursachen des Deutschen Zusammenbruchs im Jahr 1918," 12 vols. (Berlin, 1925–29, 4:218–41.

2. What Delbrück's account lacks from the perspective of the early 1920s are the primary sources, that is, Schlieffen's original war plans and the modifications of them made between 1905 and 1914. These plans did not become available to historians until after Delbrück died, and even now they have not been fully explored and explained. The matter is much more complex than anyone suspected in 1923. See Arden Bucholz, *Moltke, Schlieffen, and Prussian War Planning* (Oxford: Berg, 1991), chaps. 4–6.

3. Matthias Erzberger (1875–1921), Center Party leader and one of those behind the Reichstag peace resolution of July 1917.

4. This is the plan Schlieffen undoubtedly proposed to Kaiser Wilhelm II and his advisers. It was rejected. See Bucholz, *Prussian War Planning*, 195–209.

5. See John Keiger, *France and the Origins of the First World War* (New York: St. Martin's Press, 1983); D. C. B. Lieven, *Russia and the Origins of the First World War* (New York: St. Martin's Press, 1983).

6. In fact that was not so. The final ratios in 1914 were fifty-five divisions north and twenty-three south. Bucholz, *Prussian War Planning*, 265–66. Failure of the Schlieffen Plan is not to be found, however, in this change.

7. C. R. M. F. Cruttwell, *A History of the Great War, 1914–1918,* 2d ed. (Oxford: Clarendon Press, 1936), 499–501.

8. General William Robertson.

9. Prime Minister David Lloyd George; General Henry Wilson, who replaced Robertson as chief of staff.

10. Ferdinand Foch, Luigi Cadorna, and Howard Tasker Bliss.

11. Charles á Court Repington.

12. English Generals Herbert Gough and Julian Byng.

13. Oskar von Hutier; see Cruttwell, *Great War*, 503–7; Cyril Falls, *The Great War* (New York: Capricorn, 1959), 331–33.

14. General Douglas Haig, English commander in chief.

15. Georges Clemenceau, French prime minister and war minister.

16. General Henri Philippe Pétain, French divisional and corps commander, most notably at Verdun.

17. Delbrück quoted Ludendorff's *War Memoirs*, (Erich Ludendorff, *Meine Kriegserrinerungen, 1914–1918* [Berlin: E. S. Mittler, 1919]), 482.

18. Cruttwell, *Great War*, 510–13; Falls, *Great War*, 331–42.

19. Hermann von Kuhl, one of Schlieffen's closest associates, was in World War I chief of staff to Crown Prince Rupprecht's army group. Erich von Falkenhayn, war minister before 1914, was commander in chief from September 1914 through 1916 and then commander of the eastern front in Romania. He wrote in *PJ*, November 1922, 179.

20. General Alfred Krauss.

21. Falls agrees almost completely. *Great War*, 307–9.

22. See reading 21. Reprinted in Hans Delbrück, *Krieg und Politik*, 3 vols. (Berlin: Georg Stilke, 1918), 3:36–39.

23. Delbrück cites Ludendorff's *War Memoirs*, 484.

24. Citing Ludendorff's *War Memoirs*, 525.

25. Ludendorff was understandably in a state of shock and depression, unable to do anything, from about 18 July to the end of September. Colonel Max Bauer was Ludendorff's liaison officer. Arden Bucholz, *Hans Delbrück and the German Military Establishment: War Images in Conflict* (Iowa City: University of Iowa Press, 1985), 135.

26. Walther Nicolai, chief of the general staff's propaganda and intelligence section in 1918.

27. German troops inflicted huge casualties, the most of the war, on the attacking Entente troops from July to October, as testified by the American, French, and English cemeteries between Soissons and Reims, in northeastern France. These valley battlefields, several miles across, are virtually wall-to-wall graves. French records confirm that this period had the highest French losses for the entire war.

28. Ludendorff resigned 27 October and later fled to Sweden in disguise, fearing for his life. Martin Kitchen, *Silent Dictatorship* (London: Croom Helm, 1976), 263–66.

## Reading 24. The Peace of Versailles

Hans Delbrück, *Der Friede von Versailles*, 3d ed. (Berlin: Georg Stilke, 1930). It was published in *PJ*, August 1930, and also as a pamphlet, of which several thousand copies were sold.

1. King Alexander Obrenovich of Serbia, assassinated in June 1903 by army officers.

2. The complexities of the countermobilizations were not clear then and still are not completely unraveled. See Arden Bucholz, *Moltke, Schlieffen, and Prussian War Planning* (Oxford: Berg, 1991), chap. 6, and "Armies, Railroads, and Information: The Birth of Industrial Mass War," in *Changing Large Technical Systems*, ed. Jane Summerton (Boulder co: Westview Press, 1994), 53–70.

3. This statement is consistent with current research.

4. Presumably Delbrück is referring to the forty-eight-hour ultimatum demanding Germany sign the Treaty of Versailles.

# Index

www.ingramcontent.com/pod-product-compliance
Ingram Content Group UK Ltd.
Pitfield, Milton Keynes, MK11 3LW, UK
UKHW042257030325
455810UK00001B/20